"For a culture deeply ⟨...⟩ desperately needed resource. With contributions from a team of trusted pastors, it provides a remarkably comprehensive guide to the whole of a man's life. It rightly grounds a man's duties in his redeemed identity in Christ, offering profound wisdom for his relationships, his work, and finishing his race well."

 SCOTT ANIOL
 President, G3 Ministries, professor of pastoral theology,
 Grace Bible Theological Seminary

"A Christian man has but one ambition—to live all his days in the fear of his God (1 Peter 1:17). This is made evident in the inward motions of his heart as well as in the outward actions of his life. The value of the present volume is that it demonstrates with such clarity what this looks like in every season, relationship, calling, and condition. Here, indeed, is wise pastoral counsel for every man who desires to glorify God in all of life."

 J. STEPHEN YUILLE
 Director of Puritan publishing, Reformation Heritage Books

"*Man up* could be a barked command, a disdainful demand, a derisory snort. Not here! Here it is a reasoned, scriptural, affectionate, practical exhortation from men speaking from experience about the various ages and stages of Christian manhood. The contributors look you in the eye, speak from their heart to yours, and show you how men can serve the Lord in our generation. Listen to their words, hear their tone, consider the example set before you above all in Christ Himself. Then, *man up*!"

 JEREMY WALKER
 Pastor of Maidenbower Baptist Church, Crawley, UK

The Redeemed Man

The Redeemed Man

Edited by
Joel R. Beeke
Richard D. Phillips
Paul M. Smalley

Reformation Heritage Books
Grand Rapids, Michigan

The Redeemed Man

© 2025 by Joel R. Beeke

All rights reserved. No part of this book may be used or reproduced in any manner whatsoever without written permission except in the case of brief quotations embodied in critical articles and reviews. For more information, please contact: Reformation Heritage Books, 3070 29th St. SE, Grand Rapids, MI 49512.

ISBN: 979-8-88686-226-3

Scripture references are from the King James Version, unless otherwise noted, with the exception of the introduction and chapters 4–5, 9, 11–14, 17–19, and 21 where references are taken from the New King James Version®. Copyright © 1982 by Thomas Nelson. Used by permission. All rights reserved. (Words in italics represent the authors' emphasis.)

Printed in the United States of America
25 26 27 28 29 30/10 9 8 7 6 5 4 3 2 1

Contents

Introduction: Godly Manhood 1
Richard D. Phillips

Part 1: A Godly Man's Relationship with God

1. The Redeemed Man Repenting and Believing 9
   Joel R. Beeke and Paul M. Smalley
2. The Redeemed Man Knowing His God 21
   Conrad Mbewe
3. The Redeemed Man Committed to God's Word 33
   Paul M. Smalley
4. The Redeemed Man Growing in Grace 43
   Sinclair B. Ferguson

Part 2: A Godly Man's Relationships with People

5. The Redeemed Man Honoring His Parents 57
   Terry Johnson
6. The Redeemed Man Living in Singleness 69
   Curt Daniel
7. The Redeemed Man Loving His Wife 81
   Joel R. Beeke
8. The Redeemed Man Leading His Family 95
   Jason Helopoulos
9. The Redeemed Man Discipling His Children 107
   Richard D. Phillips
10. The Redeemed Man Growing in Family Worship 119
    Joel R. Beeke
11. The Redeemed Man Cultivating Friendships 133
    Michael A. G. Azad Haykin
12. The Redeemed Man Witnessing to Unbelievers 145
    David Strain

Part 3: A Godly Man's Work

13. The Redeemed Man Viewing Work Rightly   163
    Richard D. Phillips
14. The Redeemed Man Laboring at His Work   175
    Daniel Doriani
15. The Redeemed Man Serving in His Church   185
    Kevin DeYoung
16. The Redeemed Man Managing His Resources   197
    Jim Newheiser
17. The Redeemed Man Enjoying His Recreations   209
    Gerard Hemmings
18. The Redeemed Man Governing as a Citizen   221
    David C. Innes

Part 4: A Godly Man's Finishing Well

19. The Redeemed Man Sustaining His Health   237
    Joseph Pipa
20. The Redeemed Man Persevering in His Faith   249
    Geoff Thomas
21. The Redeemed Man Entering Retirement   261
    Derek W. H. Thomas
22. The Redeemed Man Preparing for His Death   275
    Ian Hamilton

Contributors   287

INTRODUCTION
Godly Manhood
Richard D. Phillips

IN THE DAYS when God was visiting judgment on the cities of Sodom and Gomorrah, the Lord was overheard discussing His purpose in the life of the patriarch Abraham: "For I have known him, in order that he may command his children and his household after him, that they keep the way of the LORD, to do righteousness and justice, that the LORD may bring to Abraham what He has spoken to him" (Gen. 18:19).

Abraham was called to be "the father of all those who believe" (Rom. 4:11), leading his family by the same faith through which he was saved. His life has influenced all those who looked to him and followed him and, as a result, they kept "the way of the LORD." Most significantly, the Lord said that it was by Abraham's faithfulness as a redeemed man that God's promises to him would come true: "that the LORD may bring to Abraham what He has spoken to him."

This book was written because of the conviction that just as Abraham's life was vital to God's people long ago, so also the godliness, faith, and influence of Christian men are essential to the work of God in our world today. Of course, Abraham was unique as the man whom God chose by grace to be the covenant father of the people who became the nation of Israel and, ultimately, the Christian church. But there is a definite analogy between what God intended in Abraham's life and what God seeks from the lives of Christian men today. We are to believe in Jesus Christ and live decidedly Christian lives. Redeemed men are to lead in their homes, in the church, and in society simply through living by faith and influencing others to also walk in the way of the Lord. If God long ago achieved His sovereign purpose and fulfilled His sacred promises through Abraham's faith and obedience, His work in our world also calls on redeemed men to provide Christian leadership.

The editors produced this volume because we perceived the need for a comprehensive and up-to-date guide for Christian men that is distinctively biblical in its approach. Like Caleb, who centuries ago called forth the men of Israel, our aim is to summon Christian men to embrace their calling in service to our Lord. A book like this is made necessary by the prevailing confusion of our times; men who turn to Jesus Christ today will often be coming from a world that has sown in their minds corrupt ideas of life and manhood. We therefore desired a single comprehensive book that could be handed to a believing man and speak to the whole of his life. Our prayer has been that this volume would be a treasured companion throughout the lifetime of a host of godly men, its worn pages serving as a blessing to them, to the people they know and love, and to the glory of the God of grace who redeemed us through Christ's blood.

To this end, we enlisted a remarkable group of contributors, each of whom is notable for faithful and productive ministries as pastors and scholars who teach God's Word. We realize that a high percentage of young men today have lacked appropriate male role models and therefore crave a clear path forward as men. And yet the proliferation of books, articles, and podcasts that fill the "manosphere" does not always provide a vision for manhood that reflects the truth of God's Word. It has been our privilege, then, to compile the chapters in this book, setting forth a clear and compelling case for the biblical vision of redeemed manhood.

As a comprehensive approach to biblical manhood, we intend for this volume to provide extensive treatment to topics other than the man in his role as husband and father. These roles and callings are of such great significance that they necessarily prompt a great deal of literature, and the calling of men as husbands and fathers certainly is treated in this volume. But we wanted to address the whole of a man's life, starting with the priority that must be given to his relationship with God. Here, we take to heart Jesus teaching, "I am the vine, you are the branches. . . . without Me you can do nothing" (John 15:5).

Biblical manhood inevitably begins with a saving relationship with Christ and His salvation blessings working within a man's life. The first section of this book therefore centers on a man's relationship with God. In short, godly manhood results as the fruit of union with Christ through faith by which we become the sons of God and learn to walk in the Lord's ways. A Christian must *become* in order to *do*; as such we want to emphasize the priority of conversion to faith in Christ, a growing knowledge of God, the embrace of a pattern of Christian piety that will fortify and strengthen a man, and finally the path of growth in grace that will enable everything else that is written in this book.

Having begun with a man's relationship with God, this book explores godly manhood in terms of a redeemed man's relationship with people. We prayerfully submit these vital chapters that as foundational to a life that leaves a godly legacy and bears abundant fruit for the Lord's glory. This section includes treatment of topics that often are neglected. For instance, Curt Daniel's chapter, "The Redeemed Man Living in Singleness," provides an extraordinary perspective on adult singleness that every pastor should read and that will be of enormous benefit to men in this providential circumstance. Other important chapters consider an adult man's relationship with his parents and his cultivation of male friendships, along with the vital and core chapters focused on the godly man as husband and father.

The third and fourth sections of this book also promote our aim at a comprehensive book, focusing on a man and his work and the often-neglected topic of a redeemed man finishing his life well. These chapters also are extraordinarily valuable and will enrich our thinking on these important matters.

We intentionally kept the the chapters concise. We wanted substantial treatments of each important topic, but also for the chapters to be to the point and relatively easy to read. I think our readers will appreciate both the probing nature of this material and its accessibility and brevity.

When Joel Beeke approached me about joining him in this project, he cited the example of Caleb calling out the men of Israel to stand for God in their generation (as I noted above). Our generation has a similar need for godly manhood, especially in the Christian church. Will you be such a godly man? We believe that if you have been redeemed by the blood of Jesus Christ, having trusted in His gospel, then you are equipped with the mighty Spirit of the living God in order to live for Him.

In addition to Caleb, I think of the prophet Ezekiel, who preached God's Word in a corrupt and dying generation not much different from our own. The Lord said through Ezekiel, "I sought for a man among them who would make a wall, and stand in the gap before Me on the behalf of the land" (Ezek. 22:30). We desperately need godly men today who will stand in the gap, leading and serving in line with God's Word so that truth and righteousness begin to grow. Will you be such a godly man? If you are redeemed through Christ's blood, why not be one of many men—like a strong wall—who stand in the gap against the tide of unbelief and evil that is flooding our society?

It is our privilege to provide you the counsel offered in this volume, but it is your calling not merely to study but also to live out the way of God's blessing. Only you can be the husband who will bless your wife and the father who leads your family to follow the way of the Lord. If you do—if we together as redeemed men follow Abraham's example, answer

Caleb's call, and rise up to fill Ezekiel's gap—God will not fail to fulfill His promises to His faithful people.

It is our prayer that the God of grace will restore the blessings of Christ in our time, and when He does it will have at least been in part because there were redeemed men who lived out faithful and godly manhood. The saints of prior generations are now with the Lord, their garlands already gained through godly and fruitful lives. We are the men who live today and, by God's grace, it is we who can stand up in our generation as those who know the Lord and live in the light of His truth before all the world.

PART 1

A Godly Man's Relationship with God

CHAPTER ONE

The Redeemed Man Repenting and Believing

Joel R. Beeke and Paul M. Smalley

REDEMPTION IS the act of buying back and restoring something that is lost or ruined.[1] God has been about the work of redemption since the fall of man. God saves sinners from the pollution, power, and punishment of their sins through the perfect life, atoning death, and victorious resurrection of His Son, the Lord Jesus Christ. That is the gospel. Apart from Christ, dear friend, you are lost, broken, and undone by your sin. Yet God offers a way of escape from your sin—a way of redemption. By God's grace, men lost in sin can become redeemed men.

Unless you have received that redemption—unless you have truly repented of your sins and truly believed the gospel—then your failure to meet God's standard for biblical manhood only further condemns you for your broader rebellion against His revealed will. It is impossible for you to follow the exhortations which follow in this book without a living, vital union with Jesus Christ and utter dependence on His Holy Spirit, for

---

1. We are grateful to Fraser Jones for his assistance on this chapter.

without Christ you can do nothing (John 15:5). It is only with such a great salvation that you can live a life that will truly "adorn the doctrine of God our Saviour" (Titus 2:10). With that in mind, we will consider the genuine conversion of the redeemed man in repentance and saving faith.

The Sinner's Need for Conversion

The reason why you must experience conversion is because you are a sinner. Sin is more than making a mistake; it is failing to be what God designed you to be. God created human beings in His image to bear His righteous likeness in their character, words, and work (Gen. 1:27; Eph. 4:24). The standard for righteousness is the law of God revealed in the Bible.

You have broken God's standard. The tragic news is that "all have sinned, and come short of the glory of God" (Rom. 3:23). Someone might object, "But I have kept God's commandments! I have not murdered, committed adultery, or stolen another person's property." Perhaps not, but Christ tells us that the law of God reaches the heart. It is not enough to avoid committing murder; you also must avoid selfish anger and hatred (Matt. 5:21–22). Have you cursed someone in your heart? Adultery is evil, but we commit adultery in our hearts when we engage in sexual lust (vv. 27–28). Have you lusted after someone? Have you chosen to look at pornography? We must not steal, but the heart of stealing is greed, and if you love money, you cannot serve God (6:24). Do you crave more money and more possessions?

Furthermore, you have broken God's standard for your relationships as a man. Since you are a son, God requires you to honor your father and your mother (Ex. 20:12). Have you disobeyed your parents without just cause when you were a child? Have you dishonored them with your words or actions? Have you resented their authority and resisted their good counsel?

If you are a husband, God calls you to love your wife as Christ loves the church (Eph. 5:25). Have you consistently denied yourself to serve your wife? Do you speak God's Word to her for her spiritual growth and pray with her (v. 26)? Do you listen to her and show her the same concern and compassion that you show your own body (v. 28)? These are your duties.

If you have the privilege of being a father, you are responsible to represent to your children the heavenly Father in His righteousness and mercy. Do you bring your children to God? Have you read the Holy Scriptures to your children in regular family devotions? Have you trained them to do what is right and given them consistent, loving discipline when they disobey? Have they heard their father's voice pleading in prayer for them before the throne of grace? Can they look to you as an example of a righteous and godly man?

Our problem is that we have lived for ourselves instead of loving God with all our hearts and loving our neighbor as ourselves (Matt. 22:37–40). When I (Joel) was a young man, I worked for my dad for a few summers. On my first day on the job he said, "You see that hammer there? Don't try to saw a board with it. You see that saw? Don't try to drive a nail with it." I said, "I know that, Dad." He replied, "But do you know *why* I am telling you? Because God designed us to live to His glory and to be of service to our neighbor. When we try to live for ourselves, it is like trying to saw a board with a hammer and trying to drive home a nail with a saw. It doesn't work. You will never find satisfaction in life, my son, if you try living for a purpose for which God did not make you."

What man can consider his duties to God and people, and not be humbled by his many failures? We have offended against the Most High (Ps. 51:4) and provoked His holy wrath (Rom. 1:18). His law pronounces its curse upon all lawbreakers (Gal. 3:10). We all have great cause to cry out, "God, have mercy on me a sinner!" (Luke 18:13). To be saved, we need true conversion, which consists of repentance and faith in Jesus Christ.

The Saving Repentance of the Redeemed Man

Repentance is a gift of God (Acts 11:18; 2 Tim. 2:24).[2] The Lord alone has the power to remove a heart of stone and to replace it with an obedient heart of flesh where the Spirit of God dwells (Ezek. 36:26–27). Repentance, however, is also our duty (Acts 17:30). Our inability to repent apart from God's grace does not remove our responsibility, but rather accentuates our guilt because that inability is willful and wicked.

Repentance consists of the turning of the whole person from sin to God (Joel 2:12). Repentance is what takes place in the heart of the prodigal son when he comes to his senses, realizes that life would be infinitely better at home with his father, and returns home with confession on his lips to seek mercy from the one whom he has offended (Luke 15:11–32).

Turning from sin to God involves a change in every aspect of human life.

- *intellectual change*: turning the mind from the deceit and darkness of sin and Satan (Acts 26:18; Eph. 4:22) to acknowledge the truth of God (2 Tim. 2:25)
- *emotional change*: turning the affections to grieve over sin (2 Cor. 7:10) and to delight in God and His kingdom (Matt. 13:44; 1 Thess. 1:6)
- *volitional change*: turning the will to deny oneself (Matt. 16:24) and to choose God and His ways (Deut. 30:19–20)
- *behavioral change*: turning the conduct to forsake sin (Prov. 28:13) so that by grace a person may "cease to do evil [and] learn to do well" (Isa. 1:16–17).

---

2. This and the following section are adapted from Joel R. Beeke and Paul M. Smalley, *Reformed Systematic Theology* (Crossway, 2021), 3:447–512. Used by permission of Crossway, a publishing ministry of Good News Publishers, Wheaton, IL 60187, www.crossway.org.

The spiritual exercise of repentance involves seven factors that come together in the heart of a man changed by God's regenerating grace. These factors figure prominently in David's confession in Psalm 51.

First, repentance involves *turning to the merciful God*. There can be no turning to God without trust in His goodness, forgiveness, and love in Christ (Ps. 51:1–3). The gospel declares, "Seek ye the Lord while he may be found, call ye upon him while he is near: let the wicked forsake his way, and the unrighteous man his thoughts: and let him return unto the Lord, and he will have mercy upon him; and to our God, for he will abundantly pardon" (Isa. 55:6–7).

Second, repentance involves *sorrow for sin*. The Holy Spirit works through the Word to produce new awareness of the seriousness of sin and deep sorrow for committing it (Ps. 51:3). Paul explains that "godly sorrow worketh repentance" because it grieves over dishonoring and displeasing God, in contrast to "the sorrow of the world," which regrets only the consequences of sin (2 Cor. 7:10). Truly converted men have repented because they have come to see God's glory and now love His laws more than their happiness in this world (Ps. 119:67–68, 71–72).

Third, repentance involves *heartfelt confession of sin against the righteous God*. Repentance is not a merely formal or outward confession of sin but a heartfelt grieving and forsaking of it (Ps. 32:3–5). David says, "I acknowledge my transgressions" (Ps. 51:3), which implies that he confessed specific acts of rebellion against God's law. He continues, "My sin is ever before me" (v. 3) which indicates distress and shame over sin. He acknowledges that his sins against people were, in essence, offenses against God, and that God had every right to condemn him for his guilt (v. 4). The sinner must also recognize that his problem is not just what he does but *who he is* (v. 5).

Fourth, repentance involves *praying for the grace of forgiveness*. The sinner seeks to be cleansed from the guilt of his sin and to be restored to God's favor. David says, "Hide thy face from my sins, and blot out all mine iniquities" (Ps. 51:9). Though his sins have provoked God's wrath to come like an overwhelming flood, he hides in God's mercy—the forgiveness of sins in the blood of Christ (32:5–7; 1 John 1:7, 9).

Fifth, repentance involves *praying for the grace to forsake sin and to be holy*. Repentance is not pursuit of mere forgiveness so that the sinner can keep sinning without consequences; rather, it is an authentic turning to God out of a resolution to not sin again. David prays, "Create in me a clean heart, O God; and renew a right spirit within me" (Ps. 51:10). He desires more than a transformation of behavior but a renewal of the deepest motives of his heart that enables him to turn away from sin. He does so understanding that this requires a supernatural work of new creation that only God can provide.

Sixth, repentance involves *declaring God's saving grace to others*. Those who turn back to the Lord and experience His mercies often seek opportunities to call others to seek Him too. David says that, if God will restore him spiritually, in his joy he will "teach transgressors thy ways; and sinners shall be converted unto thee" (Ps. 51:13).

Seventh, repentance involves *worshiping God with His church*. Godly sorrow for sin is only half of true conversion; the other half, as the Heidelberg Catechism tells us, "is a sincere joy of heart in God, through Christ."[3] Broken-hearted over sin and rejoicing in God, the converted sinner is released to worship God (Ps. 51:14–19). He longs to join with God's people in adoring the Lord; indeed, he desires for the saints to extol God for His mercies (32:11).

Have you turned to the God of mercy in sorrow over your sins, confessing the guilt of your wrongdoing and praying for His forgiveness and power to change? Have you discovered joy in God that moves you to tell others of His grace and to worship with His people? These are the marks of the repentance of a redeemed man.

---

3. The Heidelberg Catechism (LD 33, Q. 90), in *The Three Forms of Unity* (Solid Ground Christian Books, 2010), 99.

The Saving Faith of the Redeemed Man

The only faith that saves is faith in Jesus Christ (Acts 16:31), for Christ is the only Mediator (1 Tim. 2:5–6) and the only way to God (John 14:6). Such faith resides in the heart and moves a person to confess that Jesus Christ is Lord (Rom. 10:9–10). This is possible only by the work of the Holy Spirit (1 Cor. 12:3). Like repentance, saving faith is a gift of God, granted to His elect through hearing the gospel (Acts 11:20–21; 13:48; Eph. 2:8; 2 Thess. 2:13).

Three qualities are essential to saving faith in Jesus Christ:

- *experiential knowledge of God* (Ps. 9:10; Rom. 10:14, 17). We must know God in the heart so that we taste and relish His goodness (Ps. 34:8), so that we listen to His Word, repent of sin, keep His commandments, and love Him and one another (1 John 2:3–4, 13–14; 3:6; 4:6–8).
- *submissive assent to God's Word* (John 3:33–34). We must believe God's Word is true (John 17:17), receiving it not as the mere word of man but the Word of God (1 Thess. 2:13), believing that God is faithful (Heb. 11:1, 11).
- *confident trust in Christ*. We must receive Christ as the Lord of grace and glory (John 1:12, 14), indeed as our very life (6:35), with a faith that rests upon Him as the foundation of all hope (Isa. 28:16; 1 Peter 2:6–7).

Wilhelmus à Brakel wrote, "Faith is a heartfelt trust in Christ—and through Him in God—in order to be justified, sanctified, and glorified, leaning upon Christ's voluntary offer of Himself and upon His promises that He will perform this to all who receive Him and rely upon Him to that end."[4]

---

4. Wilhelmus à Brakel, *The Christian's Reasonable Service*, ed. Joel R. Beeke, trans. Bartel Elshout (Heritage Books, 1993), 2:295.

The spiritual exercise of faith in Christian experience takes place in the following ways.

First, *saving faith empties us of self*. To lay hold of Christ and to treasure His righteousness necessitates relinquishing one's own righteousness (Phil. 3:9). Faith teaches utter humility, the total emptiness of all within the sinner when viewed outside of Christ. The language of faith is, "I am not worthy" (Matt. 8:8, 10). Faith makes a sinner conscious of the desperate situation he is in and the tragic judgment he deserves (Ps. 130:3). Sin must become sin in his estimation if grace is to become grace. Far from being a work of merit, faith causes him to realize his demerit and makes him cling entirely to the hope of divine mercy.

Thus, faith breeds a large view of Christ and a small view of self. The law must condemn us for our willful failure to love God and our neighbors (Rom. 3:19-20) if we are to appreciate the beauty of the Savior who perfectly obeyed the law and bore the penalty of sin (5:6-10). Our unrighteousness must be uncovered if Christ's righteousness is to be discovered as our only righteousness (Ps. 71:16). Faith renounces self precisely because it embraces Christ.

Second, *saving faith comes to Christ in His fullness*. Faith is simply the means that unites a sinner with his Savior. Christ calls sinners to "come unto me" (Isa. 55:3; Matt. 11:28; John 7:37). This is not a physical motion, but a spiritual action. This coming arises from an inward conviction that Christ is suitable and sufficient for us so that the soul cries out, "Lord, to whom shall we go? Thou hast the words of eternal life" (John 6:68).

The believer finds his warrant and liberty to receive Christ in the promises of Christ. By faith, the Christian surrenders to the gospel and falls into the outstretched arms of God. Faith looks away from self to Christ. Faith flees with all the soul's poverty to Christ's riches. It moves with all the soul's guilt to Christ as reconciler and with all the soul's bondage to Christ as liberator. Saving faith lays hold of Christ and His righteousness, and experiences pardon and peace that passes understanding (Rom. 5:1;

Phil. 4:7). Faith does not receive saving benefits in abstraction from Christ but receives Christ as the One in whom all saving benefits are bestowed (Eph. 1:3; 1 John 5:11–12).

In Scripture, receiving Christ is compared to eating bread (John 6:35), drinking water (John 7:37), and putting on clothing (Rom. 13:12, 14). William Perkins compared faith to a hand by which we "apprehend" or take hold of Christ.[5] It is the empty hand of a beggar. Saving faith, then, receives and rests on Christ as He is offered to us in the gospel.

The gospel offers Christ in the fullness of His threefold office. Faith receives Christ as the divine Prophet to teach us the authoritative truth (Acts 3:22–23); as the divine Priest to give us forgiveness and reconciliation with God by His one sacrifice and perpetual intercession (Heb. 7:25; 10:10); and as the divine King to rescue us from sin and Satan, and to rule us by His Spirit through His Word (Psalm 2; Acts 5:31–32). By faith, we receive the whole Christ. His teaching heals our blindness and ignorance; His blood and intercession take away our guilt and punishment; His power delivers us from sin and misery. As Brakel said, "In Christ there is a fullness to meet all your needs and fulfill all your desires."[6]

Third, *saving faith lives out of Christ*. Faith roots and establishes the believer in Christ (Col. 2:6–7). Being united to Christ by faith, the believer possesses all of Christ's benefits and experiences them as the Spirit applies them. Faith especially lives out of Christ's death and resurrection for us, which are the heart of the gospel (1 Cor. 15:1–5). Faith does not look at itself—it is not faith in our faith but faith in Christ Himself. Faith depends on Christ's support and draws from Christ the life of the soul, bearing fruit in good works (John 15:5). By faith in Christ, the believer strives against all spiritual obstacles (1 Tim. 6:12), fighting against

---

5. William Perkins, *An Exposition of the Symbol or Creed of the Apostles*, in *The Works of William Perkins*, ed. Joel R. Beeke and Derek W. H. Thomas, vol. 5, ed. Ryan Hurd (Reformation Heritage Books, 2017), 12–14, 207.
6. Brakel, *Christian's Reasonable Service*, 2:298.

unbelieving fear (2 Tim. 1:7), worldly trust in human glory (John 5:44), and all temptations from the world (1 John 5:4–5). Through this spiritual combat, faith produces the works of love (Gal. 5:6), proving that it is a living faith (James 2:14, 17).

Conclusion

Dear friend, if you are yet in your sins, repent from your sins and believe the gospel. God has given us ample reasons to do so.

First, repent and believe because of *God's command*. When Christ proclaimed, "Repent!" it was not an option, but an imperative (Mark 1:15). This command comes to all those who hear the gospel call. If we do not repent, we are in rebellion against God (Acts 27:30). Will you not have regard to the sovereign authority of the One who made you?

Second, repent and believe because of *God's mercy*. The sovereign God could have left all mankind under the darkness of sin, but instead he gave us the light of His special revelation, the Bible, and the way of salvation in it. By that very act, He shows us that He takes no pleasure in our destruction, but that we turn unto Him and live (Ezek. 33:11).

Third, repent and believe because of *God's kingdom*. When God comes as King, it is always for salvation and judgment. Sin is the wicked determination that God will not rule us as our King. We are rebels against the Almighty. Sin reaps death—temporal, spiritual, and eternal death: "For the wages of sin is death" (Rom. 6:23). Therefore, we must repent and believe or face eternal punishment (Matt. 3:10–12). Without conversion, there is nothing but damnation for sinners (Mark 16:16; John 3:18, 36).

Fourth and finally, repent and believe because of *God's Son*. The One who commands us to repent is the Lord and lords and the King of kings. The One who commands us to repent also reaches out to us with nail-scarred hands and says, "Turn unto me, all ye ends of the earth" (Isa. 45:22). He looks with compassion upon us in our sin and guilt and calls out, "Come unto me, all ye that labour and are heavy laden, and I will give you rest" (Matt. 11:28). Therefore, conversion, which consists of repentance and faith, is not an option to enhance one's spiritual life, but a necessity for salvation, spiritual life, communion with God, fruitfulness in our daily walk, deliverance from hell, and eternal glory and happiness.

Christ calls the wicked to forsake his way and his thoughts, and promises that "he will have mercy upon him... he will abundantly pardon" (Isa. 55:7). How can you refuse this loving Savior? Why will you die? He will be ten thousand times better to you than your sins ever were. He will love you forever. He will lead you to fulfill the purpose for which God made you: to glorify God and enjoy Him forever. Then you will truly be a redeemed man, for both time and eternity.

CHAPTER TWO

The Redeemed Man Knowing His God

Conrad Mbewe

ANYONE WHO wants to understand the Christian man must not simply study what he does in his work and in his relations with other human beings. It is true that in such observations he will see something unique about such a man that may prompt him to ask, "Why is this man so different from other men?" It is in seeking answers to this question that the ultimate answer will be found in the Christian man's relationship with his God. There is an inner knowledge of God that functions as a compass, ever pointing north during all the storms and tempests of life. It sets the redeemed man's direction in life apart from all other human beings on earth.

The Redeemed Man Is Someone Who Knows God

To begin with, the spiritual knowledge that the Christian man has of his God is one that he gets only at the point of his conversion. The state of the human heart before regeneration and conversion is one of being estranged from the life of God. There is a darkness that covers the eyes. Thus, believers are urged not to walk "as other Gentiles walk, in the vanity of their mind, having the understanding darkened, being alienated from the life of God through the ignorance that is in them, because of the blindness of their heart" (Eph. 4:17–18). This is what it means to be in a state of spiritual death. Even those who are brought up in Christian homes and are taught about God from the Bible and at church will only have head knowledge of God. It is important knowledge, but it is not saving knowledge until the Holy Spirit enlightens a person's spiritual eyes.

In his discussion on the prophetic office of Christ, Wilhelmus à Brakel wrote,

> Even if by study you were to increase your natural knowledge of the truth to some degree, your knowledge will nevertheless remain natural and shrouded in darkness. Even if you were to understand the entire Bible as to the meaning of the words and their respective context, you would not understand the matter expressed by these words.... In order to be delivered from your darkness and to be illuminated with spiritual light, the Lord Jesus, this great Prophet, must take the task in hand to instruct you.[1]

The Lord Jesus Christ in His high priestly prayer spoke of salvation as coming into possession of a saving knowledge of God. He prayed, "This is life eternal, that they might know thee the only true God, and Jesus Christ, whom thou hast sent" (John 17:3). This is not mere philosophical knowledge or that which is derived from observing creation. It is a heart knowledge. It is a fruit of faith that is begotten in the heart, which in turn is a fruit of the regenerating work of the Holy Spirit. It is what was promised in the new covenant when the Lord said through the prophet Jeremiah,

> For this is the covenant that I will make with the house of Israel after those days, says the LORD: I will put My laws in their mind and write them on their hearts; and I will be their God, and they

---

1. Wilhelmus à Brakel, *The Christian's Reasonable Service* (Reformation Heritage Books, 1992), 1:525–26.

shall be My people. None of them shall teach his neighbor, and none his brother, saying, "Know the LORD," for all shall know Me, from the least of them to the greatest of them. (Heb. 8:10–11)

In one sense, salvation takes humanity back to the pre-fall days. Adam and Eve had a real and rich relationship with God when they were created, which was destroyed by the fall in Genesis 3. This relationship is now renewed in Christ. Yet, a Christian's experiential knowledge is even higher than Adam's because it includes knowing the God of all grace who pardons all our sins. By faith, therefore, a true Christian is conscious of God. This consciousness gives birth to an insatiable thirst after God that consumes him for the rest of his earthy and heavenly life.

The Redeemed Man Continues to Learn about God

One source of this ongoing knowledge is in creation. The psalmist says, "The heavens declare the glory of God; and the firmament sheweth his handywork. Day unto day uttereth speech, and night unto night sheweth knowledge" (Ps. 19:1–2). Any believer who studies creation comes away expressing amazement at whoever the One who created all this is. There is order and beauty. There is complicated symmetry and intricate balance. The very vastness of the universe itself suggests a powerful being behind it all. The Christian man is well represented by the words of the psalmist David who uttered in worship, "O LORD our Lord, how excellent is thy name in all the earth! Who hast set thy glory above the heavens. . . . When I consider thy heavens, the work of thy fingers, the moon and the stars, which thou hast ordained; What is man, that thou art mindful of him?" (Ps. 8:1, 3–4). David was lost in wonder, love, and praise as he gazed into the evening sky, admiring the beauty of the stars and the moon. That place of worship is where the Christian man often joins the psalmist.

Beyond the study of God in creation, the Christian man also learns about God through observing God's providence. As Cornelius Van Til once said, "The natural man begins his thinking from below while the redeemed man begins his thinking from above."[2] To the Christian man, therefore, nothing happens by chance, not even the most insignificant event. As Jesus once said, "Are not two sparrows sold for a farthing? And one of them shall not fall on the ground without your Father" (Matt. 10:29). This is his Father's world. The Christian man is convinced that all the great events of history were ordained by God, and He uses secondary agents to carry out His plans. All the details taking place in his life, in the life of his family, and in the life of his nation are under the control of his God. Since this God is an intelligent being who never acts capriciously, the Christian man concludes that he can learn from history and become wiser as he organizes his own life and that of his family.

Yet, above all these, the Christian man learns about God and His ways from the Scriptures. The God of creation is a God who speaks. He has revealed Himself. The Bible says, "God, who at sundry times and in divers manners spake in time past unto the fathers by the prophets, hath in these last days spoken unto us by his Son, whom he hath appointed heir of all things, by whom also he made the worlds" (Heb. 1:1–2). The words of the prophets and Jesus the Son of God are now written for us in the Bible. In the same Bible, we also have the writings of the apostles who wrote for the purpose of keeping the truth of God in its purity before the church as it had now reached fruition after the day of Pentecost. Throughout the Old and New Testaments, the Christian man recognizes that there is a rich fountain of knowledge and wisdom.

Such a man will take his family to church so that they may together be

---

2. Cornelius Van Til, "Herman Dooyeweerd and Reformed Apologetics," in *The Pamphlets, Tracts, and Offprints of Cornelius Van Til*, ed. Eric H. Sigward, electronic ed. (Labels Army, 1997), part 3, section titled, "Dooyeweerd's New Synthesis Thinking."

instructed in the ways of the Lord through the preaching of God's Word. He prays that through this regular ministry, his unconverted children will soon meet the God of glory and rejoice in His saving grace. Back home, he waters the seed that is sown at church by finding out what the children learned and by pointing out afresh some important applications to their hearts. Yet perhaps the most riveting image that the children grow up with is regularly seeing their father alone on his favorite chair poring over the sacred Scriptures. That image convinces them of the value of Scripture. They are made to realize that

> The law of the LORD is perfect, converting the soul: the testimony of the LORD is sure, making wise the simple.
>
> The statutes of the LORD are right, rejoicing the heart: the commandment of the LORD is pure, enlightening the eyes.
>
> The fear of the LORD is clean, enduring for ever: the judgments of the Lord are true and righteous altogether.
>
> More to be desired are they than gold, yea, than much fine gold: sweeter also than honey and the honeycomb.
>
> Moreover by them is thy servant warned: and in keeping of them there is great reward. (Ps. 19:7–11)

The Redeemed Man Appreciates God's Attributes

As the Christian man learns from creation, providence, and the Scriptures, he grows in his appreciation of the nature of God. He sees the kind of God who has made the universe and continues to superintend over it. As he appreciates this God, he grows in his own sense of peace, joy, and wonder despite the difficulties that may sometimes attend his life.

This is what the apostle Paul meant when he wrote, "That which may be known of God is manifest in them; for God hath shewed it unto them.

For the invisible things of him from the creation of the world are clearly seen, being understood by the things that are made, even his eternal power and Godhead" (Rom. 1:19–20). By observing creation and providence, we see the eternal power of God and appreciate His divine nature. What is missing from this self-revelation of God in creation is His forgiving grace. This grace is made manifest in His self-revelation through the Scriptures. When in the valley of discouragement Moses the man of God sought to know God beyond what he knew of Him thus far, he prayed, "I beseech thee, shew me thy glory" (Ex. 33:18). God's response was not only in actions but also in words. The words revealed something of his grace and righteousness. God said, "The LORD, The LORD God, merciful and gracious, longsuffering, and abundant in goodness and truth, keeping mercy for thousands, forgiving iniquity and transgression and sin, and that will by no means clear the guilty; visiting the iniquity of the fathers upon the children" (Ex. 34:6–7).

There is a deep longing in the soul of the Christian man to continue growing in his relationship with the Creator of the universe, the Governor of history, the Savior of His elect people, and the coming Judge of the living and the dead. He sees God to be the only true and living God, and all other gods are dumb idols. As he learns about God, he marvels at His infinity, His immutability, and His immensity. He realizes as never before that this God is eternal and altogether powerful. Then, as observed in the encounter with Moses, he is dissolved to tears at the realization that this God is gloriously good. This goodness is seen in His love, mercy, and grace toward sinners—himself included. That this thrice-holy God should pardon hell-deserving sinners is to him the apex of all the wonders of God.

It was the Puritan Thomas Goodwin who asked and answered as follows: "Now, take a man that has assurance, what is the next thing he desireth? To have much communion with God, to have much intimate converse with him; to see that God of whom he is assured, by a spiritual light revealed to his soul, to see him and to see the excellency and the glory of him."[3] Thus, the Christian man joins the seventeenth-century hymnwriter John Mason in expressing his adoring wonder at this glorious being. He says,

> *How shall I sing that majesty*
> *Which angels do admire?*
> *Let dust in dust and silence lie;*
> *Sing, sing, ye heavenly choir.*
> *Thousands of thousands stand around*
> *Thy throne, O God most high;*
> *Ten thousand times ten thousand sound*
> *Thy praise; but who am I?*
>
> *How great a being, Lord, is thine,*
> *Which doth all beings keep!*
> *Thy knowledge is the only line*
> *To sound so vast a deep.*
> *Thou art a sea without a shore,*
> *A sun without a sphere;*
> *Thy time is now and evermore,*
> *Thy place is everywhere.*[4]

This Knowledge Impacts the Redeemed Man's Life

Such knowledge inevitably impacts every aspect of the life of the Christian man. Let me demonstrate this by looking at four areas of his life.

---

3. Thomas Goodwin, *The Works of Thomas Goodwin* (Tanski Publications, 1996), 1:288.
4. John Mason, "How Shall I Sing that Majesty?" (1683).

Knowing God in Personal Life

The result of this knowledge of God turns a person into a true and godly worshiper. What Abraham Kuyper, the Christian Prime Minister of The Netherlands, once said about a Calvinist becomes true of anyone who has truly immersed himself in the knowledge of God. He wrote,

> He only is the real Calvinist, and may raise the Calvinistic banner, who in his own soul, personally, has been struck by the Majesty of the Almighty, and yielding to the overpowering might of his eternal Love, has dared to proclaim this majestic love, over against Satan, and the world, and the worldliness of his own heart, in the personal conviction of being chosen by God Himself, and therefore of having to thank Him and Him alone, for every grace everlasting.[5]

Yes, because of this knowledge, the Christian man lives everyday *coram Deo*—in the presence of God. God is everywhere. He is omnipresent. But not everyone lives with that consciousness. Yet, for the Christian man, it is this consciousness of God's presence that causes him to bow to His authority in real time. The authority of God is evidenced as he makes decisions even about the minutest details of life and living. He can say from the depth of his heart the words of the Westminster Catechism, "Man's chief end is to glorify God, and to enjoy him forever."[6] He believes it. He lives it.

Knowing God in Family Life

There is a lot that can be said here but let us restrict ourselves to two areas.

First, knowing his God results in the redeemed man wanting to

---

5. Abraham Kuyper, *Calvinism: Six Lectures Delivered in the Theological Seminary at Princeton* (Fleming H. Revell, [1899]), 86.
6. Westminster Shorter Catechism 1, in *Westminster Confession of Faith* (Free Presbyterian Publications, 1994), 287.

ensure that his wife and children also grow in knowing this God in a saving and sanctifying way. We have already noted how the desire to know God drives the man to take his family with him to church for worship and to spend time with his family in family worship. Life in the home pauses regularly as the whole family is brought together around the Bible, not to worship it but with reverence to learn about the person and ways of God. The children can see from the father's devotion and respect that this God is real and must be worshipped. The father's burning desire is that his children may come to know this God that he loves and adores. He wants them to know him in a saving way. He prays in their hearing that it might be so.

Second, the Christian man will also seek to live out his faith in full view of his family. This is especially the case in times of trouble. Like Job, in the face of devastating loss, he will say, "Naked came I out of my mother's womb, and naked shall I return thither: the LORD gave, and the LORD hath taken away; blessed be the name of the LORD" (Job 1:21). His knowledge of God is with such deep roots that he cannot disown God because of immediate temporal trials. He responds as Job later responded to his wife, who had told him to curse God, "Thou speakest as one of the foolish women speaketh. What? Shall we receive good at the hand of God, and shall we not receive evil?" (2:10). God has put granite into his being that enables him to weather the storms of life, and his family notes this example while the storms last. It adds to their conviction that the God of their father is real. He is a refuge in times of trouble.

Knowing God in Professional Life

The result of knowing this God has ramifications in how the Christian man relates to his entire working life. Whereas the man of the world sees work as a necessary evil by which he seeks to earn a living and, at the most, make himself rich, the redeemed man sees work as worship. He worships God with his hands six days a week and then on the seventh he carries some of the fruit of his sweat to the house of God as he worships

God with the praise of his lips. In this way, he is a man who does all things to the glory of God (1 Cor. 10:31).

The Christian man sees his family and working life as a stewardship from God, according to the backdrop of Genesis 1:28, where we read, "God blessed them, and God said unto them, Be fruitful, and multiply, and replenish the earth, and subdue it: and have dominion over the fish of the sea, and over the fowl of the air, and over every living thing that moveth upon the earth." The godly man exerts himself with all the strength and giftings that God has given him to fill his time with fruitful labor. This combination of family and work is best expressed in the exhortation of Ecclesiastes,

> Live joyfully with the wife whom thou lovest all the days of the life of thy vanity, which he hath given thee under the sun, all the days of thy vanity: for that is thy portion in this life, and in thy labour which thou takest under the sun. Whatsoever thy hand findeth to do, do it with thy might; for there is no work, nor device, nor knowledge, nor wisdom, in the grave, whither thou goest. (Eccl. 9:9–10)

Knowing God in Church Life

The fullest expression of the fruit of knowing his God is seen in the redeemed man's life of worship in the context of the church. We have already seen that such a man will want to take his wife and children with him to the place of worship. We have also seen that he will want to take some of the fruit of his labors with him to give to the Lord and views all his work as an act of worship. We must go further.

The Christian man prepares his soul for worship long before leaving home to go to church. Like the Puritans, he considers the Lord's Day as "the market day for the soul."[7] It is a day of mercy given by God to replenish the soul with grace for the week ahead. The profitability of the day will

---

7. See James T. Dennison, *The Market Day of the Soul: The Puritan Doctrine of the Sabbath in England* (Reformation Heritage Books, 2008).

depend on the right frame of mind and heart. So, he gathers his thoughts together around the theme of worship by meditating on the appropriate texts of Scripture, and especially the psalms that speak of God and His worship. He does so either on the previous evening or early in the morning on the Lord's Day itself. He expects Jesus's promise to be fulfilled that "where two or three are gathered together in my name, there am I in the midst of them" (Matt. 18:20). So, as important as fellowship with other believers may be, the Christian man looks forward to meeting with God during the time of worship in a way that he does not do so elsewhere.

The Christian man is also aware that he must be careful to meditate upon the word that was taught and preached so that it is not lost in the hustle and bustle of life. As in the parable of our Lord that we often call the Parable of the Sower, if one is not careful, the devil will steal the word from the heart, or it will be lost through temptations and the cares and riches and pleasures of this world. He knows if he is to profit from the word, he must have an honest and good heart that keeps the word that was preached and taught (Luke 8:4-15). It is this commitment to meditation that makes him "chew the cud" and profit the most from the word. His walk with God receives a boost each Lord's Day because of this.

During the Puritan era in New England, someone stated,

> There is one article of piety to be recommended unto us all; and it is an article which all piety does exceeding turn upon, that is the sanctification of the Lord's Day. Some very judicious persons have observed, that as "they sanctify the Lord's Day, remissly or carefully, just so their affairs usually prospered all the ensuing week." Sirs, you cannot more consult the prosperity of the town, in all its affairs, than by endeavouring that the Lord's Day may be exemplarily sanctified.[8]

---

8. Cotton Mather, *The Great Works of Christ in America* (Banner of Truth, 1979), 1:101.

The Redeemed Man Longs to Meet His God in Glory

Finally, the Christian man realizes that this life is temporal and must soon come to an end. This thought does not fill him with fear and despondency. Rather, it fills him with joy because he looks forward to meeting with his God, the God with whom he has walked since the day of his conversion. Like the apostle Paul, he says, "For I am now ready to be offered, and the time of my departure is at hand. I have fought a good fight, I have finished my course, I have kept the faith: Henceforth there is laid up for me a crown of righteousness, which the Lord, the righteous judge, shall give me at that day: and not to me only, but unto all them also that love his appearing" (2 Tim. 4:6–8).

Yet, the greatest joy is not the crown of righteousness that this man will receive. The redeemed man longs to finally meet with God forever, especially after the resurrection when his soul is reunited with his body. The apostle Paul spoke of this as the day of final comfort for the people of God. It will be the day when all our aspirations will be finally satisfied. He wrote,

> For the Lord himself shall descend from heaven with a shout, with the voice of the archangel, and with the trump of God: and the dead in Christ shall rise first: then we which are alive and remain shall be caught up together with them in the clouds, to meet the Lord in the air: and so shall we ever be with the Lord. Wherefore comfort one another with these words. (1 Thess. 4:16–18)

"So shall we ever be with the Lord." The redeemed man hears those words and says, "Amen. Even so, come, Lord Jesus" (Rev. 22:20).

CHAPTER THREE

The Redeemed Man Committed to God's Word

Paul M. Smalley

JOSHUA IS A MODEL of strong and godly manhood. But his life began in sorrow. Joshua, the son of Nun, grew up in bondage as a slave in Egypt. As a child, he watched his fellow Israelites labor under the whip of their taskmasters while groaning to the God of Abraham. Perhaps he felt the whip himself. Life in Egypt was bitter for the people of God.

Then, Moses came, proclaiming the word of the Lord. Through Moses, God sent astonishing plagues until Pharoah let the people go. Joshua's dreams came true when he walked out of Egypt as a free man. He passed through the Red Sea on dry ground with the water like a wall on either side. He saw the same water crash down on the pursuing chariots of Egypt. Then, he followed Moses to Mount Sinai and through the wilderness, experiencing God's majestic presence and miraculous provision. For forty years, Joshua served as the assistant to Moses in the wilderness (Ex. 24:13). Matthew Henry commented that Joshua "was trained up in subjection and under command. Those are fittest to rule that have learnt to obey."[1] Then,

---

1. Matthew Henry, *Matthew Henry's Commentary on the Whole Bible* (Hendrickson, 1994), 290.

Moses died. Israel stood poised to enter the Promised Land, and God had chosen Joshua to lead them forward.

We see in Joshua an example of the kind of man that Christ uses to lead people. You don't need to be a preacher for God to use you for His glory. Joshua was not a preacher or minister by vocation but a political and military leader. Yet he was a faithful servant of God, and the Lord used him to influence others. The life of Joshua foreshadowed Jesus, the greater Joshua, who obeyed God's will as the perfect Servant-King and now reigns as the supreme King. The Lord Jesus is with His people to lead them into their eternal inheritance through men like Joshua.

As men redeemed by Christ, we can learn potent lessons from the life of Joshua about the courage of a man committed to God's Word. When the Lord commissioned Joshua, He repeatedly commanded him to be strong and courageous (Josh. 1:6–9). We find in God's calling on Joshua four practical directions on how to be courageously committed to His Word. Let us consider each one in light of Joshua's example.

Strength from God's Faithfulness

The Lord said to Joshua, "Be strong and of a good courage: for unto this people shalt thou divide for an inheritance the land, which I sware unto their fathers to give them" (Josh. 1:6). God's call to courage revolves around the oath that He swore to Abraham, Isaac, and Jacob (Gen. 22:16; 26:3; 50:24). It is impossible for God to lie, and doubly impossible for Him to break His oath (Heb. 6:13–18). Therefore, we find courage by standing on God's faithfulness. John Calvin said, "There can be no courage in men, unless God supports them by his word."[2]

We need courage because sometimes obeying God requires us to do things that look foolish. We are exposed to mockery and may struggle

---

2. John Calvin, *Commentaries* (Baker, 2003), on Zech. 8:9–11.

with fear and shame because of God's Word. Consider the battle of Jericho. The city of Jericho was one of the fortified cities of Canaan that seemed invincible to the spies Moses sent into the land (Num. 13:28; Deut. 1:28; 9:1). Joshua had insisted that Israel could conquer the walled cities with God's help (Num. 14:6–9). But now Israel faced those walls, which might have risen more than twenty feet above the ground.[3] A besieging army might wait several years to starve out a city, for a frontal assault could result in a horrendous loss of life as defenders showered the attackers with deadly arrows, javelins, and stones.[4]

What brilliant tactic would Joshua use to penetrate the city? The Lord told Joshua to march his soldiers around Jericho while the priests blew trumpets, repeating this for six days. On the seventh day, they were to march around the city seven times and shout, and then, God promised, the city walls would fall down. To human reasoning, this must have seemed ridiculous. Walls do not collapse by the power of musical instruments and human voices. Imagine the soldiers looking at Joshua as they marched out on day one, two, three—six times. Did he know what he was doing? But Joshua trusted in God's covenantal faithfulness and obeyed His commands, and on the seventh day God gave the promised victory (Joshua 6). The lesson: trust in God's faithfulness and He will win the victory by His power—not ours.

Godly men have the strength to remain faithful and to lead others in

---

3. Archaeological excavations at the probable site of ancient Jericho (Tell es-Sultan) have discovered a stone revertment wall (a wall retaining an embankment) about fifteen feet high, at the base of which is a pile of bricks that appear to be the remains of an upper parapet wall of perhaps another twelve feet in height. Bryant G. Wood, "Did the Israelites Conquer Jericho?," *Biblical Archaeology Review* 16, no. 2 (March/April 1990): 44–58. Wood argued that the city enclosed by those walls, which shows evidence of widespread burning and destruction, was conquered by invaders circa 1400 BC. On the dating of the archaeological evidence, see David M. Howard, Jr., *Joshua*, New American Commentary (Broadman & Holman, 1998), 177–78.

4. Boyd Seevers, *Warfare in the Old Testament* (Kregel Publications, 2013), 137.

faithfulness because they are convinced that God is faithful. As Joshua said at the end of his life, not one of God's words has ever failed (Josh. 23:14). William Gurnall said, "What more powerful consideration can be thought on to make us true to God, than the faithfulness and truth of God to us?"[5] A man committed to the Word leans on God's faithfulness, and thus, uses the means that He ordains.

Obedience to God's Law

The Lord said to Joshua, "Only be thou strong and very courageous, that thou mayest observe to do according to all the law, which Moses my servant commanded thee: turn not from it to the right hand or to the left, that thou mayest prosper whithersoever thou goest" (Josh. 1:7). The heart and soul of Joshua's calling can be summed up in a single word: *obedience*. Joshua's work required a great deal of skill in the arts of leadership and war, but God would measure his success by the standard of his obedience to the law of God.

The Lord had revealed the core principles of that law on Mount Sinai in the Ten Commandments (Ex. 20:1–17), repeated by Moses in his final speeches to Israel (Deut. 5:6–21). Remarkably, the main qualifications Joshua needed to prosper as a leader were that he worshiped no deity but the Lord, rejected using images of divine beings, honored God's name, kept the Sabbath holy, honored his father and mother, did not destroy human life without authorization from God, remained sexually faithful to his wife, and did not steal, lie, or covet. Moses summed up the obligations of this law as requiring each of us to "love the LORD thy God with all thine heart, and with all thy soul, and with all thy might" (Deut. 6:5). Joshua took the requirements of God's moral law very seriously and urged Israel to do the same (Josh. 23:6, 11).

5. William Gurnall, *The Christian in Complete Armour*, 2 vols. in 1 (Banner of Truth, 1964), 1:374.

Furthermore, Joshua obeyed the ordinances of the old covenant. In obedience to God, Joshua had all the males in Israel circumcised (Josh. 5:2, 8)—a painful procedure, especially for adult men (Gen. 34:24–25). Israel then kept the Passover in remembrance of the exodus (v. 10). Similarly, godly men today are committed not only to keeping the moral law of God but also to observing the ordinances of the new covenant, which are baptism and the Lord's Supper.

God called Joshua to careful and consistent obedience to the law, saying, "Turn not from it to the right hand or to the left" (Josh. 1:7). Thomas Brooks said, "He who obeys sincerely endeavours to obey thoroughly."[6] The obedience of Joshua, while not perfect, was comprehensive and complete (11:15). In this, he is a model for all believers, who should make it a matter of first principle to obey God in every area of life. How this world needs men who determine that, regardless of the consequences, they will obey all God's commandments!

Are you a man who loves God's law and is careful to keep His commandments? Do you pray with your whole heart that God would give you the grace to keep his precepts diligently? A man who is committed to the Holy Scriptures is obedient to laws and statutes of the Lord.

Meditation on God's Word

The Lord next commanded Joshua, "This book of the law shall not depart out of thy mouth; but thou shalt meditate therein day and night, that thou mayest observe to do according to all that is written therein: for then thou shalt make thy way prosperous, and then thou shalt have good success" (Josh. 1:8). Someone might object that this is fitting advice for a gospel minister but not for a military commander. However, meditation is not just for theologians but for everyone who desires God's blessing (Ps.

---

6. Thomas Brooks, *Paradise Opened*, in *The Complete Works of Thomas Brooks* (James Nisbet and Co., 1866–1867), 5:328.

1:1–3). Though Joshua's responsibilities as Israel's commanding officer were enough to keep ten men busy, he had to make it a top priority to meditate daily on the Word of God.[7] Meditation, as the words "thy mouth" suggest, has to do with repeating God's Word to ourselves for the sake of deepening understanding, stirring affection, and motivating action. Biblical meditation is not emptying your mind but filling it with the Holy Scriptures to know and experience the living God.[8] Dale Ralph Davis said, "Constant, careful absorbing of the word of God leads to obedience to it. Lack of study results in lack of obedience."[9]

Joshua understood well that faith and obedience begin with knowledge of God's Word. Thus, in obedience to Moses' instruction, Joshua gathered Israel, had God's law written on a stone altar at Mount Ebal, "and afterward he read all the words of the law, the blessings and cursings, according to all that is written in the book of the law" to the men, women, children, and foreigners with them (Josh. 8:30–35). He later exhorted some of the tribes to give careful attention to God's law (22:5), repeating almost word-for-word what Moses had said to Israel (Deut. 10:12; cf. 11:22). At the end of his life, Joshua recited to Israel its history beginning with Terah, the father of Abraham (Josh. 24:1–14; cf. Gen. 11:27). Thus, Joshua is a model of making the whole Bible the object of our study and prayerful meditation.

Furthermore, we should meditate on God's Word together with our families. Joshua said, "Choose you this day whom ye will serve . . . but as for me and my house, we will serve the LORD" (Josh. 24:15). He had nurtured his family in domestic piety and expected them to continue it. Similarly, godly men edify their wives and raise up their children in the ways of the Lord by the regular practice of family worship. You do not need

---

7. Henry, *Commentary on the Whole Bible*, 290.
8. Howard, *Joshua*, 86.
9. Dale Ralph Davis, *Joshua: No Falling Words* (Christian Focus, 2000), 19.

a seminary education to read through the Bible with your wife and children, to pray together, and to sing a psalm or hymn to God each day. If you want to be a godly man, there is no substitute for setting apart times for your personal devotions and family worship—and exercising the self-control to use those times for biblical meditation instead of letting other things steal them away. This is crucial, for a man committed to the Word regularly meditates on the Holy Scriptures.

Courage Because of God's Presence

The Lord ended His call upon Joshua by saying, "Have not I commanded thee? Be strong and of a good courage; be not afraid, neither be thou dismayed: for the LORD thy God is with thee whithersoever thou goest [wherever you go]" (Josh. 1:9). Here God repeats what He said earlier in verse 5, "I will be with thee." The essence of godly courage is knowing that God is with us as we do the will of the Lord (Deut. 31:23).

Joshua's courage was tested when the Canaanites in the northern part of the land formed a coalition to destroy the Israelites. One can imagine the sober expressions that appeared on faces when the news arrived at Joshua's tent of a Canaanite army "even as the sand that is upon the sea shore in multitude, with horses and chariots very many" (Josh. 11:4). Davis notes that the text is designed to make us "begin to feel how overwhelming the enemy is, to sense . . . the almost hopeless situation Israel faces."[10] But the Lord told him, "Be not afraid," promising victory (v. 6). God was with them! That was enough for Joshua. The son of Nun did not wait for his foes to come to him but marched his soldiers to the enemy and attacked them (v. 7). "And the LORD gave them into the hand of Israel," who obliterated the enemy (v. 8).

The message of the book of Joshua is not that faithful Christians will

---

10. Davis, *Joshua*, 90.

always win every conflict they enter—whether it's a football game or a political election. The powers, pleasures, and prestige of this world are not our inheritance. Rather, the book of Joshua teaches us to take heart because God is with His people to bring them into His eternal kingdom.

Jesus Christ is the greater Joshua. God was with Christ (Acts 10:38). He died on the cross and rose from the dead so that our sins would be forgiven (vv. 39–40, 43). As a result, God is with believers in Christ, even dwelling in them by the Holy Spirit, to make sure that every one of them makes it home to their eternal inheritance. Satan and this world cannot stop God's people. By faith in Christ, we can become like Joshua and even like Jesus Himself, men of courageous faith and obedience.

Conclusion

Joshua's example calls us to be men courageously committed to God's Word. Christ is the greatest man of courage the world will ever know. Even as Jesus died on the God-forsaken cross, bearing the wrath of God against the sins of His elect, Christ still clung to the faithful, covenant-keeping God (Mark 15:34; Luke 23:46). Though Christ suffered for our sins, He Himself was pure of all sin (Heb. 4:15), like "a lamb without blemish and without spot" (1 Peter 1:19), flawless in His obedience to the Father's commands (Rom. 5:19; 2 Cor. 5:21). Christ's mind constantly meditated on the Holy Scriptures, from his youth to his severe temptations as an adult man (Luke 2:46–47; 4:1–13). Walking with God the Father, Jesus could confidently say, "He that sent me is with me: the Father hath not left me alone; for I do always those things that please him," and, "I have kept my Father's commandments, and abide in his love" (John 8:29; 15:10). Jesus waged a war infinitely more difficult than Joshua's calling and overcame by faith and obedience (Rev. 5:5, 9). And now He has entered His glory.

Jesus says to us, "Follow me. Follow me in the path of trusting the covenant Lord to keep His promises. Follow me in careful obedience to God's commandments. Follow me in daily meditation on the Word of God. Follow me in a life of courage because God promises to be with His people." Yes, Jesus says, "Follow me," promising to be with us Himself, our Immanuel, the God-man, the All-Sufficient One who will never leave us or forsake us! If we follow Him to the death, we will find ourselves part of a glorious kingdom that death cannot steal away.

When death comes to you, will you be found faithful? Joshua finished his course and departed from this world long ago. But the greater Joshua, Jesus Christ, rose from the dead and is alive today. He is the preeminent Servant-King. By His Spirit, Jesus Christ is able to make us like Him, placing the same commitment to His Word in our hearts that He put by His Spirit thousands of years ago in the heart of Joshua.

No one can follow Jesus fully while being carried along on "flow'ry beds of ease," as Isaac Watts wrote. No, the Christian must be "a soldier of the cross." This leads us to pray,

Sure I must fight, if I would reign:
Increase my courage, Lord;
I'll bear the toil, endure the pain,
Supported by thy word.[11]

And in the last day, when all our striving and suffering is done, Jesus Christ will say to each one who has followed Him in faith and obedience, "Well done, good and faithful servant," and will welcome him into the inheritance of eternal joy (Matt. 25:21).

Will you be a man committed to God's Word? Will you be a man of godly courage?

---

11. Isaac Watts, "Am I A Soldier of the Cross" (1724).

CHAPTER FOUR

The Redeemed Man Growing in Grace

Sinclair B. Ferguson

WHEN SCRIPTURE describes growth in grace it often uses horticultural imagery. The classic Old Testament example is that of the blessed man who is "like a tree planted by the rivers of water, that bringeth forth his fruit in his season; his leaf also shall not wither; and whatsoever he doeth shall prosper" (Ps. 1:3).

The "redeemed man" is called to be good soil in which the seed of the word of God takes root, grows, and bears fruit (Mark 4:8, 20); or like a fruit-bearing branch in the Vine that is pruned in order to bear even more fruit (John 15:2, 5)—the "fruit of the Spirit" (Gal. 5:22). In a word, the redeemed man "grows in grace."

But how does this growth, this transformation, take place? Instinctively we may think of Paul's teaching in Romans 12:1–2, or perhaps his more autobiographical account in Philippians 3:3–21, or his most comprehensive exposition in Colossians 3:1–17—all passages that dig into the roots of the process of spiritual maturation.

The wording of the title assigned for this chapter, however, alludes to the teaching of another apostle, namely Simon Peter. They are embedded in his last recorded words: "*grow in the grace* and knowledge of our Lord and Savior Jesus Christ" (2 Peter 3:18).

In fact, these words bookend Peter's whole letter. He begins by pointing to the foundation of salvation in the grace of God in Christ (and wishes it to be "multiplied"—2 Peter 1:2); he concludes by urging his readers to grow in that multiplied grace. Their salvation is all of grace; as his friend the apostle John writes: "of His fullness we have all received, and grace for grace" (John 1:16). The gospel is a story of grace from beginning to end. Therefore, spiritual growth is growth *in grace*.

Much of 2 Peter is devoted to warnings against false teachers and their teaching. Peter also addresses the positive elements of "our common salvation." He bookends his letter with two synonymous exhortations. For "grow in grace" at the end (2 Peter 3:18) is virtually the equivalent of "add to your faith" at the beginning (1:5). Furthermore, we are to be "giving all diligence" to the task (v. 5). The noun "diligence" comes from a favorite apostolic root meaning to hurry, to "take pains" (as our forefathers would have said), to be eager and enthusiastic.

It is important here to reflect on what the New Testament means by "grace." Our thinking here can sometimes (perhaps often) be unhelpfully influenced, even controlled, by a long tradition of misunderstanding in the Christian church.

In the late-medieval church, "grace" was seen virtually as a commodity, a kind of substance that was infused into the individual by means of the sacraments administered by the priest. The sixteenth-century Reformers, as it were, took the application of God's grace out of the hands of priesthood and sacraments and restored it to where it properly belongs, namely in the hands of the Holy Spirit.

But John Calvin, and the best Reformed theologians after him, did something else that has sometimes been forgotten. They understood *that there is no such "thing" as "grace"!* Grace is not an impersonal, mysterious commodity that is transferred to us. No! Grace is *Jesus Christ Himself*. But unfortunately, the old medieval mindset has not been entirely or finally exorcised from the evangelical mindset.

John Owen comes to our aid here. He points us to the apostolic benediction in 2 Corinthians 13:14 (words many of us thankfully still hear on a weekly basis): "Yea, Paul is so delighted with this, that he makes it his motto . . . 'The *grace* of our Lord Jesus Christ be with you all.' Yea, he makes these two, '*Grace be with you,*' and, '*The Lord Jesus be with you,*' to be equivalent expressions."[1]

Grace is Jesus Christ Himself. We cannot over-emphasize this. In essence, therefore, to grow in grace by adding to faith is nothing more or less than developing communion with the Lord Jesus Himself and experiencing and manifesting its effects on our character. The redeemed life is characterized by the atmosphere of a gracious lifestyle. Peter—a man's man surely—slowly came to discover what this is. It is, in Pauline terms, the fruit of the unfolding of the ultimate purpose of God for us, the good towards which all things in our lives work, the fruit of predestination, calling, justification and glorification—namely that we should be "conformed to the image of His Son, that He might be the firstborn among many brethren" (Rom. 8:28–30).

To grow in grace, to "add to your faith," means, therefore, becoming more like our Lord Jesus Christ.

How, then, does this take place?

There is a common pattern to the apostolic teaching here:

1. The Christian life is built on the solid *foundations* of God's grace in Christ.
2. This grace in Christ carries *implications* that lead to holiness.
3. These implications are strengthened by powerful *motivations*.
4. All of this leads to *exhortations* to grow in grace and knowledge of Christ.

---

1. John Owen, *Communion with God the Father, Son, and Holy Ghost*, in *The Works of John Owen*, ed. William Goold (1850–1853; repr., Banner of Truth, 1966–1968), 2:47.

This is exactly the pattern Peter follows in 2 Peter 1:2–11. He himself helps us respond to his exhortation to "grow in grace" by showing us what it means to be "adding to your faith."

Solid Foundations

The gospel has its own "grammar." In the language of grace, indicative statements—declarations and expositions of what God has done for us and what is true about us in Christ—are always foundational to imperative statements urging us to respond. Unless we build our spiritual house on the rock it will not be able to stand. So here, we grow in grace only if we have put down roots into the gracious Christ. Those foundations and roots are magnificently described here:

> His divine power has given us all things that pertain to life and godliness, through the knowledge of Him who called us by [or perhaps, to his] glory and virtue, by which have been given to us exceedingly great and precious promises, that through these you may be partakers of the divine nature,[2] having escaped the corruption that is in the world through lust. (2 Peter 1:3–4)

Here Peter outlines what is already true of us. God has powerfully called us into union with Christ. In that union we have been set apart for God once-for-all time, and set free from our natural bondage to sin. We have died to its dominion; it no longer reigns over us (Rom 6:6–8, 14; 1 Peter 2:24–25).

Not only so, but we have been anchored to the promises of God through which the restoration of the fractured image of God begins, so that we once again reflect the glory for which we were created but of

---

2. By "partakers of the divine nature" here is not meant that the Christian is deified but, as in Hebrews 12:10, we come to share in the qualities and characteristics and express in human form the "communicable" attributes of God, such as holiness.

which we have fallen short in sin (Rom. 3:23). Everything necessary to reproduce "godliness" in us has been provided for us in Christ. Long-term, progressive growth in grace is now a real possibility for us.[3] The "grace" that Peter tells us we have received in Christ (2 Peter 1:2) enables us to fulfil his closing exhortation to grow in grace (3:18)—that is, become more like Christ.

Our first priority, therefore, if we are to grow in grace, is to appropriate the multiplied grace of Christ in which we are to grow. Only when our roots are sunk deeply into the soil of the divine indicatives will we be able to grow in the joy of obedience to the rigorous and vigorous divine imperatives that follow.

The Logic of Implications

Notice Peter's logic: it is on the basis of these indicatives that the imperatives flow. Peter says, "But also for this very reason, giving all diligence, add to your faith virtue, to virtue knowledge, to knowledge self-control, to self-control perseverance, to perseverance godliness, to godliness brotherly kindness, and to brotherly kindness love" (2 Peter 1:5–7).

"For this very reason . . ." (2 Peter 1:5)—that is, on the basis of, and energized by divine power, promises, knowledge, and calling these certain implications follow. We need to be fed before we can grow. To live as though we belong to the new humanity we must first be "partakers of

---

3. The distinction between these two dimensions to sanctification is reflected in the *Westminster Confession of Faith* (13.1): "They who are effectually called and regenerated, having a new heart and a new spirit created in them, are further sanctified, really and personally, through the virtue of Christ's death and resurrection, by His Word and Spirit dwelling in them: the dominion of the whole body of sin is destroyed, and the several lusts thereof are more and more weakened and mortified, and they more and more quickened and strengthened in all saving graces, to the practice of true holiness, without which no man shall see the Lord." *Westminster Confession of Faith* (Free Presbyterian Publications, 1994), 61–62.

the divine nature" (v. 4). Clearly this is a quite different logic from false "higher life" conclusions that are sometimes drawn from the principle that salvation is by grace.

The present writer remembers an awkward occasion when as a very young guest minister seeking to distinguish Paul's teaching on union with Christ from mistaken "higher life views" quoted the following words, with the intention of exposing their unbiblical thinking:

> Buried with Christ, and raised with him too;
> What is there left for me to do?
> Simply to cease from struggling and strife,
> Simply to walk in newness of life.
> Glory be to God!

The response to these words was a hearty chorus of "Amen"! In sharp contrast, however, the truth is that it is only when we have been embraced by the grace of Christ that struggling and strife really begin in earnest against the world, the flesh, and the devil. Growing in grace, adding to faith, calls for specific and determined commitment.

But does the fact that we have to "add" to faith imply that faith itself is inadequate? Is this not a contradiction of the gospel?

The verb Peter uses, translated as "add" (*epichorēgeō*) is not drawn from the world of mathematics but from Greek drama. At the heart of the Greek verb is the root of our word "chorus." The verb originally meant to lead the chorus, or to supply whatever was necessary for it. That background suggests a helpful picture: growing in grace is essentially a matter of supplying what faith requires in order for us to grow in grace. And what faith in Christ requires is more knowledge of Christ.[4] This is what

---

4. The function of the chorus in a Greek drama was to respond to the central characters and to comment on the drama of the play. We might stretch the metaphor here by saying that being a Christian is a matter of responding in faith to Christ and living a life that is a running commentary on all that He has done for us.

the redeemed life is—reflecting on, interpreting, and responding to the grace of God expressed for us in Christ and in us through the Holy Spirit. Peter's thinking is therefore a diameter removed from the idea that we have to complete something that is lacking in the work of Christ. No. Nevertheless the work of Christ for us does need to come to completion in us. And this the Holy Spirit accomplishes as he enables us to "add" to our faith by working out Christ's salvation into every aspect of our lives. Paul's logic is similar: we are to work out our salvation because God has worked for us in Christ and is working in us by His Spirit (Phil. 2:5–13).

But we must not think that growth in grace is accomplished by adding together fifty percent of our activity to God's fifty percent, thus making up the whole. No, God is one hundred percent engaged, and so are we. Any alternative is false logic, not biblical logic. He is saving us; but that salvation means we are beginning to live out, willingly, freely, personally, and universally, a saved lifestyle.

There is a further implication of the fact that Peter is not speaking here mathematically. He suggests that we add to our faith seven characteristics: virtue, knowledge, self-control, perseverance, godliness, brotherly kindness, and love (2 Peter 1:5–7). But it would be a mistake to think that these are to be "added" one by one. For all these qualities are in fact reflections of the life and character of the Lord Jesus. They are *all* to be added because "adding" to faith is feeding faith on the whole Christ. Indeed, we cannot really add one of them without adding each of the others. They may not all manifest themselves in each of us in the same proportions or to the same degree. But like "the fruit of the Spirit"—an equivalent idea in Paul (Gal. 5:22–23)—they are a multi-dimensional yet single reality. They all grow, or are added, together in the ongoing process in which the Spirit transforms us into Jesus's likeness.

Limited space prohibits the examination of each of these Christ-like characteristics. But for purposes of illustration it may be worth reflecting on the one occupying the central position—perseverance.

Growing in perseverance is essential to developing all these qualities. Peter uses the compound word *hupomonē*—combining the ideas of "remaining" and "under." Picture the Olympic Games weightlifting competitions. Competitors lift enormous weights over their heads without their arms bending or knees buckling. They "remain underneath" the almost overwhelming load. This is a vivid picture of *hupomonē*. You can tell that these men have been well fed, well guided by their trainers, and have spent time in the gymnasium!

This is what the Christian life is like. The faith that perseveres is well nourished, spending time in the gymnasium with the Trainer. Strong faith is not produced by leisurely living! Its growth involves testing, opposition, challenge, and stress (Rom. 5:1–5). Jesus Himself "learned obedience by the things which He suffered" (Heb. 5:8). As it was with the Master, so it will be with His servants and friends.

Two further comments are in order here. The first is that there is nothing spectacular about what we are to "add." Nothing is said here about possessing great gifts, or a highly regarded public ministry. These may be the temporary calling of some, but what is to be added to faith is the universal responsibility of all believers. Its development always follows a similar pattern, and its consequences are eternal.

The second is that we should remind ourselves again that the qualities listed here are all reflections of the character of Jesus. Of course, it is important to grow in our understanding and appreciation of the *categories* in which He is rightly described. He is indeed consubstantial with the Father, possesses two natures united in one person, has experienced two states (humiliation and exaltation), exercises three offices (prophet, priest, and king), and accomplished propitiation, justification, reconciliation, and victory.

But these are categories to aid our understanding; we must never lose sight of His actual personal qualities. These are described here. And *that* is what we are to become. And the way we do so is by growing in our knowledge of Him and in intimacy with Him. The more we gaze upon Him, especially as He is revealed to us in the Gospels, the more this will take place. For it is when "with unveiled face, [we are] beholding as in a mirror the glory of the Lord [in His Word, we] are being transformed into the same image from glory to glory, just as by the Spirit of the Lord" (2 Cor. 3:18).

This is plenty of incentive for us to grow in grace. But Peter adds to it.

Powerful Motivations

We have noticed the logic inherent in Peter's thinking. It is "for this very reason" (2 Peter 1:5)—that is, God's lavish grace in Christ—that we are to add to our faith. But he now provides a double motivation to encourage us further.

First, "For if these things are yours and abound, *you* will be neither barren nor unfruitful in the knowledge of our Lord Jesus Christ" (2 Peter 1:8).

What an encouragement this is! And the fact that it is a promise that comes *via* Simon Peter, of all the apostles, itself means a great deal to us because we know that, like us, he failed badly. When he did so he became spiritually "barren." But divine power was made available to him and (even if not yet perfectly) he bore rich fruit. This letter is part of that fruit.

But even more significantly, these words are God's infallible word. They are not only Peter's promise to us; they are God's promise.

Second, there is another motivating word here: "For he who lacks these things is shortsighted, even to blindness, and has forgotten that he was cleansed from his old sins" (2 Peter 1:9).

And although expressed negatively, this warning not to forget is in fact an encouragement to remember. But to remember what?

The Christian must never forget to remember "that he was cleansed from his old sins." Some commentators take this to be a reference to baptism. Peter had spoken of that in his previous letter.[5] But perhaps he is looking back to Jesus's words on the evening of the crucifixion when He had washed Peter's feet. He should have remembered the significance of that cleansing. But he had forgotten it, fallen asleep in Gethsemane, reacted violently to Jesus's arrest, and eventually denied his Master three times. He had been shortsighted, looking only to the present. He had failed to "add" to his faith "virtue . . . knowledge . . . self-control . . . perseverance . . . godliness . . . brotherly kindness . . . love." Thankfully, he learned from his failure that night. And he wants to encourage us to learn from it too.

Closing Exhortations

In the light of this teaching (notice the "Therefore," 2 Peter 1:10), Peter exhorts us once again to concentrate: "Therefore, brethren, be even more diligent to make your call and election sure, for if you do these things you will never stumble; for so an entrance will be supplied to you abundantly into the everlasting kingdom of our Lord and Savior Jesus Christ" (vv. 10–11).

He is not urging us to accomplish something to guarantee our election by God, but to live in a way that expresses the reality of our salvation. For without some measure of obedience, some indications of God's grace in our lives, we will either become vainly presumptuous or begin to doubt that we are really Christians and were ever elect. Only when we want holiness is it clear that we also want heaven. What possesses us to think that we would be happy being transformed *then* into the likeness of Christ (1 John 3:2) if we do not want to be like Him *now*?

But what if we do desire to grow in grace and to add to our faith? Then,

---

5. 1 Peter 3:21. He likens baptism to the way Noah and his family "were saved through water" (v. 20). So for the Christian, baptism "now saves us" (v. 21)—not by water's natural effect of washing away dirt, but by its spiritual significance.

Peter assures us, "you will never stumble" (2 Peter 1:10) and you will have an abundant entrance into Christ's heavenly kingdom—yes, "abundant" (v. 11).

But surely Peter did "stumble"! He probably means this here in the sense of ultimate failing.[6] Yes, there may be times we feel we have stumbled with John Bunyan's pilgrim into the Slough of Despond. But Peter assures us, if we have been cleansed from our sin, justified by grace, are recipients of the glorious promises of God, and are seeking to add to our faith, we will never lose our grip on Christ. For we are being "kept by the power of God through faith" (1 Peter 1:5)—the very faith to which we are to "add" as we grow in grace.

This, then, is how the redeemed live, in the knowledge of the riches of God's grace in our Savior Jesus Christ on whom we moment by moment fix our gaze.

No wonder Peter wrote, "For this reason I will not be negligent to remind you . . . grow in the grace and knowledge of our Lord and Savior Jesus Christ" (2 Peter 1:12; 3:18).

---

6. In a similar way, in Rom. 11:11, Paul asks whether his kinsmen have stumbled so badly they have stumbled completely, and denies that this is the case.

PART 2

A Godly Man's Relationships with People

CHAPTER FIVE

The Redeemed Man Honoring His Parents

Terry Johnson

THERE ARE A NUMBER of cultural trends that mitigate against a high esteem of parents. We might include the usurping of parenting by so-called "experts," the professionalization of childcare, and the dominance of peer groups and pop culture. At the top of the list is the propensity to blame shift.

Far too often, social pathologies are explained or excused in terms of a domineering mother or an abusive or absentee father. Why is so-and-so a murderer? Why did he commit rape? Why did he rob a store? He had an overbearing mother who suppressed his personality, squashed his individuality, didn't allow him to express himself, and made him feel dependent, isolated, and frustrated until finally he exploded. Or perhaps it was his absentee father—he was the problem. He was never there. He starved his children emotionally. It has become all too typical for parents to be assigned the blame for whatever problem society may be experiencing. They are at fault for our pathologies, whatever they might be.

Abigail Shrier in *Bad Therapy* catalogs how the assumption that all children have experienced "trauma" during their childhood and youth and are in need of "therapy" has driven the "Social-Emotional" philosophy of education that places so-called "emotional health" above learning actual facts and skills.[1] "Repressed memories" of parental abuse are aggressively brought to the surface. The result is a generation where many people view themselves as victims of abuse, permanently damaged, without agency, and without the resilience that characterized previous generations. Most of the blame for the personal wreckage is placed on the doorstep of the caretakers of their childhood and youth—their parents.

In contrast to our propensity to blame our parents, God's law calls us take responsibility for our lives, and the fifth commandment in particular says we are responsible to honor our parents. What does that mean for us today, a time when parents and the elderly have never been more dishonored?

What the Fifth Commandment Says

The Lord commanded His people, "Honor your father and your mother, that your days may be long upon the land that the LORD your God is giving you" (Ex. 20:12).

To "honor" (Hebrew *kāvēd*, Greek *timaō*) means to "prize highly," to treat as important, to reverence, to glorify, even to "fear" (Lev. 19:3; Prov. 4:8; Mal. 1:6).[2] It is used of a proper response to God in worship (Ps. 86:9). "A son honors his father," is presented as a truism and as that, which of course, all sons do (Mal. 1:6). The opposite of "honor" is to "despise" and

---

1. Abigail Shrier, *Bad Therapy: Why the Kids Aren't Growing Up* (Sentinel, 2024).
2. Wright defines *kāvēd* as "to give weight to, regard as of high value and worth, to glorify." It is the opposite of "to make light of, regard as of no value, despise." Christopher J. H. Wright, *The Story of God Bible Commentary: Exodus* (Zondervan, 2021), 369n22. Motyer points to its use in connection with "what is important or substantial (Gen 13:2; Ezek 27:25), serious (Gen 18:20; Is 24:20, NIV, 'heavy'), dignified and possessing status (Job 14:21; 2 Sam 6:20)." He concludes, "The honoring of parents therefore gives them the important seriousness and dignity that is their right." J. A. Motyer, *The Message of Exodus: The Days of Our Pilgrimage*, The Bible Speaks Today: Old Testament (InterVarsity Press, 2005), 227n29.

"lightly esteem" or show "contempt," whether by word, tone of voice, or gesture (1 Sam. 2:36; Ezek. 22:7; Mal. 1:6;). "Children are to show honor to their parents," said the English Puritan Thomas Watson, "by a reverential-esteem of their persons," demonstrated "inwardly, by fear mixed with love," and "outwardly, both in word and gesture."[3] They are to be honored not because they are worthy of honor or have earned honor, but simply because of their role, status, or position as parents.

Then follows the promise: "that your days may be long upon the land" (Ex. 20:12). If applied *nationally,* it promises the secure possession of the land of Canaan over a long period of time. The implication is that well-ordered families are the key to a strong, healthy, well-ordered society.[4] If applied *individually*, it promises longevity. Long life is a blessing because life is a blessing. One's last days may be difficult, but that may be the case at any age. "Life itself is a blessing, and a longer life is a further blessing," said the Dutch theologian Wilhelmus à Brakel.[5] The Bible celebrates those who live to "a good old age" (Gen. 15:15).[6] The longer one lives, the more potential opportunities one has to contribute to the growth and success of Christ's gospel kingdom, no minor aspiration for God's servants.[7]

3. Thomas Watson, *The Ten Commandments* (Banner of Truth, 1965), 128. Gestures such as rising up, bowing, keeping silence are mentioned by James Durham, *A Practical Exposition of the Ten Commandments* (Reformation Heritage Books, 2017), 237.
4. According to Brevard Childs, "that your days may be long," "not only envisages a chronological extension of time, but points to the rich blessing of the society which is in harmony with the divine order." Further, "to this extent, the commandment does touch on the relation of authority and order between God and His representative within the life established by the commandment." *The Book of Exodus: A Critical, Theological Commentary* (Westminster Press, 1974), 419.
5. See Wilhelmus à Brakel, *The Christian's Reasonable Service*, trans. Bartel Elshout, ed. Joel R. Beeke (Reformation Heritage Books, 2012), 3:191; see also Robert L. Dabney, *Lectures in Systematic Theology* (Zondervan, 2015), 399–400.
6. See also Gen. 25:8; Judg. 8:32; 1 Chron. 29:28; Job 42:17.
7. See Thomas Boston, *Body of Divinity*, republished as *Commentary on the Shorter Catechism*, 2 vols. (1853; repr., Still Waters Revival Books, 1993), 2:257.

Deuteronomy's version of the Ten Commandments adds the phrase "that it may be well with you in the land which the LORD your God is giving you" (Deut. 5:16). This is a promise of prosperity.[8] Your crops will grow, your herd will multiply, and your family will be healthy; you will experience the rich and full blessings of God.[9] Where will their blessing be experienced? "In the land," the land of Canaan, "which the LORD your God is giving you." On the other hand, "Cursed is the one who treats his father or his mother with contempt" (27:16).[10]

Does the promise of longevity and prosperity have application outside of the Promised Land? Does it apply to us today? The apostle Paul universalizes the promise: "Children, obey your parents in the Lord, for this is right. 'Honor your father and mother,' which is the first commandment with promise: 'that it may be well with you and you may live long on the earth'" (Eph. 6:1–3).[11]

As B. B. Warfield has pointed it, the word "earth" universalizes the promise.[12] Even in the New Testament, there is a connection between righteousness and prosperity. Covenant keeping is rewarded. Jesus promises a hundredfold "now in this time, houses . . . and lands" (Mark

---

8. "Of course, long life is not a blessing without prosperity." John Frame, *The Doctrine of the Christian Life* (P&R, 2009), 575. See also J. Douma, *The Ten Commandments: Manual for the Christian Life* (P&R, 1996), 167.

9. On the blessings of prosperity see Deut. 5:32–6:3; 28:1–14; on the connection between obedience and "life" see Frame's list: Lev. 18:5; Deut. 4:1; 5:29; 6:3,18, 24; 10:13; 12:28; 30:15–20; 1 Kings 3:14; Neh. 9:29; Psalm 1; Isa. 55:3; Ezek. 18:9; 20:11; Amos 5:4–6; Mal. 3:8–12; Matt. 19:17.

10. Beyond this, the law from Sinai required, "Whoever curses his father of his mother shall be put to death" (Ex 21:17; see Matt. 15:4; Mark 7:10; Prov. 19:26; 20:20).

11. The Greek word *gē*, sometimes rendered "land," is rightly translated as "earth" in Eph. 6:3 in many English versions (such as the KJV and the NKJV). *Gē* is the prefix in our English word geology, the study (*logos*) of the earth (*gē*).

12. B. B. Warfield, "The Foundations of the Sabbath in the Word of God," in *Selected and Shorter Writings*, ed. John E. Meeter, 2 vols. (Presbyterian and Reformed, 1970), 1:333.

10:29–31; see also 1 Tim. 4:8; 1 Peter 3:8–12). "God takes special notice of your conduct towards your parents," Thomas Boston observes.[13] Though Christ is not promising to make the faithful wealthy in earthly goods, he is reminding us that our heavenly Father delights to give full provision when His people walk in obedience to His commands. A society in which people honor their parents is generally a society that flourishes. Gray hair, in such a world, is "a crown of glory... found in the way of righteousness" (Prov. 16:31; see also 17:6; 20:29). "We should not absolutize this promise" of the blessing of God, said J. Douma, "but neither should we downplay it."[14]

What the Fifth Commandment Requires

What positive actions and attitudes does the fifth commandment require of the redeemed? What, conversely, does it forbid?

Reverence

First, the Fifth Commandment requires that the redeemed man *reverence* his parents. The law of God says, "Every one of you shall revere his mother and his father, and keep My Sabbaths: I am the LORD your God" (Lev. 19:3).

Parents are to be honored and treated with reverence. The children of the devout woman will "*rise up* and call her blessed" (Prov. 31:28). When Joseph's shepherd father Jacob came into his presence, he was not embarrassed at his old humble father, though "every shepherd is an abomination to Egyptians" (Gen. 46:34), but "bowed down with his face to the earth" (48:12). When Solomon's mother came to speak to him when he was on his throne, he rose and "bowed down to her" (1 Kings 2:19). We are to honor their office (as parents), their achievements, and their sacrifices.

---

13. Boston, *Body of Divinity*, 222, citing Col. 3:20.
14. Douma, *Ten Commandments,* 167. The promise, he continues, "can never be understood in an absolute sense" (167).

Boston joined the obligation to reverence to that of fear. Parents are due their children's "singular love" and fear: "Their fear is to be squared with love and their love salted with fear."[15]

Respect

Second, closely associated with reverence, the redeemed man is to *respect* his parents. The redeemed are to cherish their wisdom, listen to their advice, and appreciate their labor. "My son, hear the instruction of your father, and do not forsake the law of your mother" (Prov. 1:8).[16]

"Children must let their parents speak first, answer respectfully, be quiet when parents are speaking to them, say 'thank you' when they receive something from them, and the like," said Douma.[17] "From those we respect, we expect to learn," observes John Frame, "and we are willing to change out of respect for their words." We show honor to our parents, he continues, "in our demeanor, our respectful way of listening, our willingness to hear teaching or rebuke, our gentle manner when we must exhort."[18]

Respect for parents carries over to our view of the elderly. Biblical religion values and honors the elderly. Young people are to "rise before the gray headed and honor the presence of an old man" (Lev 19:32; see Isa. 3:5). The righteous will "bear fruit in old age," a phrase that has become a daily prayer for many of those who are aging (Ps. 92:14). They have much to contribute. We are promised of the messianic kingdom, "*old men shall dream dreams*" (Joel 2:28; Acts 2:17; see Zech. 8:4). Though age does not guarantee wisdom—there are plenty of old fools (Job 32:9; Ps.

---

15. Boston, *Body of Divinity*, 2:220.
16. We are told the same repeatedly in Proverbs. See Prov. 2:1; 3:1, 11, 20; 4:1, 10, 20; 5:1; 6:1, 20; 7:1, 24 (essentially, all of chaps. 1–7); 13:1; 15:5; 19:27; 23:15–26; 27:11.
17. J. Douma, *Ten Commandments*, 172.
18. Frame, *Doctrine of the Christian Life*, 579.

119:100)—yet typically with age comes wisdom. The accumulated wisdom of the aged is to be respected.

As we move into the New Testament, Paul's charge to Timothy assumes this same measure of deference towards the elderly generally and to fathers specifically. "Do not rebuke an older man, but exhort him as a father, younger men as brothers" (1 Tim. 5:1). The Apostle assumes that respect is due the "older man" that is not due to "younger men." The latter can be treated as "brothers" whereas the older man is to be treated with the higher respect that is due to a father. We are obligated to honor our parents specifically and the elderly generally until they leave this world.

Gratitude

Third, the redeemed man owes his parents *gratitude* for all they have done. "Great is the pain, cost, and care, which parents must undergo for their children," said the Puritan layman Edward Leigh. "If love be in them, no pains, cost, or care will seem too much."[19] Our parents changed our diapers, fed, comforted, and held us. They stayed up with us when we were afraid or sick, applying damp cloths to our feverish foreheads, enduring sleepless nights. They taught us to walk, to use utensils, to tie our shoes, and to ride our bikes. They clothed us, housed us, and educated us. They fielded our questions, put up with our mischief, and endured our teen years. They laughed with us, were anxious for us, cried with us, and celebrated with us. They gave us life itself. "They were the instruments of their being," said Leigh.[20] Joel Beeke and Paul Smalley include in their list of those things for which we should be grateful the passing on to us of "the dignity of their name and a network of supportive relationships in their community."[21]

---

19. Edward Leigh, *A Systeme or Body of Divinity* (by L. M. for William Lee, 1654), 1114.
20. Leigh, *Body of Divinity*, 1112.
21. Joel R. Beeke and Paul R. Smalley, *Reformed Systematic Theology, Volume 3: Spirit and Salvation* (Crossway, 2021), 3:922.

Parents are not directed to "repay" their children, but children are to do so for parents (1 Tim. 5:4). "Repay" indicates something owed for all that parents have poured into their children in time and energy, and in various forms including financial, emotional, educational, and especially spiritual. "Children never can equal a parent's love," Watson said, "for parents are the instrument of life to their children, and children cannot be so to their parents."[22] This is a given among the classic authors. It is a "law of nature," said the English dissenter Thomas Ridgeley, that "under God, children derive their being from their parents; and they are obliged to honor them from a sense of gratitude for that love, tenderness, and compassion which they have shown to them."[23] The ledger of debt is overwhelmingly in the direction of what children owe parents. "We can never make a full recompense," says Boston, of our parents, "but, after all, must die in their debt." He complains of those "who look on what they do for their parents in a magnifying glass, while they are blind to what their parents have done for them."[24] Our debt to our parents should temper any disappointments arising from parental flaws and lead us to search for something for which we may be grateful, that "in everything" we may "give thanks" (1 Thess. 5:18), and lead us to "patiently bear with their weaknesses and infirmities."[25]

Honor as Adults

Fourth, the redeemed man is to *honor* his parents *when he becomes an adult*. "Once grown," Douglas Kelly insists, "adult children are still to be careful to honour their parents."[26] Indeed, according to C. J. H. Wright,

22. Watson, *The Ten Commandments*, 131.
23. Thomas Ridgeley, *A Body of Divinity*, republished as *Commentary on the Larger Catechism*, 2 vols. (1855; repr., Still Waters Revival Books, 1993), 2:368.
24. Boston, *Body of Divinity*, 2:222.
25. Beeke and Smalley, *Reformed Systematic Theology*, 3:923.
26. Douglas F. Kelly, *Systematic Theology, Volume 3: The Holy Spirit and the Church* (Christian Focus, 2021), 311.

honoring parents would "apply to several adult generations, not just children." Its "wider concern," he argues, "is with societal well-being and long-lasting economic viability."[27] The relationship between parents and children changes when they become adults and form independent households. Adult children no longer are required to obey their parents. Yet they are required to continue to honor them. What does that mean? Fundamentally it means that they continue to show them respect. "To honor is to *show deference toward parents*," Douma maintained.[28]

The Scriptures say, "Listen to your father who begot you, and do not despise your mother when she is old" (Prov. 23:22; see also 10:1; 15:20; 19:26; 20:20; 30:11, 17). Notice the setting: "when she is old." The proverb counters the temptation to despise elderly parents. Notice as well the emphasis upon the mother. Why? Because children—and young men specifically—tend to be embarrassed by being so closely mothered.

"As people are ready to break over the hedge where it is lowest," Boston warned, "so children are most apt to despise their mother." He attributes this to the principle that "familiarity breeds contempt," children being so much in the presence of and under the direction of their mothers when young.[29] Hence the warning to sons (which applies to daughters as well) "not to despise your mother when she is old," even if she continues to tell you to be careful, to put on your jacket, and not to drive too fast. Rather, let her children "rise up and call her blessed" (Prov. 31:28). Likewise, sons are not to disregard or curse their fathers. According to Childs, "lying at the heart of the original prohibition was a command which protected parents from being driven out of the home or abused after they could no longer work."[30]

---

27. Wright, *Exodus*, 369, citing Prov. 4:10; 13:1; 15:5; 19:18.
28. Douma, *The Ten Commandments*, 172.
29. Boston, *Body of Divinity*, 2:220; see also Douma, *Ten Commandments*, 162, citing Lev. 19:3 and Prov. 23:22.
30. Childs, *Exodus*, 382. See Ex. 21:15, 17; Lev. 20:9; Deut. 27:16.

We can be specific:
1. Adult children should not speak to or of their parents harshly, contemptuously, or rudely.
2. Fathers and mothers should be treated with honor and according to their distinctive roles, even in conflict. Honoring aging parents means "bearing with their infirmities," says Boston, "and covering them with the wings of love."[31]
3. Expectations should be minimal. Parents paid their children's bills for eighteen or twenty-five or maybe thirty years. Parents owe their children nothing. Children owe their parents everything. Whatever they do for adult children as adults and married, and for their children's children, is a matter of grace.

Support

Fifth, the redeemed man is to *support* his parents as they age. Abandonment and isolation ever have been the fear of the elderly. The expectation accompanying the birth of Obed to Boaz and Ruth was that he would be "a restorer of life and *a nourisher of your old age*" (Ruth 4:15). Children are to enrich the lives of their aging parents. They are to honor their aging parents with their love, their wealth, and their personal sacrifices. It may be costly to do so. It may be a nuisance, or interfere with plans, or prove exhausting, annoying, or exasperating. Yet this is what it means to honor parents.

Jesus criticizes the Pharisees for evading the responsibility financially to support their parents under the guise of "Corban"—that is, of devotion to God (Mark 7:9–13). Christ says, "You no longer let him do anything for his father or his mother" (v. 12). The expectation clearly is that to "honor" one's parents is to support them financially in their old age. Furthermore,

---

31. Boston, *Body of Divinity*, 2:221.

any care and support that we give to our parents should be motivated by love.

As the eldest son, Jesus ensured proper care of His widowed mother (John 19:26–27). What he had been responsible to do up to this point in His life, He transferred to "the disciple whom He loved," the apostle John. Again, the apostle Paul admonishes in the strongest language children and grandchildren concerning their responsibility to care for elderly parents and grandparents, to "repay their parents" for the sacrifices that they made on behalf of their children (1 Tim 5:4, 8). "Children sin," says Ridgeley, "by neglecting to maintain them if they need it, especially when they are aged." He continues: "By this conduct they appear to have no sense of gratitude for past favors, nor regard to that duty which nature obliges them to perform."[32] This support might include finances, housing, medical care, mental stimulation, and emotional support.[33]

Support includes the responsibility to protect them. We must guard parents physically, emotionally, spiritually, and especially care for their *reputations*. We must not indulge criticism or ridicule of our parents, but speak highly of them whenever possible (Eph. 4:29). "The duty of rendering honor continues throughout life," say Beeke and Smalley, "a duty that extends to one's father-in-law and mother-in-law."[34] It is evil to turn one's spouse against his or her own family. As we just noted, Jesus targets the dishonoring of parents as among the great hypocrisies of Pharisees and scribes, who for the sake of this tradition and self-interest fail to give parents the material assistance they deserve (Matt. 15:1–9; Mark 7:1–13).

Conclusion

The Old Testament warns of a time when adult children will be in conflict with parents, as well as their spouses (Mic. 7:6). Jesus echoes this passage

---

32. Ridgeley, *Body of Divinity*, 2:374.
33. Frame, *Doctrine of Christian Life*, 581.
34. Beeke and Smalley, *Reformed Systematic Theology*, 3:924.

and applies it to the impact of His mission (Matt. 10:34–35). This dishonoring of parents, Brakel said, "is an assault upon God, human society, and is contrary to nature—so that it is the most abominable of all abominations, even being repulsive in a natural sense."[35] Further, he insisted, "If there is a spark of natural love in you, you will be motivated to honor and obey them."[36]

It is vital that we provide a model for our children in our treatment of our parents how we wish to be treated when we grow old. The Bible commentator Alan Cole points out that "those who build a society in which old age has an honoured place may with confidence expect to enjoy that place themselves one day."[37]

---

35. Brakel, *The Christian's Reasonable Service*, 3:192.
36. Brakel, *The Christian's Reasonable Service*, 3:193.
37. Alan Cole, *Exodus: An Introduction and Commentary* (Inter-Varsity Press, 1973), 158.

CHAPTER 6

The Redeemed Man Living in Singleness

Curt Daniel

I WRITE THIS ESSAY as a lifelong Christian bachelor to my fellow single Christian brothers.[1] It is for Christians, not non-Christians; for men, not women. However, I write for all kinds of single Christian men: for the never married, the divorced, and the widowed.

Most men will marry at some time. The average age of marriage, thirty, is rising, and the rate is declining due to cohabitation ("living together"), divorce, homosexuality, and other factors. Half of all first marriages and more than half of second marriages end in divorce. Singleness is an issue that needs to be addressed biblically, wisely, and compassionately.

Loneliness

When God created the first man, He said, "It is not good that the man should be alone" (Gen. 2:18). Adam needed a wife to propagate the human race and care for the garden of Eden. He felt the natural desire for

---

1. The most in-depth scholarly study of Christian singleness is Barry Danylak, *Redeeming Singleness* (Crossway, 2010). An excellent booklet is Joel R. Beeke and Paul M. Smalley, *How Should I Live as a Single?* (Reformation Heritage Books, 2023).

a wife and was lonely even before he sinned. Loneliness is not a sin. Most single men are lonely and want to be married. They want to love and be loved. As Rachel (Gen. 30:1) and Hannah (1 Samuel 1) wept and prayed for a child, many men weep and beg God for a wife. The loneliness can be unbearable. They attend friends' weddings and rejoice with them, then go home to a lonely little apartment. Ecclesiastes 4:9–10 says, "Two are better than one.... Woe to him that is alone."

The loneliness increases as men pass through the stages of life, worrying that they will never marry and that no one will care for them in their old age. Sometimes, they are more concerned about their careers, and it catches up with them in middle age. They feel like orphans. Friends and relatives often ignore or misunderstand them and resemble Job's "friends." They rarely say, "You must be very lonely. I'm sorry," but instead, "You're too picky. You won't commit. You're too self-centered. It's your own fault you're not married," or conversely, "Be glad you're single and independent." Friends mean well but often are overzealous and unwise in trying to match us, even with obvious mismatches. Hopes rise and are dashed. Prospects are fewer and fewer. We hurt. Others may wonder if we're homosexual. Prolonged loneliness can lead to severe depression. Hope is vanishing as the decades pass. Most divorced and widowed men have children and grandchildren, but the never married have no one. There is a world of difference between being single at twenty-five and at fifty or older.

Nevertheless, the lonely Christian man has a friend in Jesus, who was also a lonely man. He was "a man of sorrows, and acquainted with grief" (Isa. 53:3). He sympathizes with the lonely Christian as no one else can. He cares (1 Peter 5:7). Brothers, take your tears to Jesus. Offer them to Him as a sacrifice of love and worship and say, "I still love you, Jesus." He stores up your tears in His bottle (Ps. 56:8), for they are precious to Him. When you go through the deep waters of loneliness, He will be with you (Isa. 43:2). The loneliness of being single can be a kind of martyrdom.

God will reward you a hundredfold for every tear. Jesus wept (John 11:35) and knows what it is like. Let your loneliness draw you close to the Good Shepherd.

Loneliness can be a thorn in the flesh (2 Cor. 12:7). A thorn is not a thorn unless it hurts. It can be the cross you are called to carry. Crosses have splinters and nails. Some men unwisely marry just to escape the loneliness or out of fear of being all alone in old age. Others become bitter against God. Some even think God broke a promise to give them a wife when it is presumption to believe a promise God did not make. A wife is a gift of grace, not an earned reward. Perhaps God has not given you a wife because He mercifully knows you are not ready and would ruin the marriage.

One may ask, "But doesn't Psalm 37:4 say, 'Delight thyself also in the Lord: and he shall give thee the desires of thine heart'?" Yes, but learn the lesson of Gethsemane. Christ prayed for the cup of suffering to pass, He wept and begged the Father, but His main prayer was "Not my will, but thine, be done" (Luke 22:42). That was His delight in the Lord. He was answered (Heb. 5:7). Imitate Jesus.

"God setteth the solitary in families" (Ps. 68:6). Single men and women are in the family of God and should actively be part of a local church. It helps. Also, remember the advice of Elisabeth Elliot, thrice married and twice widowed: "Turn your loneliness into solitude, and your solitude into prayer."[2]

The Gift of Singleness

God has bestowed on some Christians the gift of singleness. Jeremiah and several other prophets never married (Jer. 16:2). The apostle Paul

---

2. Elizabeth Elliot, *Loneliness* (Nashville: Oliver Nelson, 1988), 127. Note the subtitle: "It can be a wilderness. It can be a pathway to God."

was a lifelong bachelor.[3] Preachers like Augustine, Richard Sibbes, Isaac Watts, and J. Gresham Machen, and missionaries like David Brainerd, Amy Carmichael, and Mary Slessor never married. John Murray didn't marry until he retired at sixty-five. Nancy Leigh DeMoss was satisfied to serve God as a single woman until after she turned fifty and met and married Robert Wolgemuth. John Calvin was married only nine years before his wife and only child died. When an enemy said this was God's judgment for his sin, Calvin acknowledged God's providence in giving and taking away the child but replied, "I have myriads of children in the whole Christian world."[4]

Angels never marry (Matt. 22:30). They are all masculine: masculine personal pronouns are used for them, they have masculine names like Michael and Gabriel, and they always appear as men and not as women in the Bible. Masculinity is not just physical but about personality. Further, all three members of the blessed Trinity are masculine. The Holy Spirit is not a mother goddess, the wife of God the Father, or the mother of Jesus. The second person of the Trinity became a man and never married. He had the gift of singleness to the perfect degree.

Few Christian men seriously consider staying single to serve God better. Shortly after being saved at age twenty, I took 1 Corinthians 7 seriously. I was willing to serve God as a bachelor or a married man, whichever God chose. I did not take a vow of singleness. I have always desired a wife, but in His providence, the Lord has kept me as a single pastor. Young Christian men should read 1 Corinthians 7 and Matthew 19:8–12 repeatedly and commit themselves to whatever God wills. In 1 Corinthians 7, Paul clearly

---

3. Some Christians mistakenly think Paul had once been married and his wife either died or divorced him. First Corinthians 7 clearly teaches that Paul was not married. There is no evidence that he had ever been married.
4. "Dederat mihi Deus filiolum, abstulit: hoc quoque recenset inter proba liberis me carere. Atqui mihi filiorum sunt myriades in toto orbe Christiano." John Calvin, *Responsio ad Balduini convitia* (S.I., 1562), fol. D iv r. to D iv v. I am indebted to Karin Maag at the Meeter Center of Calvin University for this citation.

teaches there is a superiority to being single for some Christians (vv. 1, 7–9, 26, 38, 40), yet they should marry if they cannot resist sexual immorality (vv. 2, 9). Some should stay single; others should marry (vv. 20, 24, 27). It is not a sin to marry (vv. 2, 9), nor to stay single if that is God's will (v. 28). Yet Paul warns there will be "troubles" for them if they marry (vv. 28, 32–35), which may hinder their serving God. Single Christians often serve God better without the responsibilities of a wife and children (v. 34). Some Christians must not marry, such as those who have been unbiblically divorced (vv. 10–11; Matt. 5:32). God does not command all men to get married. Singleness is not a sin.

The single man has more time and finances, and can travel more. But God neither commands nor forbids a man to marry in order to serve Him, including full-time ministry as a pastor or missionary. Just as a married man may confess that he could never have served God so effectively without his wife, so others know they could not have served God so well if married. We need both married and unmarried ministers.

When a Christian knows his spiritual gift and uses it effectively, that is his ministry in which he serves God. Sadly, many Christians do not even know what their gift is, nor are they using it. The gift of singleness helps one serve God with other gifts. One less-appreciated area is the ministry of prayer, like single women in Scripture (Luke 2:37; 1 Tim. 5:5). They are prayer warriors like George Mueller and my late godly mother, who prayed an hour or more daily as a widow. Unfortunately, some single men are not serving God but themselves, their careers, and their hobbies. They misuse their time and finances. On the other hand, many godly couples serve God together, like Aquila and Priscilla (Acts 18:26), Jonathan and Sarah Edwards, and many others. Brothers, aim to be like them if you marry.

How can a man know he has this gift of singleness? First, pray. Next, study 1 Corinthians 7 and Matthew 19:12 and examples in Scripture and church history. If you are married, you do not have this gift. If single, you may have it temporarily or permanently. Do you desire to be married? If God has not provided a spouse for you for a protracted period, it may well be that He has given you this gift. But don't take a rash vow of singleness! Having the gift does not necessarily mean you will never desire a wife, though that is sometimes the case. Some with the gift still earnestly want to be married. Ask yourself, *Do I prefer to be married but am willing to stay single, or do I prefer to stay single to serve the Lord but am willing to marry if God wills?* (See Philippians 1:21–24 for a similar principle.) Sometimes, God says in His providence, "Marriage is one of the greatest gifts I can give My children. But it is not for you. I have something better for you that My married children often do not appreciate"—the opportunity to have deeper communion with Christ.

Communion with Christ

Just as afflictions are blessings in disguise that can draw us closer to Christ, so are the loneliness of singleness and the gift of being single. The single Christian man has more time and fewer hindrances to pursue this wonderful opportunity. Some have done so, such as the bachelor missionary David Brainerd. Some married couples have as well, such as Jonathan and Sarah Edwards. Edwards had a perceptive observation on Christ the unmarried man: "How greatly are we inclined to the other sex! Christ has a human nature as well as we, and has an inclination to love those that partake of the human [nature] as well as we. That inclination which is in us it turned to the other sex, in him is turned to the church, which is his spouse."[5] Jesus knew it was the Father's will for Him to stay unmarried, so His manly desire is directed to His bride, the church. Similarly, in His providence, God may show His will that a Christian man who desires a

---

5. Jonathan Edwards, *Miscellany* 189, in *The Works of Jonathan Edwards, Volume 13, The "Miscellanies": (Entry Nos. a–z, aa–zz, 1–500)*, ed. Thomas A. Schafer (Yale University Press, 1994), 332.

wife not have a wife. God then calls on him to redirect that natural desire to a higher spiritual desire fulfilled in our love for Christ, our heavenly Husband.

Edwards also said, "We should receive Christ as the spouse and husband of our souls, passing by all others, choosing him above all, in that near relation to be our nearest friend and companion, to the exclusion of all others."[6] In conversion, we pledge, "*I do* (receive Christ)," and "*I will* (love, honor, and obey Him)." Scripture often speaks of our relation to Christ as bride to Him as husband (Psalm 45; Song of Solomon; Isa. 54:5; 62:5; 2 Cor. 11:2; Eph. 5:25–33; Rev. 19:9, 21:2; 22:17).[7] Edwards observed, "Heaven and earth were created that the Son of God might be complete in a spouse."[8] We were engaged in the eternal covenant of redemption, betrothed in the covenant of grace in conversion, and will be married to Him at the second coming.

The essence of marriage is mutual love between husband and wife. So also with Christ and His bride. He initiates love; we respond with love (1 John 4:19). The conduit of this love is the Holy Spirit (Rom. 5:5), who is the *arrabon* engagement ring (Eph. 1:14). This is an even greater blessing than justification or adoption. We are to commune with Him in our hearts (Ps. 4:4). Too few Christians appreciate this marvelous blessing. Some even mock it. A preacher friend once said, "Yeah, I know about that spiritual romance thing." Nevertheless, others throughout the ages have treasured it. Samuel Rutherford had an astonishingly intimate love

---

6. Jonathan Edwards, unpublished sermon #318, on Rev. 3:20, in *The Works of Jonathan Edwards Online, Volume 49, Sermons, Series II, 1734* (New Have, Conn.: The Jonathan Edwards Center at Yale University, n.d.), L. 7r, http://edwards.yale.edu.
7. I especially recommend Edward Pearse, *The Best Match* (Soli Deo Gloria, 2014) and Thomas Vincent, *The True Christian's Love to the Unseen Christ* (Soli Deo Gloria, 2015).
8. Edwards, *Works*, 13:271–72.

for Christ. John Owen, John Gill, Charles Spurgeon, and many others preached on it from the Song of Solomon.

Instead of the joy of sexual intimacy with a wife, a single Christian man can enjoy true spiritual ecstasy with Christ, our heavenly spouse. Edwards describes it in his *Personal Narrative*.[9] His wife, Sarah, also experienced it as being "in love with Christ."[10] This wonderful experience is described in 1 Peter 1:8: "Whom having not seen, ye love; in whom, though now ye see him not, yet believing, ye rejoice with joy unspeakable and full of glory." Human marriage is temporary; spiritual marriage is eternal. The joys of spiritual intimacy with Christ far exceed those of human marriage. They are heaven on earth. It is the best antidote to the loneliness of being unmarried. Christ longs to have this communion with us now and especially at the heavenly wedding at the second coming. Do we long for it too?

Practical Advice

I close this chapter with some practical points on living as a single Christian man.

General Principles

1. Learn what the Bible says about marriage, divorce, separation, remarriage, and singleness, especially in 1 Corinthians 7.
2. Don't be obsessed with getting married. Serve God, pray, seek, wait.
3. Are you willing to marry or stay single as the Lord wills?

---

9. Jonathan Edwards, *Personal Narrative*, in *The Works of Jonathan Edwards, Volume 16, Letters and Personal Writings*, ed. George S. Claghorn (Yale University Press, 1998), 790–804, especially 800–804.

10. Jennifer Adams, ed., *In Love with Christ: The Narrative of Sarah Edwards* (Corner Pillar, 2010). See also Sharon James, *Sarah Edwards: Delighting in God* (10Publishing, 2023).

4. Don't waste your singleness. Serve God.
5. Learn to apologize and forgive.
6. Pray for the woman God will bring to you. She is praying for you.
7. Don't give up hope. God may yet provide a wife for you in His time.
8. Learn the true meaning of love from Ephesians 5, 1 John 4, and 1 Corinthians 13. Imitate Christ's love. Know the difference between love and lust.
9. Develop good spiritual disciplines and spiritual fruit while single, which may become more difficult when married.
10. Above all, live to the glory of God, whether single or married.

Relating to Women

1. Don't covet another man's wife (Ex. 20:17).
2. Be a true Christian gentleman, neither wimpy nor macho. Be truly manly—a real lady wants a real man. Be polite, kind, patient, and strong.
3. Never use violence with a woman. Control your temper. Don't marry a woman with an anger problem or who nags you (Prov. 21:19).
4. Never insult or lie to a woman. Know how to compliment her on her spiritual virtues more than her physical appearance (1 Peter 3:3–5). Yet, know how to "sweet talk" your wife. See the Song of Solomon.
5. Treat every Christian woman as a sister and older ones as mothers (1 Tim. 5:2).
6. Watch your eyes, speech, and hands when you are with a woman.
7. Never be alone with a woman in your bedroom or hers. Avoid a woman who is chasing you, especially for sex. Remember Joseph.

Developing a Right Perspective on Finding a Spouse

1. Know what the Bible says to look for in a godly wife (Proverbs 31) and what a godly husband should be (Eph. 5:25–33). Ignore what the world says.
2. Don't marry an unbeliever. If you are an unbeliever, don't marry a Christian, or you will lead her to disobey God.
3. Don't set unrealistic standards of what you are looking for in a wife. Don't marry for beauty alone, for it will fade (Prov. 31:30), yet she should be beautiful in your eyes. There should be that indefinable romantic fire.
4. Remarriage after divorce or the death of a spouse is not the same as being married for the first time. Wait at least a year before dating again. Unpacking the emotional baggage and healing the wounds isn't easy. Beware of the rebound effect. Don't marry a woman who was unbiblically divorced (Matt. 5:32).
5. Do not marry only for sex or to have children. The inability to have either is not an impediment to getting married.
6. Don't overreact to being hurt in the past by staying away from marriage.

Dating and Courtship

1. Always put Christ first in your singleness, dating, courting, and marriage.
2. Pray and read the Bible together when dating. Talk about spiritual things and experiences.
3. See her in a variety of situations, not just in church.
4. Observe how she respects her parents.
5. Enjoy legitimate pastimes together, but avoid certain kinds of entertainment (ungodly television, movies, and music). Learn to laugh together.

6. Don't keep a lady waiting and wondering if you will ask her out again.
7. Don't say, "I love you," unless you are nearly ready to say, "Will you marry me?"
8. When engaged, spend more time and effort preparing for a marriage that will last a lifetime than a wedding that will last an hour. Don't elope.
9. Avoid all sexual sins. Most if not all discussion of sexual matters should wait until marriage. Is she modest? Are you?
10. Be on the same page doctrinally, spiritually, and practically.
11. Avoid bossy "feminists." Seek a woman who has "a meek and quiet spirit" (1 Peter 3:4) and is willing to submit to your loving leadership (1 Tim. 2:11–12; Eph. 5:22–24).
12. A woman who is immoral before marriage may well be the same after marriage. The same holds true for you, so prayerfully submit your sexual desires to the Lord and ask Him for the grace to control them before and after marriage.
13. When engaged in Christian dating or courting, gradually and kindly take the lead; do not force your will on her.
14. What do your parents and closest Christian brethren think of the one you are dating? If they have serious reservations, back off and rethink things. Better to break an unwise engagement than a marriage. Don't marry against the wishes of your parents or hers.
15. Use the Golden Rule when politely and gently breaking off a relationship. Do to her how you would want her to do to you.

Considering Marriage to a Particular Woman

1. Are you financially able to support a wife? Are both of you free of major debt?
2. When deciding whether to propose, don't resort to dreams,

visions, voices, omens, "fleeces," signs, or "personal prophecies" that say to marry a specific person.
3. Are you each other's best friend? Do you like and love each other?
4. Be willing to give up much of your independence when you get married.
5. Don't give away your heart too quickly. But when getting married, do it wholeheartedly and without reservation.
6. "Cool" people make poor spouses. Aim for godliness, not worldliness.
7. Do you agree on what constitutes biblical worship? And the biblical practice of the sacraments?
8. Before getting married, think deeply about what "for better, for worse, in sickness and in health" means. Consider your wedding vows seriously before taking them. Would you still love her if she became disabled or disfigured?
9. True love in marriage isn't best shown on Valentine's Day with flowers and candles but when you tenderly and sacrificially care for her when she is ill or elderly.
10. Are you willing to die for her? Protect her from other men?
11. Are you able to teach her the Bible?
12. Don't court a woman too long without proposing marriage—fish or cut bait.

CHAPTER SEVEN

The Redeemed Man Loving His Wife

Joel R. Beeke

ONE OF MY FAVORITE stories is the account of the pastor who visited a newly-married parishioner who was deeply in love with his wife.[1] The pastor said to the young man, "Brother, I am concerned that you love your wife too much; I think you may be making an idol of her." The young man became quite upset. He went home in confusion and said to himself, "I love God above all, but should I not love my wife with passion?" He then thought to himself, "I must be a good Berean and test what my pastor says by the Scriptures." So, he began searching the Bible until he came

---

1. I am grateful to Fraser Jones for his work in adapting this chapter from various addresses, chapters, and books I have written on marriage, including Joel R. Beeke, *Friends and Lovers: Cultivating Companionship and Intimacy in Marriage* (Cruciform Press, 2012); *How to Lead your Family* (Reformation Heritage Books, 2025); "The Puritan Marriage," in *Living for God's Glory: An Introduction to Calvinism* (Reformation Trust, 2008), 317–32; Joel R. Beeke and Paul M. Smalley, "Puritans on Marital Love," *Puritan Reformed Journal* 12, no. 1 (January 2020): 155–67; Joel R. Beeke, "The Puritans on Marriage and Child-Rearing: The Teaching of William Gouge," in *Growing in Two Families: Living God's Way in Home and at Church*, ed. Joel R. Beeke and Paul M. Smalley (Reformation Heritage Books, 2025), 17-32. Used with permission from Cruciform Press and Reformation Trust.

across this verse from Ephesians: "Husbands, love your wives, even as Christ also loved the church, and gave himself for it" (5:25). The young man thought to himself, "I don't give my whole self to my wife the way that Christ gave His whole self to the church. The problem is not that I'm loving my wife *too much*; I do not love her *enough*!" So, he went back to his pastor and said, "Pastor, look at this passage. The Lord calls me to love my wife like Christ—and that is a standard I could never meet! I have not loved her absolutely nor laid down my life for her as Christ has for the church." The pastor looked at the text and said, "You're right, brother; go home and keep showering your wife with love."

As the Puritan William Gouge observed, all the duties of a husband are comprised under just one word—*love*.[2] In utter dependence on the Holy Spirit, the redeemed man must strive to love his wife with love that is spiritual, superlative, sacrificial, sympathetic, serving, sanctifying, sharing, sexual, and stable.

The Spiritual Love of the Redeemed Man

The redeemed man strives to love his wife in a *spiritual* way. The deepest fellowship is spiritual fellowship, in which you share your life with your wife in the presence of the living God (1 John 1:3). As the Puritan William Whately observed, love that is built on physical appearance, wealth, or talents instead of mutual communion with Christ rests on a "sandy" foundation that is easily "blown down by some storm."[3] Whately went on to say, "Spiritual love, that looks upon God, rests upon his will, yields to his commandments, and resolves to obey it, cannot change itself, because the cause thereof is unchangeable."[4] Mutually enjoying the means of grace is

---

2. William Gouge, *Of Domesticall Duties* (London, 1622), 350. Throughout this chapter, spelling and punctuation from archaic quotations have been modernized.
3. William Whately, *A Bride-Bush, or A Wedding Sermon* (London, 1617), 7.
4. Whately, *A Bride-Bush, or A Wedding Sermon*, 7.

one of the sweetest ways in which a husband and wife can experience their unity as two who have become one physically, emotionally, and spiritually (Gen. 2:24; Eph. 5:31).

Dear Christian husband, first, *love your wife spiritually by leading her in the means of grace*. Read the Scriptures with her, sing psalms with her, observe the Sabbath with her, worship God with her, discuss sermons with her, initiate spiritual conversation with her, fellowship with her, and celebrate the sacraments with her. If you stop conversing with her about spiritual matters—the most intimate matters in life and in death—your marriage will gradually decay; but if you keep the flame of spiritual vitality alive, God will be glorified, and your marriage will be strengthened. Share your spiritual experiences with your wife. Share with her your spiritual concerns, frustrations and triumphs, pilgrimage and progress. Discuss how the Lord is working in your life by His Word and Spirit.

Second, *love your wife spiritually by leading her in private prayer*. It is vital for a husband to lead his wife in times of prayer and private devotions that are separate from family worship with the children. When you are praying for each other, sometimes even to the point of tears, you will come to treasure each other like no one else on earth. Plus, it is difficult to be upset with a woman who has just prayed for you!

Set aside time every day to approach the throne of grace together. The apostle Peter assumes that Christian couples pray together (1 Peter 3:7). Pray for your wife in her presence; let her feel your love, strength, and boldness at the throne of grace. Let her feel that you carry her upon your heart just as the high priest carried the names of the tribes of Israel upon his heart (Ex. 28:29).

Marriage fulfills its deepest purposes and achieves its greatest stability only when grounded in the Christian faith and the fear of God. Whately summarizes this well: "Let man and wife pray together, let them confer with each other of their heavenly country, let them sing a psalm together, and join in such religious exercises; so shall their hearts be knit together fast and firm to God first, and so to each other."[5] As they do so, he continued, "bright beams of God's image will shine forth, and show themselves in each of them, and that is lovely and alluring, and will make them amiable to each other. These will nourish the spirit of holiness in them, and that kindles love."[6]

The Superlative Love of the Redeemed Man

The redeemed man strives to love his wife in a *superlative* way—more than anyone else on the face of the earth.

First, *love your wife superlatively by loving her absolutely* (Eph. 5:25)—with all of your being and with passion, even to the point of doting upon her. As Whately writes, the Christian man should love his wife so dearly that both of them are persuaded that the other is "the only fit and good match that could be found under the sun for them."[7] Because of parental love, a godly parent would not trade his child for another parent's child, even if that child were better looking and more talented; similarly, a godly husband would not trade his wife for another who is better looking and more gifted.[8]

Second, *love your wife superlatively by esteeming her above yourself* (Phil. 2:3). Never do anything that destroys love. Do not allow any other relationship to take priority over your friendship with her. Your spouse should be closer to you than your parents, your siblings, and your friends. Avoid criticizing her in front of anyone else. Never criticize her in a cruel way. Cover her sins much as bandages cover sores, so they may heal. Sandwich loving, constructive criticism between compliments.

---

5. William Whateley [Whately], *A Bride-Bush, or, A Direction for Married Persons* (London, 1623), 49.
6. Whately, *A Bride Bush, or, A Direction for Married Persons*, 49.
7. Whately, *A Bride-Bush, or, A Wedding Sermon*, 8.
8. Whately, *A Bride-Bush, or, A Wedding Sermon*, 8.

Third, *love your wife superlatively by showing her kindness*—incredible kindness in practical ways—and love her dearly just as she is. Respect her, honor her, tell her how much you love her (every day!), and shower her with verbal, physical, emotional, and spiritual affection. Seldom walk by her as she works in the kitchen without stopping to give her a hug or a kiss. Write her love letters. Give her a warm card. Tell her that she is God's precious gift to you. Tell her that outside of your spiritual rebirth, she is the best thing that ever happened to you. Tell her that you love her more than anyone else in the world besides the Lord. Learn her love language. Learn the way she thinks and study her likes and dislikes. Appreciate her and treasure her.

This superlative love, wrote Isaac Ambrose, is "a sweet, loving, and tender-hearted pouring out of their hearts, with much affectionate dearness, into each other's bosoms."[9] It is an entire love, a full love, a love that pours itself out between spouses without reservation in a variety of expressions, gestures, looks, and actions.

Fourth, *love your wife superlatively by heaping praise and compliments on her*. Compliment her with affection in your voice, with love in your eyes, and in the warm arms of embrace. Compliment her when she shows effort to do good, even in her areas of weakness. Praise her in the presence of others, especially your own children, as the wise husband does for his wife (Prov. 31:28). I have never met a couple whose marriage was in deep trouble while they were still complimenting each other every day.[10]

Fifth, *love your wife superlatively by striving to please her* (1 Cor. 7:33). According to Whately, this "pleasingness" is "a disposition of the will and earnest desire of the heart to give all content [satisfaction] to each other, so far as they may possibly do it, without sinning against God."[11]

---

9. Isaac Ambrose, *Media: The Middle Things*, in *The Compleat Works of That Eminent Minister of God's Word, Mr. Isaac Ambrose* (London, 1689), 130 (10.6.1).
10. This assumes, of course, that neither spouse has committed a grave sin such as adultery.
11. Whately, *A Bride Bush, or, A Direction for Married Persons*, 54.

He concludes, "Next to the pleasing of God, make your main business to please each other."[12]

The Sacrificial Love of the Redeemed Man

The redeemed man strives to love his wife in a *sacrificial* way. Paul explains that "Christ . . . loved the church, and gave himself for it" (Eph. 5:25). Jesus voluntarily died as the surety, substitute, and representative of His elect people. He stood under the curse of God for our sins. In giving Himself, Christ gave His most precious treasure, for He is of infinite value. He died on the cross for the unworthy, ungrateful enemies of God (Rom. 5:10).

Likewise, the love of a husband must reflect the care that Jesus Christ has for His church. He loved her, laid down His life for her, and continues to protect and provide for her physical and spiritual needs by His providence, Word, and Spirit. Many men say that they would willingly die for their wives. If you would truly die for your wife, you will live for her also. You will joyfully help her with some household chores and childcare duties as you are able, listen to her cares and anxieties, sympathize with her distresses, and serve her in her needs and desires—even when you least feel like doing so.

The Sympathetic Love of the Redeemed Man

The redeemed man must love his wife in a *sympathetic* way. Paul writes that husbands must love their wives in the same way they love their own bodies. The sacred one-flesh union is so intimate that loving your wife is essentially loving yourself (Eph. 5:28). Christlike love involves "nourishing and cherishing" your wife in the same way that you care for your

---

12. Whately, *A Bride Bush, or, A Direction for Married Persons*, 59.

physical body and in the same way that Christ cares for the church (vv. 28–29). If you have a serious wound on one of your limbs, you will seek immediate help. If a sliver falls into your eye, you will try to remove it immediately. In the same way, the Lord wants you, Christian husband, to give to your wife the same focus, attention, and promptness that you give to your own body. When your wife is hurting, sit beside her and, without delay, care for her where it hurts.

The word that Paul uses for "nourisheth" (Eph. 5:29) is the same word that he uses for fathers caring for their children (translated as "bring them up," 6:4). Just as you give your body the food and water it needs, you should serve your wife in her spiritual, physical, and emotional needs. The other word Paul uses, "cherish," literally means "to provide warmth"—or be comforting and soothing.

One of the best ways that a husband can show love to his wife is by exercising patience toward her. Husbands often want to fix their wife's problems instead of providing them with emotional fulfillment by listening and seeking to understand. It is also a common vice among some men to grow harsh or gruff toward their wives because of their emotional fragility. This is precisely what Paul warns against when he commands husbands not to grow bitter against their wives (Col. 3:18). Exercising patience and cultivating the skill of careful listening is part of showing sympathetic love to your wife. She should feel emotionally safe and secure in your home and in your heart.

The Serving Love of the Redeemed Man

The redeemed man strives to love his wife in a *serving* way. Husbands and fathers have both the right and responsibility to be images of the King in their homes. Dear Christian husband, provide your wife with biblical, tender, and clear servant leadership, not ruthless authoritarianism (Matt. 20:25–27). Sadly, some men today believe that biblical headship grants them license to command their wives like servants. This perspective is patently unbiblical, un-Christlike, and un-Christian. It is the opposite of gospel leadership.

Although the husband is the head of the household, a godly man should—with rare exceptions—not lead his family against his godly wife's desires. As Gouge said, "Though the man be as the head, yet is the woman as the heart."[13]

Rather, a loving husband and a submissive wife can usually agree on nearly all the daily decisions they discuss. In a godly marriage, the husband will seed to exercise his headship by making a decision that is contrary to the wishes of his wife. Headship does not mean always having one's own way. Often, a godly husband will make decisions contrary to his own desires from a spirit of love and out of deference to his wife. The point is that he always does what he believes, in the presence of God, is for the good of his wife and family—no matter his selfish desires. One day, God will call husbands and fathers to account for these decisions.

The key here is self-denial for the good of the other person. A man should not constantly trump his wife's desires. In fact, it will often work in reverse. For example, if I say to my wife, "Let's go out for dinner tonight," but we have a difference of opinion about where to eat, I should never respond by saying, "I'm the head of the home, so we're going to the restaurant that *I* choose." Instead, I should often say to my wife, "I love you so much that I will choose what you want tonight." In a healthy marriage, she might say, "No, let's do what you want!" That is how it ought to work.

The Sanctifying Love of the Redeemed Man

The redeemed man strives to love his wife in a *sanctifying* way. Like your Savior, love your bride with the goal of making her holy. Christ gave

---

13. Gouge, *Of Domesticall Duties*, 271.

Himself for His bride "that he might sanctify and cleanse [her] with the washing of water by the word" (Eph. 5:26). Christ's sacrifice aimed at purifying our lives from sin so that we would be holy for Him. He applies His sacrifice to us in the living water of the Holy Spirit and the living truth of His Word. Paul viewed his gospel ministry as a priestly work of presenting the nations holy to the Lord, sanctified by the Holy Spirit (Rom. 15:16).

The most important gift you can give your wife is not money, a house, a car, jewelry, or even yourself. The best gift you can give her is to bring her to God so that she can glorify Him and enjoy Him forever. Therefore, speak the Word of God to her. Do not make her feel like she must badger you into being a spiritual leader. Pour your heart into leading your family to Christ. Invest time into your wife's spiritual growth. Do what is necessary so that she has time to read the Word and fellowship with other godly women.

Pray for your wife at least once every day. Your wife is the companion that the Lord has given to you during your earthy pilgrimage (Mal. 2:14). Can you not spend a few minutes every day in private prayer for her? Praying regularly for your wife is part of your duty to dwell with her according to knowledge (1 Peter 3:7). Know her needs, desires, hopes, fears, dreams, likes, and dislikes. Supplicate for her specifically. It is remarkable how the Lord often uses a healthy prayer life to soften your heart and make you more sensitive to your wife's needs and wants.

The Sharing Love of the Redeemed Man

The redeemed man strives to love his wife in a *sharing* way. The essence of marital friendship is "the personal bond of shared life."[14] Another word for friendship is "fellowship," which in the Bible often translates

14. Joel R. Beeke, *Friends and Lovers: Cultivating Companionship and Intimacy in Marriage* (Cruciform Press, 2012), 11.

the Greek word *koinōnia*. This word means "sharing" or "communing" with each other: sharing each other's joys, bearing each other's burdens, and being involved in each other's lives.

First, *share yourself with your wife*. There is no substitute for spending time with your wife. You are not a friend to her if you work so many hours that you never have time together. Friendship cannot be warmed up by thirty seconds in the microwave. Friendship is costly. It costs you yourself, your commitment, and your vulnerability. There are no rush orders in friendship. It must be baked slowly and continually if we want a truly delightful flavor.

One aspect of sharing your minds and hearts is discussing major decisions together and waiting until you have unity before moving ahead. Any decision that significantly affects your time or money, or that involves a major change for your family's life, home, work, or church, should be made only after talking together about it, praying together, and coming to a point of unity.

Be a good sounding board when your wife needs to talk. If you are a good listener, you can listen to her for ten or twenty minutes about her concerns, and she often will be satisfied even if you offer her no solutions. That does not mean that your wife never needs counsel. But more often she just wants to know that you are there for her. She wants to connect with you.

Second, *share your trust with your wife*. Maintain strict discretion and confidentiality with the secrets she shares with you. Build trust with her on a romantic level as well. For example, do not yield to resentment if your wife is not as slim as she was before having multiple children. Do not covet or make comparisons with another man's wife. Never flirt with another woman or offer any reason for suspicion. Keep your heart open to your wife so that when she wants to speak with you, you will not respond with a deaf ear or a critical spirit.

Third, *share your life with your wife*. The more your lives overlap, the closer your friendship will become. Find activities to enjoy together. Walk together, talk together, cycle together, travel together, and find hobbies to pursue together. Ask your wife about her day and tell her about yours. Mark date nights on the calendar. Encourage spiritual conversation at the dinner table, as was common in the home of Martin and Katie Luther. In these shared experiences, apply the Word of God with wisdom to every situation that you face as a family and to your shared hopes, fears, and dreams as a couple. Feed your wife with the Word of God amid the rhythms of life.

The Sexual Love of the Redeemed Man

The redeemed man strives to love his wife in a *sexual* way. The Bible often refers to sexual intimacy using the biblical idiom "to know" your spouse (Gen. 4:1). If you believe that your wife is God's image-bearer, then you will want to know her, cherish her, and care for her, much as you long to know God and express your love for Him.

First, *love your wife sexually by leading in a healthy relationship.* Sex starts in the kitchen, as it were. What I mean is that what happens in your bedroom is in many ways determined by how you relate to each other throughout the day—beginning with breakfast in the morning. Sex does not *make* a good marriage; it is the *fruit* of a good marriage. Sexual intimacy in marriage is the culmination of the entire relationship.

Second, *love your wife sexually by learning what pleases her and giving yourself to her.* Most wives long for their husbands to provide leadership, affection, conversation, appreciation, trustworthiness, financial support, and fatherly commitment to the children. So, husband, do not expect your wife to respond to your sexual advances if you give her little time beforehand for personal conversation, especially telling her how much you love her and appreciate her work around the house.

Give your wife your thoughts, your time, your talk, your tenderness, and your touch. Remember that your wife longs for a deep emotional bond with you. Stop measuring out your love in small spoonfuls according to what she has done for you lately. Start pouring out your love by the bucketful according to the infinite riches of Christ's love for you. If you touch your wife's heart often through kind words and trustworthy deeds, you will likely be delighted to discover what happens when you do touch her body. Keep touching her heart while you touch her body. Speak words of love to her. Praise her. And touch her body in ways that will touch her heart. Learn what she likes. Patiently give it to her. It might involve considerable kissing or a backrub before you reach something explicitly sexual. But it will give your wife a much more profound sexual satisfaction.

Third, *love your wife sexually by denying yourself for her*. Selfishness kills lovemaking. No matter how good-looking a man may be, he will provoke weariness and disgust from his wife if all he wants to do is take and never give. One key to enjoying good sex is going to bed as one called to serve. You do not exist for yourself; God made you to glorify Himself by serving others. Is that not what the gospel teaches us through the example of Christ? He made Himself a servant, then humbled Himself to the point of death (Phil. 2:6–8). He did not come to be served but to serve, giving His life as a ransom for many (Mark 10:45). Christ is the model for husbands in loving their wives (Eph. 5:25). So, husbands, before reaching for your wife, remember that you are called to give yourself up for her.

Fourth, *love your wife sexually by loving her exclusively*. Keep your eyes and thoughts only for your wife. Do not diffuse your sexual passions to anyone but her; let your love flow with full force to your bride alone (Prov. 5:15–23). Follow the example of the loving husband of whom Thomas Hooker said, "The stream of his affection, like a mighty current, runs with full tide and strength toward his wife."[15] Love your wife with a particular and exclusive love in which no other woman may share. Reserve that love as a seal on your hear (Song 8:6). With this love, you are not just avoiding adultery; you are intentionally pouring out your

---

15. Thomas Hooker, *A Comment upon Christ's Last Prayer in the Seventeenth of John* (London, 1656), 187.

affections upon your wife in rich and regular ways. Say to her, "You have ravished my heart" (cf. 4:9). You may not realize how important it is for your wife to know that you have forsaken all others to love her alone until death separates you—but it is crucial. Neither can you estimate the security and happiness your children receive as they see you love their mother with an exclusive, committed love.

The Stable Love of the Redeemed Man

Finally, the redeemed man strives to love his wife in a *stable* way. Christian husband, love your wife with a strong, fervent, and steady love—not with a love that waxes and wanes with the tide of beauty, dress, or riches, or fluctuates with the emotions and lusts of the flesh. This love, Daniel Rogers wrote, is not "raised suddenly in a pang of affection, ebbing and flowing . . . but a habitual and settled love planted in them by God, whereby in a constant, equal, and cheerful consent of spirit they carry themselves [towards] each other."[16] Similarly Gouge said,

> Man and wife therefore are each to other an especial pledge of God's favour, and in this respect above all others under God to be loved. If this be the ground (as it ought to be) of their mutual love, their love will be fervent and constant. Neither will the want, or withering of any outward allurements, as beauty, personage, parentage, friends, riches, honours, or the like, withhold or withdraw, extinguish or extenuate their love: neither will any excellencies of nature or grace in other husbands and wives draw their hearts from their own to those other: nor yet will the love of a former yoke-fellow dead and gone, any whit lessen the love of the living mate.[17]

---

16. Daniel Rogers, *Matrimonial Honour* (Edification Press, 2010), 137–38. For the original and unabridged quotation, see Daniel Rogers, *Matrimoniall Honour* (London, 1642), 150.
17. Gouge, *Of Domesticall Duties*, 226.

Conclusion

As we open the pages of God's Word, we see a beautiful, divine design for marriage that is at once refreshing and well-ordered, promoting both the glory of God and the flourishing of man. It is precisely this design that is under attack today but which God calls His redeemed children to embrace. We can do so by loving our wives in a way that is spiritual, superlative, sacrificial, sympathetic, serving, sanctifying, sharing, sexual, and stable.

We live in a world that is spiritually dark and has been so since the fall. That spiritual darkness impacts marriage, one of the beautiful institutions that God created in the beginning. Let us return to the old paths of God's Word, for therein we will find rest for our souls (Jer. 6:16). By faith in the Lord Jesus Christ and utter dependence upon the Holy Spirit, may we seek to live lives that reflect our redemption, that allow us to shine as lights in this dark world, open doors for evangelism, and bring glory to our triune God forever. Amen.

CHAPTER EIGHT

The Redeemed Man Leading His Family

Jason Helopoulos

A YOUNG MAN approached me for pastoral counsel. The weight of the world clearly sat on his shoulders. His drooping head and bent frame belied his youth. We sat down together, and his countenance was far from calm. I made a quick assessment before he even spoke a word: trouble, weariness, guilt, and pain were his companions. The room remained quiet while he stirred up the confidence to speak. Finally, he raised eyes filled with tears and asked, "How do I lead my wife and children?" He grasped the responsibility, the "how-to," and delight evaded him.

Maybe you find yourself like this young man: your Christian family feels rudderless in the chaotic seas of this world. The church in our day surely shares some of the blame for not addressing this great need. And as fathers and husbands, we also bear responsibility. A returned emphasis upon Christian husbands and fathers leading their families well in Christ is one of the chief necessities of our day. Our families yearn for it, the church craves it, and our society misses it (though it may not realize it).

A Leader Leads

When God formed Adam from the dust of the ground, he established him as the leader in his family. This responsibility falls upon each husband on his wedding day and only matures as children are born from this union. The Lord entrusts our wives and children to our care. They are sheep to be led, and we are the shepherds.

Paul echoes this reality in the New Testament, "For the husband is the head of the wife" (Eph. 5:23). It proves important that the apostle never questions the reality of the husband's headship (or leadership). Thus, he issues no command for the husband to "exercise" headship over his wife and children. God wrote man's leadership into creation. It provides the foundation for his marriage, leads to the genesis of his children, and serves as the calling upon his life. Biblically, the reality that a man leads his family is beyond debate. Thus, it makes sense why the apostle Paul does not address the reality of leadership in the home but rather the way a husband or father exercises leadership in the home (Eph. 5:25–6:4).

All of us are sheep and our faithful Shepherd leads us; this is what shepherds do. In that most famous of psalms, Psalm 23, David pictures the Lord as our shepherd. "He *leadeth* me beside the still waters. . . . He *leadeth* me in the paths of righteousness for his name's sake" (Ps. 23:2–3). Shepherds lead, whether the flock is in the field, the church, or the home. It is true whether the shepherd is Christ or mere men. The question is never whether a man actually leads his family, it is whether he leads it well.

The young man who came to me years ago knew innately that he led his family. He came from a non-Christian background. The Scriptures were relatively new to him, but he knew his responsibility. The problem was that he possessed no knowledge of how to accomplish his responsibility. And thus, he lost sight of the great privilege he enjoyed.

Dear brother in Christ, the Lord has called you to shepherd the members of your family. It is a distinct privilege and a wonderful delight.

He called you. He did not call that other brother or father in the faith whose gifts and abilities you might admire and esteem. You are the man for this job!

Leadership will look different from home to home according to our gifting and personality. No redeemed husband or father needs to be the most commanding figure or manifest uncanny charisma. Neither does he need to be the smartest of men. In fact, your wife may be smarter than you—and your teenagers will definitely think they are smarter than you! No personality type, gifting, or ability defines a leader. But some characteristics are to mark our shepherding leadership for it to serve our families in Christ well.

A Leader Follows

Before we even consider leading, let us realize that first we must follow. He is no faithful Christian husband who does not first see himself as the bride of Christ. He is no faithful Christian father who does not first see himself as a child of the heavenly Father. He is no faithful shepherd who does not first see himself as a sheep. If we would lead, first we must follow.

This "following" mindset of dependence upon God serves as the single greatest sign of health in a redeemed man. And where a shepherd lacks health, the sheep will suffer. Everything flows from our relationship with the great Shepherd of the sheep, Christ (John 10). Ours is a relationship of dependence. We know that we are not our own (1 Cor. 6:19). We've been purchased by another. We "are Christ's" (1 Cor. 3:23). Even as he bought us, so we understand that we serve Him. Thus, the redeemed man leading his family well in Christ primarily concerns himself with Christ. The words of our Savior echo through our ears and grip our hearts, "I am the vine, ye are the branches: he that abideth in me, and I in him, the same bringeth forth much fruit: for without me ye can do nothing" (John 15:5). The greatest service we render to our family is our own faith in Jesus

Christ, which yields union with Him and the holiness that enables us to lead in a godly way.

Paul graciously encouraged Timothy regarding his leading in the church to keep a close watch on his *life* and doctrine (1 Tim. 4:16); so must the shepherd of the home. Where we lack life in the great Shepherd, the flock under our care will lack life. When we are malnourished, they will lack nourishment. Where our zeal for Christ shrinks, it should not shock us that their commitment to Christ shrivels.

With the psalmist, your prayer today might be, "Wilt thou not revive us again: that thy people may rejoice in thee?" (Ps. 85:6). Leading our family begins with us. And we begin with following Christ. As Paul said so we honestly desire to say to our wives and children, "Be ye followers of me, even as I also am of Christ" (1 Cor. 11:1).

A Leader Cares

Shepherds know their sheep in a caring way. Peter commands husbands, "Husbands, likewise, dwell with them with understanding, giving honor to the wife, as to the weaker vessel, and as being heirs together of the grace of life, that your prayers may not be hindered" (1 Peter 3:7). Peter instructs them to live in an understanding way in the midst of all the mess and joy of life, in the down times and high times, in sickness and health. How? By living in true knowledge with her. He says, "Dwell with them with understanding." There is a lot to understand about a wife, as any husband can attest! Surely, Peter is referring to understanding God's purpose in marriage, the struggles of one's wife, what helps her and hurts her, and her strengths and weaknesses. But Peter goes on to say that part of knowing her is awareness that she is a weaker vessel. He refers here to the average physical strength of women versus men. But it also seems the context lends itself to understanding that he needs to be emotionally sensitive as he cares for her, not dealing with her harshly. Overall, the point is that he is to show her honor.

Isn't that an interesting command to someone who occupies authority? Show her honor. I imagine that a butler at the White House, upon being hired, receives pretty in-depth lectures upon showing honor to the President of the United States. The President sits in the place of leadership. Yet, I dare guess that the President does not receive the same instruction about the butlers. Christian leadership is different; it possesses a different ethic.

Why? At least in this text, there are two reasons. The word translated as "vessel" means jar or container. The New Testament writers employ it multiple times in reference to human beings as vessels created by God for His purposes (Acts 9:15; 2 Tim. 2:21). This isn't a demeaning term when Peter applies it to the wife. Rather, Peter's point is that God created her, even as He created the husband, with purpose. It is a joint purpose—to serve God. And she, like him, a vessel made with a purpose, remains frail and weak. Just a jar. Just a vessel. Thus, as a godly husband leads, living with her in an understanding way becomes a way of life. This makes for a grace-saturated Christian marriage—one of mutual care, love, and concern. And we could extend it to the family—this makes for a grace-saturated Christian home—one of mutual care, love, and concern.

The second reason Peter gives soars with greater importance. He says treat your wife with honor, because you are "heirs together of the grace of life." Peter sets Christian marriage on the highest plane possible. Christian husbands and wives possess the same eternal inheritance. Not only are they created with the same purpose, but they possess the same promises and will receive the same glory. This teaching puts everything in its proper place. The Christian husband leads his family as pilgrims on the path to the same celestial city, with eyes fixed on the same prize. This makes our Christian families wholly different from all those around us.

We lead our homes not simply focused upon the immediate or even the next forty years, but eternity. As leaders of our Christian families, we aren't simply trying to make it through the day together but trying to make it to heaven together. He put us together for a reason. We are frail vessels helping one another along the way seeking to finish the race (1 Tim. 4:6–8).

A Leader Provides Materially

If we drove down a country road and saw a flock of sheep unkept, starving, simply wool draped over stick frames, we would ask, "Where is the shepherd?" Why? Because where there is lack of provision for the sheep, it serves as a commentary upon the shepherd who bears responsibility. Shepherds provide for their sheep. As David makes clear, the great Shepherd abundantly provides to the point that his sheep "shall not want" (Ps. 23:1). And He has provided for you, redeemed man. Our provision for others flows from His provision to us. Because we have received much, we seek to give much.

Paul says to Timothy, "If any provide not for his own, and specially for those of his own house, he hath denied the faith, and is worse than an infidel" (1 Tim. 5:8). In context, Paul was instructing Timothy concerning the care of widows in the church. Paul, though, expands this field of care to "those of his own house." And then he issues a strong condemnation.

Why would a lack of provision by a Christian man for his family make him "worse than an infidel?" Calvin wrestles with this question in a sermon on 1 Timothy 5. He rightfully notes that natural law instructs us in this necessity as even animals provide for their own.[1]

If beasts know this responsibility, men with the ability to reason naturally know this truth even more readily. This evidences itself when even an unbeliever provides for members of his family. Thus, a redeemed man

1. John Calvin, *Sermons on First Timothy*, trans. Robert White (Banner of Truth, 2018), 586.

who fails to provide demonstrates that he has sunk lower than an unbeliever. We know it by nature and redemption.

Provision lies at the very heart of leading our families well in Christ. This means a man must work and labor to such a degree that provision flows. May no one ever pass the sheep of our pasture and wonder, "Where is the shepherd who should be caring for them?" Of course, circumstances arise that may prevent adequate provision. Jacob was not neglectful or a poor shepherd of his family when drought entered the land of Canaan, resulting in scarcity. Many of our ancestors faced want during the Great Depression through no fault of their own. However, these examples are far from normative circumstances. As we lead our families, we engage with all the ability and strength the Lord grants to provide for them.

A Leader Provides Spiritually

But as shepherds of people, it is not enough to provide for material needs. Families lacking spiritual provision dwell in even greater jeopardy than those lacking material provision.

Spiritual provision proves to be the most required because it addresses the greatest need. If a shepherd witnesses one sheep being attacked by a wolf and another limping from a thorn in its foot, he will expend himself with vigor to fight off the wolf. The thorn needs removing, but the wolf is more of a threat. The thorn presents immediate pain; the wolf threatens death. Material provision is not insignificant, but it is not the most significant. Our family's spiritual needs have eternal consequences.

If Paul employed such strong language for a redeemed man who looked past his responsibility to provide materially, how much greater must the condemnation be for the Christian man who fails to provide for his household spiritually?

Healthy sheep almost always reflect a caring and intentional shepherd. Know your sheep, love your sheep, and provide the food your sheep require. Our great Shepherd spoke clearly, "Man shall not live by bread alone, but by every word that proceedeth out of the mouth of God" (Matt. 4:4). In Psalm 78, Asaph challenges the nation to pass along that "which we have heard and known" (v. 3). These are things "our fathers have told us. We will not hide them from their children, telling to the generation to come the praises of the LORD, and His strength and His wonderful works that He has done" (v. 4 NKJV). The psalmist continues in verses five and six, "For He established a testimony in Jacob, and appointed a law in Israel, which He commanded our fathers, that they should make them known to their children; that the generation to come might know them, the children who would be born, that they may arise and declare them to their children."

One generation blesses the next generation by feeding them spiritually. But the blessing doesn't stop there; it continues to flow down to those who follow. It cascades with one generation impacting the next. Notice, it begins with fathers telling their children. We lead by providing spiritual sustenance.

Thus, the faithful shepherd of a Christian family provides by leading his little flock to church week-in and week-out. The gathering of God's people is not an add-on to their life together. Neither is public worship a small portion of the husband or father's leadership in the home. Rather, it serves as the centerpiece of how he cares for his little flock. We lead by placing them in the way of God's means of grace week after week. The Christian family lives life from Lord's Day to Lord's Day, committed to "not forsaking the assembling of ourselves together" (Heb. 10:25). We do this because we know that in corporate worship, God particularly ministers, provides, and lavishes grace upon those gathered to read, preach, pray, confess, sing, and see (in the sacraments) His Word. The sheep eat and drink of that which is everlasting. The promises of Christ are heard and experienced, "Blessed are they which do hunger and thirst after righteousness: for they shall be filled" (Matt. 5:6); and "I am the bread of life:

he that cometh to me shall never hunger; and he that believeth on me shall never thirst" (John 6:35). The Christian family is a church-going family.

Spiritual provision necessitates more, though. Worship is not only to be found in the church but also the home. The Christian father and husband provides spiritually for his family by leading them in regular and consistent family worship. As worship centers the Christian church, so worship centers the Christian home. From the foot of Mount Sinai to the temple to the synagogue to the private dwellings in Acts, we see God's people worshiping the true and living God. Redeemed people worship. As a Christian church without worship is suspect, so a Christian home without worship is equally suspect. What we most love, we center our lives upon.

As redeemed men, we desire above all else for our wives and children to be able to say about us, "My husband/dad wasn't a perfect man, but I always knew he loved Christ and loved us. And because both of those things were true, he kept pointing us to and centering us upon Christ." If our love for football, good food, hunting, or playing board games most marks our leadership in the home, we leave behind a legacy that is no more than a vapor. All of these things are fine in and of themselves, but they are empty of eternal significance. As a pastor, husband, and father myself, I truly know of no better way to point your family to and center your family upon Christ than the practice of regular family worship.[2] Without this consistent practice, we tend to think we do this much more often than we truly do.

This spiritual provision is not difficult. In family worship, a father or husband gathers his family before God for a few minutes of Bible reading, prayer, and singing. It never needs to be long, especially with young children. It never needs to be complex, especially in the beginning. It simply needs to be done. In family worship, we place our family and

2. See Jason Helopoulos, *A Neglected Grace: Family Worship in the Christian Home* (Christian Focus, 2013).

ourselves in the way of God's means of grace. Spiritual beings need spiritual food. Let the redeemed man shepherd his family well by providing daily spiritual food.

A Leader Protects

A man provides protection for his wife and family in three ways.

First, *he protects them physically*. A shepherd not only provides but protects. Sheep are vulnerable. Predators abound. David rests in the protection of the great Shepherd, "Yea, though I walk through the valley of the shadow of death, I will fear no evil: for thou art with me; thy rod and thy staff they comfort me" (Ps. 23:4).

As a shepherd, a father and husband protects those under his care physically. The Christian family in this world needs protection because numerous wolves seek to devour. His strength stands guard. His life, if need be, is readily sacrificed for theirs. Our wives and children should know without hesitation that their physical safety, as far as it concerns us, is assured. They sleep well at night, they walk confidently in the streets, and they play without fear in the neighborhood, because they know our nearby presence. Our strength becomes their strength.

But again, our concern for their protection soars above the physical to include the spiritual.

Second, *he protects them spiritually by the Word*. Husbands and fathers protect by leading their family members deep in the things of Christ. We train them to think biblically about the world around them. We aim to see the lens by which they view the world as the lens of Scripture. The more they know, the better protected they will be.

Third, *he protects them spiritually by prayer*. Often, we view prayer as preparation for the real work of leading. However, prayer is not preparation for the work, it is the work. The man who prays for his family loves his family and protects his family. Pray for their minds to understand and their hearts to receive the Word. We can labor as a Christian husband or father upon the hard ground of their heart, but it will remain stony until His grace makes it fertile. Pray that the Lord prepares that ground for the sowing of His seed (Matthew 13). And pray that when the seed of His Word falls upon their hearts, they embrace it.

A Leader Looks to God's Grace

The redeemed man, above all, leads by knowing and living in grace. We not only follow the Lord but depend upon Him. The soil is ours to tend, but not ours to make fruitful. We sow the seed but cannot cause it to take root. We prepare for the rain but cannot shower the ground. We know our ability and competence in leading is limited. We depend upon His ever-flowing grace. In fact, every redeemed leader in the home regularly fails, leads his family astray, and sins against them. In such moments (or even seasons), we have yet another opportunity to lead well by asking forgiveness, demonstrating the need for repentance, and displaying the joy-filled life dependent upon God's free grace.

Over and over, we simply serve our family by leading them in the grace of Christ to the gracious Christ. Whether in success or failure, whether in faith or repentance, whether in strength or weakness, we seek to lead them down the path to the One they truly need. We want to be good shepherds, but we want them to know the care, provision, and protection of a much better and greater shepherd than we shall ever be.

Entrust your wives and children to Him. In a world filled with temptations, rampant sin, a fierce adversary, loud voices to divert, and our own failures and sins, we trust in a sovereign God who holds all in His hands. He is not idle, nor is He asleep (Psalm 121); He is at work. He leads and shepherds.

CHAPTER NINE

The Redeemed Man Discipling His Children

Richard D. Phillips

EVERY PASTOR has heard same the lament from parents of Christian children who strayed from the faith after growing up. "Pastor, I don't know what happened. We took our child to church and had him attend Sunday School as a child. We sent him to Christian camp and put him in a Christian school. How could our child not continue in the faith?"

You may have noticed that while the actions cited by this concerned parent are all commendable, they also involved other people leading their children to faith in Christ. They were relying on the church to lead their child, along with Christian camp counselors, teachers, and others. God has certainly ordained the church to nurture the faith of believers and their children, and many other Christian organizations can play a valuable role. But notice that the parent made no mention of his personally discipling the child to faith in Jesus.

In the introduction to this book, I cited the important statement the Lord made about His servant Abraham: "I have known him, in order that he may command his children and his household after him, that they keep the way of the LORD, to do righteousness and justice, that the LORD may bring to Abraham what He has spoken to him" (Gen. 18:19).

While this verse speaks informatively about men in general, it instructs us specifically about God's calling on fathers to disciple their children. Believing fathers must "command" their children—a statement not about a certain style of parental leadership, but rather about the duty and authority of fathers to lead their sons and daughters into godliness. Fathers are given authority by God to command their children, which Ephesians 6:1 reinforces in its instruction: "Children, obey your parents in the Lord, for this is right."

We should especially notice the Lord's intention of a man's family leadership: "that the LORD may bring to Abraham what He has spoken to him." In God's economy, the Christian family is a chief means by which God's gospel purposes come to fruition in our world. God made great promises to Abraham, specifically the promise to grant him an abundance of offspring to be a holy nation before the Lord. And the Lord would employ Abraham's leadership of his family to bring this promise about! While Christian fathers do not play the great redemptive-historical role granted to Abraham as the covenant father of all the faithful (Rom. 4:11), the same idea can be applied to our homes and families. God has promised to be our God and the God of our children, and the discipling leadership of Christian fathers is a primary way in which He brings this blessed situation to pass.

Training and Admonition

When we speak of fathers discipling their children, we mean the personal ministry and leadership that guides sons and daughters into a personal embrace of the Christian faith. I find that a large percentage of Christian parents have embraced the biblical command to discipline our children, with the result that many families enjoy compliant and relatively obedient children. But, in addition to *disciplining* children so that they are taught to obey, parents also have the vital duty of spiritually *discipling* their children. This duty is made explicit in Ephesians 6:4, "And you, fathers, do not provoke your children to wrath, but bring them up in the training and admonition of the Lord." Here we find the companion to the Bible's command for children to obey their parents in Ephesians 6:1. Children have the duty to obey, and parents (fathers especially) have the duty to train and nurture their children in the Christian faith.

Christian parents do not control the regenerating grace of the Holy Spirit which is necessary for our children to be born again to salvation. But we are granted authority and the duty to lead our children deliberately into knowing the importance and necessity of saving faith. Some nominal Christians may take a different view, stating, "We don't want to shove religion down the throats of our children." To the absolute contrary of this spiritually neglectful posture, biblically faithful parents understand their duty to teach biblical truth to their children and impress upon them the necessity and blessing of their personal faith in Jesus. This duty is enshrined in one of the vows asked of Christian parents when they present their children for baptism. Having acknowledged their own and their child's need of Christ's cleansing blood and the renewing grace of the Holy Spirit, parents are asked:

> Do you now unreservedly dedicate your child to God, and promise, in humble reliance upon divine grace, that you will endeavor to set a godly example, to pray with and for your child, to teach the doctrines of our holy religion, and that you will strive, by all the means of God's appointment, to bring your child up in the nurture and admonition of the Lord?[1]

This solemn vow concerns the personal discipleship that parents are to grant to their children. The final statement is drawn explicitly from

1. See *The Book of Church Order of the Presbyterian Church in America* (Committee on Discipleship Ministries for the Office of the Stated Clerk of the General Assembly of the Presbyterian Church in America, 2019), sec. 56-5.

Ephesians 6:4—parents must raise their children "in the training and admonition of the Lord." This command provides the essential calling of Christian parents in discipling their covenant children.

The first of a father's two responsibilities, *paideia*, means training with an aim to proper conduct and behavior. Parents teach their children how to act in public, how to be polite and respectful, how to treat their siblings and friends, and many other vital life skills. I well remember my father giving me specific instructions about how to answer the telephone. We were an Army family, and I was to answer the phone with this greeting: "Colonel Phillips's residence; this is Ricky speaking. How may I help you, Ma'am or Sir?" My father knew exactly how he wanted me to perform this task, and he carefully explained why. He had me practice when the phone rang, gave me corrections when I erred, and praised me when I performed well. Even today, the sound of an old-fashioned telephone makes me want to stand straight, grasp the receiver firmly, and announce my father's name and rank!

The second term, translated "admonition," is the Greek word *nouthesia*, which has the primary idea of instruction. Like *paideia*, this word carries the idea of giving correction, especially with respect to what we must believe. Christian parents are required by the Lord to instruct their children in what the Bible teaches doctrinally and what conduct the Bible requires ethically.

This exhortation means that parents are to teach their children the Word of God. For starters, this duty will have fathers ensure that their families attend churches where the Bible is faithfully taught. But a father also is personally to read and explain the Scriptures to his sons and daughters. Our children are to learn the great truths of God's Word at our knees and at the table where our hands open God's Book.

What truths must fathers teach their children? One way to view the curriculum that we must teach our children during the long years of their upbringing is to work our way through the books of the Bible. Like

Genesis, we teach our children that we were created by the eternal God to know and serve Him, that Adam and Eve fell into sin, and that God made His covenant of grace with the patriarchs with a specific eye to our own salvation. Like Exodus, we teach our children the covenant history of God's people, including their bondage in Egypt and God's great redemption through Moses. Like Leviticus, we teach God's way of forgiving and cleansing sin through the blood of the atoning sacrifice. Like Deuteronomy, we instruct our children to worship one God—the true and living God—and to be faithful to His ways; knowing and living by His moral law. Like Amos, we must instruct our children that God not only judges the ungodly but also professing Christians who do not repent. Like Jonah, we communicate God's redeeming mercy for a world lost in sin. Like Ezekiel, we tell of God's renewing grace in our hearts and provide a vision of the eternal glory that is to come. In the Psalms we cultivate hearts that long to worship; in Proverbs we communicate life-saving wisdom for living in a sinful world. Like Daniel, we teach of Christ's kingdom that overthrows the powers of this world and celebrate the godly valor of those believers who face worldly temptation and danger. Like Jeremiah, we teach our children about the truth and power of God's Word: "I am ready to perform My word" (Jer. 1:12). And like Isaiah, we fill our children's hearts and minds with the wonder of God's gift of His Son, the atoning work of the Suffering Servant, and the grace of our loving Lord to redeem a people for eternal life.

You may be thinking, "That's a lot for me to teach my children!" It certainly is—and we haven't even yet discussed the New Testament, in which we walk the paths of Galilee together with Jesus, stand at the foot of His cross, gaze in wonder at the light of the open tomb, and sit at the apostles' feet to learn the doctrines of grace. Can there be a more exciting calling than for a father to teach the Word of God to his sons and daughters, all the while communicating his personal trust and adoration of the Savior?

Structure versus Good Intentions

I can anticipate objections to this rigorous call to the discipleship of our children. Some will reply, "But I'm not a trained Bible teacher!" To this I answer, "My dear friend, you are the father of children. You must now become a motivated student of God's Word if you have not already been one. Only you can be the father to your children. But you do not have to be a trained scholar, just a biblically literate Christian man who loves and knows God's Word. So, pay attention during the sermon, and make use of the many excellent family devotional guides that are available today.[2] What blessing awaits you as you stroll the paths of biblical redemption with your children at your side!"

How about this objection: "When am I supposed to do all this teaching? Where will we find the time?" Here we encounter something close to the heart of the matter. To this question I ask my own: "What are your priorities as a father for your Christian children?" Do you lie awake dreaming of sons who become sports stars or daughters who are beauty queens? Do you want your boys to be expert hunters or your daughters to be star students? There is of course nothing wrong with having this-world ambitions for your children and to coach them up in wholesome things that are exciting to you. But where does their Christian faith and walk with the Lord fit into these ambitions? If our hearts and minds are conformed to God's Word, our chief priority and ambition for our children will be for them to walk in faith before the Lord.

I have a motto that says, "Structure beats good intentions." While this precept is true in a variety of matters, it is eminently true of the discipleship of our children. If we are serious about raising our children in

---

2. For example, consider the *Family Worship Bible Guide*, ed. Joel R. Beeke, Michael P. V. Barrett, Gerald M. Bilkes, and Paul M. Smalley (Reformation Heritage Books, 2016). This book contains devotional thoughts and questions for every chapter of the Bible.

the training and admonition of the Lord, then we will structure time for family worship. Along with weekly attendance at a faithful church, family worship is the cornerstone for the discipling of our sons and daughters. Most families who practice family worship choose a meal when all are together and use it to enjoy a brief time of Bible study, prayer, and singing. Perhaps you might read through a book of the Bible, passage by passage, discussing its meaning and sharing with your children what it means to you and what it suggests to them. Or perhaps you will make use of one of the many suitable devotional guides that are available for family worship. Prayer should be offered for all present, as well as for pressing needs in the church or community. Ideally, the family will sing a hymn or psalm together, bonding in joyful singing to the Lord, perhaps learning a hymn or psalm during the week.

Our family was blessed as well by taking some time for relaxed family reading on Sabbath day afternoons. I have found that a key to enjoying the Lord's Day is to have a productive spiritual activity after the midday meal and before the evening worship service. What a blessing it was for me to read C. S. Lewis's *Narnia* series aloud to my children on Sunday afternoons (not having been raised as a Christian, I had never read these books before!). We also read through John Bunyan's *The Pilgrim's Progress* during these times. Our Sunday afternoon reading was relaxed and easy-going and is a treasured memory from our years of raising our children.

Another practice we followed was a more extensive family worship time one evening during the week. Each child had his or her own Psalter and we would sing three or four psalms. We tried to make this singing fun by taking requests of favorites and singing creatively—often we would have boys sing one verse followed by girls on the next, and similar engaging approaches. I then would lead a more extensive time of Bible teaching and discussion, after which we would engage in a longer time of prayer than was our daily habit. Sometimes we would have each family member share a burden on his or her heart, so that each child (and parent) was prayed for by the whole family. Sometimes we would devote prayer for our church's missionaries. The whole service would take about an hour and once we got this practice going, our children proved to be able to handle it and enjoy the time together with the Lord.

Speaking for myself, I fear that if we did not have these regular worship practices, weeks and even months might have gone by without me ever having a serious discussion with my children about the Lord. Life for families is so busy, with school, sports, music lessons, and social engagements, that if we did not make an intentional priority for family worship, I shudder to think how I would have discipled my children.

Some of you may be thinking: this approach involves a lot of effort and time. Yes, it does! And it should, because it involves the discipleship of our dear children into a personal faith in our Lord! Remember, structure beats good intentions! Think about the discipline that goes into a child developing athletic prowess or musical excellence. I assure you that the discipleship of our children is of more importance and demands a serious, structured effort by parents. Paul urged this very priority: "For bodily exercise profits a little, but godliness is profitable for all things, having promise of the life that now is and of that which is to come" (1 Tim. 4:8).

While family worship gives us time to disciple our children spiritually, Deuteronomy 6:4–7 calls on fathers to make all our time work to this end. In verses 4–5, Moses lays out the heart of the old covenant faith: "Hear, O Israel: The LORD our God, the LORD is one! You shall love the LORD your God with all your heart, with all your soul, and with all your strength." In the next two verses, he gives a primary strategy for passing on this faith to our children: "And these words which I command you today shall be in your heart. You shall teach them diligently to your children, and shall talk of them when you sit in your house, when you walk by the way, when you lie down, and when you rise up" (vv. 6–7).

This is not to say that we can *only* talk about the Lord and His salvation. But it does mean that we should regularly bring to our children's minds all the great things that God has done for us in Jesus Christ. To disciple our children, we must ourselves be active disciples of Jesus; in order to share our faith with them we must daily nurture our relationship with the Lord. As we do, we will never run short of things to talk about when it comes to Jesus and God's Word. In short, Christian fathers must not only communicate the truths of the Bible, but also a passion for God's Word, a holy confidence in scriptural truth, and an expectant reliance on the saving work of Christ and the ministry of the Holy Spirit.

A Heart for Our Children

Before closing this chapter on fathers discipling their children, I want to avoid giving the impression that discipleship only or even mainly involves a transfer of information. To the contrary, discipleship integrally involves a close relationship in which a father walks with his children with their hearts joined together. To this end, I often think of what I consider the key verse in the book of Proverbs. We tend to think of Proverbs as a book of miscellaneous tidbits of wisdom. But Proverbs is the record of the instruction given to a beloved son by his devoted father. The spirit of the book is provided in Proverbs 23:26: "My son, give me your heart."

With this plea in mind, a father's discipling relationship with his children requires that he develops a close and personal bond early in the child's life. When it comes to a child's obedience, Christians realize disciplining must begin while the boy or girl is little. Similarly, I have found it essential that during a child's growing years leading up to adolescence they form a close, warm, and trusted relationship with their father. By the time a child has passed through puberty, if the father has not yet connected with him or her and developed a close and loving relationship, it will be very hard to do so later. Much of the serious work of character development and the nurture of faith will take place during the teenage years, but the foundation of the parental discipling relationship is laid years earlier, when the child learns to trust and value the parent's guidance.

It is with this relationship in mind that Ephesians 6:4 not only tells parents to "bring them up in the training and admonition of the Lord," but first states: "And you, fathers, do not provoke your children to wrath." A Christian father is not to exercise authority in a harsh, demeaning, or severe manner that will inevitably lead the child to frustration. Fathers must cultivate patience and tenderness towards their children—and when they fail in this respect, they should be quick to repent and seek forgiveness. Of course, child-raising can be frustrating to parents and sinful children will do things that make a father angry. Much prayerful effort must therefore be given to restraining anger and developing self-control, lest a father so alienate small children that the vital bond of trust he will need in later years is damaged or broken.

Fathers bond with their children by spending time with them, paying loving attention to them, and showing excitement about their growth in life. It is in this manner that playing catch in the yard or playing board games on a rainy afternoon can be vital to the Christian nurture of our children. We must connect with our sons and daughters, invite them to share in the things we think are exciting, and take part with them in things that they like to do. "My son, give me your heart," pled the father in Proverbs. The first step in gaining the child's heart is to give them our own.

Proverbs 23:26 has a second line: "And let your eyes observe my ways." The discipleship of children relies not only on formal instruction but also on the even more revealing example that a father provides. It is not necessary for a father to be perfect—nor can any of us attain this standard! But it is essential that our children observe a sincere and fervent faith in the Lord and a personal dedication to God's Word, prayer, and worship. Is the father spiritually growing by showing a willingness to repent of his sins and by seeking after spiritual graces? And does the father forgive the sins of others cheerfully, showing that he is grateful for Christ having forgiven his own sins?

Glory Begun Below

In his hymn, "Come, We that Love the Lord" (1806), Isaac Watts penned memorable lines that inspire our calling as fathers to the discipleship of our children:

> *The men of grace have found*
> *Glory begun below;*
> *Celestial fruits on earthly ground*
> *From faith and hope may grow.*

Can there be a higher privilege than that given to a Christian father—together with his wife—to disciple his children, by God's grace, into saving faith? When we have grown old, I am sure that most men will have many or at least some regrets. But we will never regret a devoted commitment to the spiritual nurture of our dear children, nor the bonded relationship that this discipleship required, nor yet the results as our children stay connected to their parents through the shared bond of their faith in Jesus Christ. And what a joy it will be to watch our children giving us the compliment of imitating how we discipled them in their own discipleship of our grandchildren! Not only will these joyful family bonds continue all through our present lives, but they will extend into eternity, when we all will be brothers and sisters with the true and living God as our Father, basking in the glory of heaven that begins with God's grace here below in our earthly homes.

CHAPTER TEN

The Redeemed Man Growing in Family Worship

Joel R. Beeke

WHEN MY parents commemorated their fiftieth anniversary, all five of us children decided that each of us would express thanks to our father and mother for one thing.[1] Remarkably, though we did not consult with each other beforehand, all five of us thanked our father for his leadership of our family worship. My brother said, "Dad, the oldest memory I have is of tears streaming down your face as you taught us from *The Pilgrim's Progress* on Sunday evenings how the Holy Spirit leads believers.[2] At the age of three God used you in family worship to convict me that God is real. In later years, I could never seriously question the reality of God, and I want to thank you for that."

Family worship is deeply rooted in our theology. Our God is a triune God, a God of familial relationships in His one, uncreated essence. His fatherly love overflows into the world He created because God created us

---

1. This chapter is adapted from Joel R. Beeke, *Family Worship* (Reformation Heritage Books, 2009). Used with permission.
2. John Bunyan's *The Pilgrim's Progress* is a classic Puritan book describing the Christian life through the allegory of a man on a dangerous journey from the City of Destruction to the Celestial City.

in His image. God deals with the human race through covenant and headship, where fathers such as Abraham lead and represent families in God's promises. In the New Testament, we see families converted together and called to grow in holiness together in the life of the church.

As Douglas Kelly concludes, "Family religion, which depends not a little on the household head daily leading the family before God in worship, is one of the most powerful structures that the covenant-keeping God has given for the expansion of redemption through the generations, so that countless multitudes may be brought into communion with and worship" of the living God through Jesus Christ.[3]

Let us examine the subject of leading family worship under four headings: duty, general guidelines, specific suggestions, and motivations.

The Duty of Family Worship

Given the importance of family worship as a potent force in winning untold millions to gospel truth throughout the ages, we ought not be surprised that God requires us as heads of households do all we can to lead our families in worshiping the living God. Joshua says,

> Now therefore fear the LORD, and serve him in sincerity and in truth: and put away the gods which your fathers served on the other side of the flood, and in Egypt; and serve ye the LORD. And if it seem evil unto you to serve the LORD, choose you this day whom ye will serve; whether the gods which your fathers served that were on the other side of the flood [back in Ur of Chaldees], or the gods of the Amorites, in whose land ye dwell [here in Canaan]: but as for me and my house, we will serve the LORD. (Josh. 24:14–15)

---

3. Douglas Kelly, "Family Worship: Biblical, Reformed, and Viable for Today," in *Worship in the Presence of God*, ed. Frank J. Smith and David C. Lachman (Greenville Seminary Press, 1992), 110.

Joshua does not make worship or service to the living God optional. Joshua enforces the service of God in our families with his own example. He has such command over his family that he speaks for the entire household: "as for me and my house, we will serve the LORD," he says. The word translated as *serve* includes not only serving God in every sphere of our lives, but also in special acts of worship.

According to Scripture, God should be served in special acts of worship in our families today in the following three ways:

First, *daily instruction in the Word of God*. God should be worshiped by daily reading and instruction from His Word. As Moses says, "These words, which I command thee this day, shall be in thine heart: and thou shalt teach them diligently unto thy children, and shalt talk of them when thou sittest in thine house, and when thou walkest by the way, and when thou liest down, and when thou risest up" (Deut. 6:6–7).

Second, *daily prayer to the throne of God*. Does not the command to "pray without ceasing" (1 Thess. 5:17) include when we are with our families? Our families must daily pray together unless providentially hindered. Paul says, "For every creature of God is good, and nothing to be refused, if it be received with thanksgiving: for it is sanctified by the word of God and prayer" (1 Tim. 4:4–5). If you want to eat and drink to the glory of God (1 Cor. 10:31), you must sanctify your food and drink by prayer. And just as we pray that our food and drink may be sanctified and blessed to the nourishment of our bodies, so we should pray for God's blessing of His Word to the nourishment of our souls (John 17:17).

Third, *daily singing the praise of God*. Psalm 118:14–15 says, "The LORD is my strength and song, and is become my salvation. The voice of rejoicing and salvation is in the tabernacles [or tents] of the righteous: the right hand of the LORD doeth valiantly." That is a clear reference to singing. The psalmist says this sound *is* (not simply *ought to be*) in the tents of the righteous.

The Lord is to be worshipped daily by the singing of psalms in our homes. As a result, God is glorified, and our families are edified. Since these songs are God's Word, singing them is a means of instruction, enlightening the understanding. Singing promotes devotion as it warms the heart. The graces of the Spirit are stirred up in us, and our growth in grace is stimulated. "Let the word of Christ dwell in you richly in all wisdom; teaching and admonishing one another in psalms and hymns and spiritual songs, singing with grace in your hearts to the Lord" (Col. 3:16).

Dear brothers, we must implement family worship in our homes. God requires that you worship Him not only privately as an individual, but also publicly as the church, and socially as families. The Lord Jesus is worthy of it, God's Word commands it, and conscience affirms it as your duty.

Your family owes its allegiance to God. God has placed you in a position of authority to guide your children in the way of the Lord. You are more than friends and advisors to your children; as their teacher and ruler in the home, your example and leadership are crucial. Clothed with holy authority, you have a duty to do what God said of Abraham: "For I know him," God said, "that he will *command* his children and his household after him, and they shall keep the way of the LORD, to do justice and judgment; that the LORD may bring upon Abraham that which he hath spoken of him" (Gen. 18:19).

General Guidelines for Family Worship

I want to give you some directions to help you establish and maintain God-honoring family worship in your homes.

First, *family worship will require some preparation*. You should pray for God's blessing upon that worship. Have your Bibles ready and a Scripture passage selected. Catechisms and books of questions and answers for children are very helpful. A good daily devotional can also be used. Sometimes you might read through a book like John Bunyan's *Pilgrim's Progress* or *Holy War* and discuss it together. Choose some psalms and hymns that are easy to sing. Pick a place to gather, such as the supper table or the living room. Set the times for family worship, ordinarily at breakfast and supper but as it fits your family's needs. Whatever times you set, carefully guard those times like a precious jewel.

Second, *during family worship, aim for brevity*. Don't provoke your children. If you worship twice a day, try ten minutes in the morning and twenty in the evening. Be consistent. It is better to have twenty minutes of family worship every day than to try for extended periods on fewer days— say forty-five minutes on Monday, then skipping Tuesday.

Third, *don't indulge excuses to avoid family worship*. Even if you have been sinning—perhaps you lost your temper—still lead family worship; just begin it with heart-felt confession and repentance. If you are tired, deny yourself out of love for God and your family. After all, Christ was bone-weary when He went to the cross for you, yet He carried on. Shouldn't we carry on in response to His love as well?

Fourth, *lead family worship with a firm, fatherly hand and a soft, penitent heart*. Speak with hopeful solemnity. Talk naturally yet reverently during this time, using the tone you would use when speaking to a deeply respected friend about a serious matter. Expect great things from a great covenant-keeping God.

Specific Suggestions for Family Worship

Allow me to offer some specific advice that will be helpful for leading family worship, especially for fathers who have never led it before.

1. Advice for the reading of Scripture.
- Have a plan for reading through the whole Bible in reasonable portions over a period of time. Ordinarily ten to twenty verses are a good amount for each time together.
- Involve the family, so that everyone who can read gets to read.

Encourage family members to read clearly so that all can hear and understand.

2. Advice for biblical instruction.

- Be plain in your meaning.
- Encourage family dialogue by asking questions, especially of older children.
- Be pure in doctrine. Don't abandon doctrinal precision when teaching young children; aim for simplicity *and* soundness.
- Be relevant in application. You might tell your children why a passage is special to you, or illustrate it with some experience from Scripture, history, or your life.
- Be affectionate in manner. Show warmth, love, and urgency as a God-fearing father.

3. Advice for praying.

- Be short. With few exceptions, don't pray for more than five minutes. Teach with your eyes open; pray with your eyes shut.
- Be direct. Spread your needs before God, plead your case, and ask for mercy. Name your teenagers and children and their needs.
- Be varied. Remember and stress the various ingredients of true prayer: adoration, confession, thanksgiving, supplication.
- Be a trainer. Train even your young children to pray and give them opportunities to do so in family worship.

4. Advice for singing.

- Sing doctrinally pure songs. There is no excuse for singing doctrinal error no matter how attractive the tune might be.
- Sing the Bible's psalms first and foremost without neglecting sound hymns. The Psalms are the richest gold mine of deep, living, experiential, scriptural piety.

- Sing heartily and with feeling. Meditate on the words you are singing. On occasion discuss a phrase that is sung.

Office-Bearing Leadership in Family Worship

Office-bearing has far-reaching implications for leading family worship in our homes. As God's appointed representatives to our wives and children, we should serve them as prophets, priests, and kings. Of course, fathers are not mediators of God's saving grace—only Jesus Christ is the Prophet, Priest, and King in that sense, and every man, woman, and child may draw near to God by faith in Christ alone. However, husbands and fathers serve their families with prophetic truth, priestly prayer, and kingly care according to the measure of authority that Christ has delegated to them. Thus, we are to reflect Christ's threefold office as we lead our families, and especially so in engaging them in family worship. But how are we to do this? Let's briefly examine the use of each of these offices in relation to family worship.

Prophet

Here are five guidelines for teaching as God's prophet in family worship:

Teach the whole Bible. Declare to your children the whole counsel of God (Acts 20:27). Teach them Bible stories and Bible doctrines, and apply both to their daily lives by addressing the mind, the conscience, the heart, and the will of each of your children. Major on the basics, teaching your children about each Bible book, showing them its major theme, and how it leads us as needy sinners to Jesus Christ, and then grows us in being His disciples.

Teach by catechizing. Thoroughly biblical creeds, catechisms, and confessional doctrinal standards (such as the Belgic Confession of Faith, the Heidelberg Catechism, the Canons of Dort, and the Westminster

Confession of Faith and Shorter and Larger Catechisms) are valuable tools that assist us in communicating divine truths to our children. They provide clear, concise definitions of basic doctrines that our children can easily memorize, and that can also, by the Spirit's grace, convict their consciences of sin, call their hearts to true faith, and stir their wills to bring forth godly fruit.

Teach with passion. A true prophet cannot help but speak (Jer. 20:9; Amos 3:8; 1 Cor. 9:16). Similarly, we as fatherly prophetic teachers must instruct our children diligently (Deut. 6:6–7)—that is, with passion, being more moved and excited to teach them about some aspect of Jesus Christ's mediatorial work than about the score of a ballgame.

Teach with love. Our children must understand we love their souls more than anything else on earth. J. C. Ryle said, "Love is one grand secret of successful training. Soul love is the soul of all love."[4] Proverbs continually uses the phrase "my son," showing a godly father's warmth and love for his children. Many times, my dad wept as he taught us the truths of God and often said with tears, "Children, I cannot miss any of you in heaven one day."

Teach by example. In addition to being our chief prophet, Jesus was and is the living Word (John 1:1, 14), revealing God not only in His words but also in His life and His deeds. We are always teaching our children, whether we know it or not, for they are always reading the book of our lives. Beside the Bible, your life is the most important "book" your children will ever read.

Priest

To be parent-priests in our homes, we must establish and maintain family worship, which has often been called in priestly terms, "the family altar," reminding us that we must daily consecrate ourselves and our children to

---

4. J. C. Ryle, *The Duties of Parents* (Triangle Press, 1993), 9.

God's service primarily through family prayer. Priestly prayer is a critical aspect of family worship. Here are three guidelines for praying as God's priest in family worship:

Pray by adoration. Pray worshipfully by expressing one or more titles or attributes of God as you begin your prayer, and then praise Him for who He is. Help your children to recognize that the family is bowing before the thrice holy God the universe: Father, Son, and Holy Spirit. Demonstrate to them that prayer is not something we do alongside family worship, but that it is an act of worship itself.

Pray by confession. Confess the depravity of your nature, as well as your and your family's original and actual sins humbly before God in the presence of your children. Your children need to see and hear a broken and contrite spirit exuding from you, as well as to witness you, by faith, pleading for God's forgiveness through Christ's blood.

Pray for and with your children. Our prayers as fathers cannot compare to Christ's perfect intercessory prayers for us, but we can and do share in His priestly work by praying for our children. We ought to bring our children before God privately, even as we also pray for them collectively and individually during family worship. By the Spirit's grace, a father's daily prayers can leave a transforming and lasting impression upon a child.

What an amazing privilege Christ has granted us to be priests in our families to God's glory. Seek grace to make your home a holy temple in which you lift up prayers for your loved one like sweet-smelling incense to the throne of grace. Usually, the more you exercise your priestly ministry of intercession by the Spirit's grace, the more you will discover the presence of the living Savior and Lord in your family.

King

Like David, Jesus Christ serves as King of His people by ruling over us and destroying our enemies (2 Sam. 8:13–15). He is supreme in His authority and sovereign in His power. He alone as King can bind our conscience with sacred obligations and change our hearts, so that His people will one day reign with Him as kings (Rev. 1:6; 5:10). Christ delegates a measure of His authority to fathers to rule as His servants in the home. Here are three guidelines for guiding family worship as God's appointed fatherly kings.

Be faithful in family worship, leading it every day. Like Joshua, be determined to worship the Lord, together with your family (Josh. 24:15). Don't ever allow your children's or your own feelings to stand in the way of conducting family worship. Of course, you are to be friends with your children, but you are *more* than that; in the Lord, you are their authority figure who represents the King. In response to God's divine command, you are responsible to ensure that family worship is a daily, intentionally biblical and edifying occurrence in your home.

Exercise family worship with kingly guidance that is just, wise, and loving. You have the right and responsibility to be an image bearer of the King of kings in your home without denigrating the essential equality of your children as fellow human beings created in the image of God. An important part of your ruling your own house well (1 Tim. 3:4–5) is to lead family worship well. You are in charge, guiding the discussion, asking questions, and guiding your children in the paths of truth.

Require attendance at and attention during family worship. God's worship is not an optional activity. Unless lawful reasons prohibit, all children should be present when the family gathers to worship God. During family worship, Proverbs 4:1 must be adhered to: "Hear, ye children, the instruction of a father, and attend to know understanding." The truths we are conveying are of utmost important; hence, we must insist on attentive hearing of God's Word in our home. All potential distractions should be removed. Do not allow cell phones to be checked during family worship, and if the phone rings, let it ring. Your sacred time with God in family worship is the most important part of your day, for your audience with Him is more important than having time with anyone else.

Motivations for Family Worship

Every God-fearing father should establish and maintain family worship in the home for the following reasons.

First, *lead family worship for the eternal welfare of your loved ones.* God uses means to save souls. Most commonly He uses the preaching of His Word. But He also may also use family worship. Fathers, use every means to have your children saved. Pray with them, teach them, sing with them, weep over them, admonish them, and plead with them. Remember that at every family worship you are ushering your children into the very presence of the Most High. Remember, too, that life is but a vapor (James 4:14), and soon your opportunity will be past.

Second, *lead family worship for the satisfaction of a good conscience.* The sorrows of parenting are heavy enough when fathers have faithfully discharged their duty yet still have a prodigal child. But who can bear the reproach of a stinging conscience that condemns us because we never brought them up in the fear of the Lord? It is much better if we can say to our children: "We taught you God's Word, wrestled for your soul, and lived a God-fearing example before you. Your conscience will bears witness that Christ is the center of this home. We sang together, prayed together, and talked together. If you turn away from this light and these privileges, and insist on going your own way, we can only pray that you will come to your senses before it is too late."

Third, *lead family worship for assistance in child-rearing.* Family worship helps promote family harmony in times of affliction, sickness, and death. It offers greater knowledge of the Scriptures and growth in personal piety both for yourself and your children. It nurtures wisdom in how to face life, openness to speak about meaningful questions, and a closer relationship between father and children. Strong bonds established in family worship in early years may be a great help to teens in years to come. These teens may be spared from much sin when recalling family prayers and worship. In times of temptation, they may say, "How can I offend a father who daily wrestles with God on my behalf?"

Fourth, *lead family worship because of love for God and His church.* Godly parents want to glorify God and serve His church. They want to give the church spiritually stalwart sons and daughters. Pray that your sons and daughters may be pillars in the church. Blessed is the parent who can one day see among the crowd of worshipers their own sons and daughters. Family worship is the foundation of such a future.

Conclusion

All God-fearing fathers feel guilty about their failures and inadequacy in leading their families in God's worship. So let me offer a few words of encouragement to you who are anointed to bear the threefold office of Christ in your home.

You may feel like a certain father who was discouraged because things were not going well with his children. He did not know what to do. A friend saw what was happening and said, "Remember that the essence of parenting is to make disciples. The One with all authority in heaven and on earth said, 'I am with you.'" So let me remind you, father, that if you become discouraged in trying to lead your family in worship, the Lord Christ says to you, "I am with you alway, even unto the end of the world" (Matt. 28:20).

We cannot exercise the offices of Christ apart from Christ. Apart from Him you can do nothing. But if you abide in Him you will bear much fruit. Look to Him. Rely upon His Holy Spirit, who anoints you out of His fullness. Take your guilt, shame, and sins as a father to your great High Priest. Wash your conscience in His precious blood. Cry out to the Lamb who was slain so that you can love your children as He does. Remember that He who prays for you is seated at the right hand of God. Even as you exercise kingly authority to defend and discipline your children, be much in prayer to the King of kings. Pray that He would conquer Satan and make your children willing to serve Him. Your weakness can become the platform where His strength is displayed.

Faith in our "chief Prophet and Teacher," "only High Priest," and "eternal King," as the Heidelberg Catechism says,[5] will make you confident and active. Therefore, in His name, teach your family. Love them. Sacrifice for them. Evangelize them. Pray for them. Rule them. Protect them. Draw them to worship God. Persevere in faithfulness as a father.

Perhaps you have failed to lead your family in God's worship or have been passive. You have fallen short of providing leadership in your home. It is never too late to start evangelizing your children or to speak to them about spiritual things. It is never too late to confess your own sin to them, even after they have moved out of the home. It is never too late for you to find grace and mercy from the great Prophet, Priest, and King. Perhaps God will grant you the opportunity to help your children by instructing your grandchildren in the ways of God. Use every opportunity you are given to influence the grandchildren God has given to you. If you have never been a spiritual leader in your home, today is the day to begin.

---

5. The Heidelberg Catechism (LD 12, Q. 31), in *The Three Forms of Unity* (Solid Ground Christian Books, 2010), 78.

CHAPTER ELEVEN

The Redeemed Man Cultivating Friendships

Michael A. G. Azad Haykin

THE ENGLISH ANGLICAN writer C. S. Lewis has an ingenious little book entitled *The Screwtape Letters*, a commentary on spiritual warfare from the point of view of our enemy. In it there is one letter from the senior devil Screwtape to his nephew Wormwood in which Screwtape rejoices over the fact that "in modern Christian writings" there is to be found "few of the old warnings about Worldly Vanities, the Choice of Friends, and the Value of Time."[1] Now, whether or not Lewis was right with regard to a scarcity of twentieth-century Christian literature about "Worldly Vanities" and "the Value of Time," he was undoubtedly correct when it came to the topic of friendship. For a large part of the twentieth century, Christian reflection on friendship was something of a rarity and was a definite departure from a long tradition within the halls of the Christian Faith that saw friendship as vital to Christian living.

---

1. C. S. Lewis, *The Screwtape Letters*, Letter 10, in *The Best of C. S. Lewis* (Canon Press, 1969), 43.

The Christian Tradition of Friendship

Four vignettes help to reveal this tradition. In the ancient church, alongside the importance of showing love to all men and women—family, friends, acquaintances, even enemies—friendship was highly valued. In fact, the emphasis placed on the unity in Christ of all Christians encouraged a high degree of spiritual intimacy that resembled, and even surpassed, the intimacy considered by Graeco-Roman paganism to be essential to the experience of genuine friendship.[2] Gregory of Nazianzus, a leading fourth-century Greek Christian theologian, thus wrote of his friendship with Basil of Caesarea during their time together as students in Athens in the 350s:

> In studies, in lodgings, in discussions I had him as companion. . . . We had all things in common. . . . But above all it was God, of course, and a mutual desire for higher things, that drew us to each other. As a result we reached such a pitch of confidence that we revealed the depths of our hearts, becoming ever more united in our yearning.[3]

Given this estimation of friendship, it is not surprising that Gregory was convinced that "if anyone were to ask me, 'What is the best thing in life?,' I would answer, 'Friends.'"[4]

In the Middle Ages, Aelred of Rievaulx, an English Cistercian monk, penned a classic on this subject, *Spiritual Friendship*. For Aelred, genuine

---

2. Carolinne White, *Christian Friendship in the Fourth Century* (Cambridge University Press, 1992), 57.
3. Gregory of Nazianzus, *De vita sua*, 225–35, trans. Denise Molaise Meehan, *Saint Gregory of Nazianzus: Three Poems*, The Fathers of the Church, vol. 75 (Catholic University of America Press, 1987), 83-84.
4. Cited in White, *Christian Friendship*, 70. On Gregory's understanding of friendship, see also David Konstan, *Friendship in the Classical World* (Cambridge University Press, 1997), 163–65.

friendship must "begin in Christ, continue in Christ, and be perfected in Christ." And such spiritual friendship is to be highly prized: "In human affairs nothing more sacred is striven for, nothing more useful is sought after, nothing more difficult is discovered, nothing more sweet experienced, and nothing more profitable possessed. For friendship bears fruit in this life and in the next."[5]

And at the beginning of the modern era, John Calvin, who has had the undeserved reputation of being cold and harsh and unloving, also had a rich appreciation of friendship. The French Reformed historian Richard Stauffer reckoned that there were few men at the time of the Reformation "who developed as many friendships" as Calvin.[6] Two of his closest friends were his fellow Reformers William Farel and Pierre Viret. Calvin celebrated his friendship with these two men in his preface to his *Commentary on Titus*, where he stated:

> I do not believe that there have ever been such friends who have lived together in such a deep friendship in their everyday style of life in this world as we have in our ministry. I have served here in the office of pastor with you two. There was never any appearance of envy; it seems to me that you two and I were as one person. ... And we have shown through visible witness and good authority before men that we have among us no other understanding or friendship than that which has been dedicated to the name of Christ, has been to the present time of profit to his church, and has no other purpose but that all may be one in him with us.[7]

---

5. Aelred of Rievaulx, *Spiritual Friendship* 1.9, 2.9, trans. Mary Eugenia Laker (Cistercian Publications, 1977), 53, 71.
6. Richard Stauffer, *The Humanness of John Calvin*, trans. George H. Shriver (Abingdon Press, 1971), 47.
7. Cited in Stauffer, *Humanness of Calvin*, 57. On Calvin's friendships, see especially Machiel A. van den Berg, *Friends of Calvin*, trans. Reinder Bruinsma (Eerdmans, 2009).

This brotherly friendship can be seen in the extant correspondence of these three men: 163 letters from Calvin to Farel; 137 from Farel to Calvin; 204 letters from Calvin to Viret; and 185 from Viret to Calvin. Not only did they frankly discuss theological problems and ecclesiastical matters, but they also demonstrated an openness in relation to the problems of their private lives.

Finally, in the early summer of 1783, John Sutcliff, the minister of the Baptist cause in Olney, Buckinghamshire—a town remembered today for its connections with the hymnwriters and best of friends, John Newton and William Cowper—sat down in his study to write a brief note to a friend in Bicester, Oxfordshire. A few short sentences at the outset of this letter sum up the entire tradition of Christian thinking about friendship that we have been noting:

> I embrace an opportunity of sending you a line as a token of love. The friendship I received from you and others at Bicester has made an impression on my heart, that I trust will never wear away. Christian friendship is the sweetest of all connections. It is the very life and soul of every other. Souls joined together with this heavenly cement are eternally united. Such acquaintance and intercourse are begun here below, but are to ripen and be perfected in the heavenly world. There, distance of place or difference of sentiment will never interrupt the communion of saints.[8]

Again, we see high praise for the surpassing excellence of Christian friendship. But exactly how does the "heavenly cement" of friendship, as Sutcliff put it in this letter, actually bind Christians together? To answer this question, let's turn to a friendship that comes from Sutcliff's own era

---

8. John Sutcliff, Letter, May 22, 1783, in *Christian Watchman and Reflector* (March 2, 1854): 35. For more on Sutcliff's experience of Christian friendship, see Michael A. G. Haykin, *One Heart and One Soul: John Sutcliff of Olney, His Friends, and His Times* (Evangelical Press, 1994).

and from among his own Baptist community, namely, the friendship that developed and flourished between two eighteenth-century Welsh Baptist pastors, Benjamin Francis and Joshua Thomas.[9]

"Queries and Solutions"

For forty-three years Thomas was the pastor of Leominster Baptist Church, in Herefordshire. In the keeping of this church, there is an unpublished manuscript that records the precious friendship between Thomas and Francis, pastor of the Baptist work in Horsley, Gloucestershire, from 1757 till his death. The manuscript, entitled "Queries and Solutions," is actually a transcript drawn up by Thomas of letters that passed between him and Francis from 1758 to 1770.[10]

The practice of Francis and Thomas appears to have been for one of them to mail two or three queries periodically to the other. Then, some months later the recipient mailed back his answers, together with fresh questions of his own. These answers were commented on, the new questions answered, and both the comments and answers mailed back along

---

9. For Benjamin Francis, see Thomas Flint, "A Brief Narrative of the Life and Death of the Rev. Benjamin Francis, A.M.," annexed to John Ryland, Jr., *The Presence of Christ the Source of Eternal Bliss. A Funeral Discourse... Occasioned by the Death of the Rev. Benjamin Francis, A. M.* (Bristol, 1800), 33–76; Geoffrey F. Nuttall, "Letters by Benjamin Francis," *Trafodion* (1983): 4–8; Michael A. G. Haykin, "Benjamin Francis (1734–1799)," in *The British Particular Baptists, 1638–1910*, ed. Michael A. G. Haykin (Particular Baptist Press, 2000), 2:16–29. I have also benefited from Gwyn Davies, "A Welsh Exile: Benjamin Francis (1734–99)" (Unpublished ms., 1999), 3 pages.

For Joshua Thomas, see Eric W. Hayden, *Joshua Thomas: A Biography*, in *The American Baptist Heritage in Wales*, ed. Carroll C. and Willard A. Ramsey (Church History Research and Archives Affiliation, 1976), Part Two.

10. There is also a copy of this manuscript in Bristol Baptist College: MS G.98.5; Bristol Baptist College Library, Bristol, England. On this correspondence, see Geoffrey F. Nuttall, "Questions and Answers: An Eighteenth-Century Correspondence," *The Baptist Quarterly* 27 (1977–1978): 83–90.

with new queries, and so forth. All in all, there are sixty-eight questions and answers in two volumes—fifty-eight in the first volume and the remaining ten in the second volume. On only one occasion during these years from 1758 to 1770 was there a noticeable gap in correspondence. That was in 1765 when Francis lost his wife and his three youngest children.

It is noteworthy that at the beginning of the correspondence the two friends sign their letters simply with their names or initials. However, as time passes, their mutual confidence and intimacy deepens, and they begin to write "yours endearingly" or "yours unfeignedly" and even "yours indefatigably" or "yours inexpressibly." It was in October 1762 that Thomas first signed himself "your cordial Brother Jonathan," and in the following February Francis replied with "your most affectionate David." From this point on this is the way the two friends refer to each other.

Francis and Thomas saw in their friendship a reflection of that between David and Jonathan. In a key biblical passage that describes the friendship of the latter, 1 Samuel 18:1–3, we read that "the soul of Jonathan was knit to the soul of David, and Jonathan loved him as his own soul.... Then Jonathan and David made a covenant, because he loved him as his own soul." The knitting together of the souls of Jonathan and David, and their eighteenth-century counterparts, Francis and Thomas, bespeaks the sharing of innermost thoughts and feelings and is charged with deep intimacy. But it is equally noteworthy that four years passed before Francis and Thomas began to speak along these lines. Deep and meaningful friendships do not happen overnight nor are they wrought in the twinkling of an eye. They take time to deepen and mature.

On Prayer

The questions and their answers are extremely instructive as to the areas of personal theological interest among mid-eighteenth-century Calvinists. For instance, the question is asked, "When may a Minister conclude that he is influenced and assisted by the Spirit of God in studying and ministering the word?"[11] Queries are raised about the eternal state of dead infants,[12] how best to understand the remarks in Revelation 20 about the millennium,[13] and about whether or not inoculation against that dreaded killer of the eighteenth century, smallpox, was right or wrong.[14]

Let's look closer at those questions and answers that relate to prayer, one of the most vital areas of the believer's walk with God, but about which men are often reluctant to talk. "How often should a Christian pray?," Francis asked his friend on one occasion.[15] Thomas has an extensive answer to this important question. He deals first with what he calls the "ejaculatory kind" of prayer—prayers that arise spontaneously during the course of a day's activities—and then the prayers offered during times set apart specifically for prayer, what a later generation of Evangelicals would call "the quiet time."

In response to Thomas's answer, Francis confesses to his friend,

> I wish all our Brethren of the Tribe of Levi were so free from lukewarmness, on the one hand, and enthusiasm, formality & superstition on the other, as my Jonathan appears to be. I am too barren in all my Prayers, but I think mostly so in Closet prayer (except at some seasons) which tempts me in some measure to prefer a more constant ejaculatory Prayer above a more statedly Closet prayer, tho I am persuaded neither should be neglected. Ejaculatory prayer is generally warm, free, and pure, tho short: but I find Closet prayer to be often cold, stiff or artificiall, as it were, and mixt with strange impertinences & wandrings of heart.

11. "Queries and Solutions," Vol. 1, Query 5.
12. "Queries and Solutions," Vol. 1, Queries 17 and 22.
13. "Queries and Solutions," Vol. 1, Query 18
14. "Queries and Solutions," Vol. 1, Query 45.
15. "Queries and Solutions," Vol. 1, Query 44.

Lord teach me to pray! O that I could perform the Duty always, as a duty and a privilege & not as a Task and a Burden![16]

Here, Francis begins by emphasizing his concern that his prayer-life be marked by a zeal that was free from that bugbear of the eighteenth-century, "enthusiasm," or fanaticism. He was also concerned that it not be marked by "formality," a concern he picks up at the very end of this quotation, where he expresses the hope that his prayers not be "a Task and a Burden." In other words, he is longing for prayer that is "warm, free, and pure," that is, sincere—his experience of "ejaculatory prayer." On the other hand, he confesses that he struggles with his regular times of devotion. They are often marred by praying that is "cold, stiff, or artificiall" and that cannot maintain its focus on God. In another of Francis' comments about his praying we find the same honesty and humility repeated: "How languid my faith, my hope, my love! How cold and formal am I in secret Devotions!"[17] These remarks surely stem from deep-seated convictions about the vital importance of prayer, and prompt Francis to cry out, like the first disciples, for his Lord to teach him to pray.

Francis's frank remarks about his own struggles with prayer also have their root in Francis's belief that because the Lord had led him to seek Christ at a very young age—and, in his words, "overwhelmed me with Joy by a sense of his Love"—he should be more eager to pray out of a sense of gratitude. Instead, he confessed, "A stupid, indolent, sensual or legal Temper sadly clog the Wings of my Prayers."[18] He well knew the "Opposition, or at least Disinclination I find in my wicked Heart too often unto Prayer, as if it were to perform some very painful service."[19]

16. "Queries and Solutions," Vol. 1, Remarks on [Thomas's] answer to Queries 43 & 44.
17. "Queries and Solutions," Vol. 1, Remarks on [Thomas'] answer to Query 48.
18. "Queries and Solutions," Vol. 2, Remarks on Queries 7–8.
19. "Queries and Solutions," Vol. 2, Remarks on Queries 7–8.

Thomas sought to encourage Francis by reminding him that

> closet prayer [is like] the smoke on a windy day. When it is very calm the smoke will ascend and resemble an erect pillar, but when windy, as soon as it is out it is scattered to and fro, sometimes 'tis beaten down the chimney again and fills the house. Shall I not thus give over? Satan would have it so, and flesh would have it so, but I should be more earnest in it.

Francis told his friend that he sought to pray to God twice daily, but he confessed that his difficulties with following a discipline of a set time for prayer stemmed from his being away from his home a lot of the time. He also admitted that he had taken up "an unhappy Habit of Sleeping in the Morning much longer" than he should have. And this cut into valuable time for prayer. But he did not try to excuse such failings.[20]

Though much has changed since Francis's day, yet this struggle with sin and poor habits that hinder prayer and devotion remains the same. And yet, there must have been times when Francis knew the joys of experientially fellowshiping with God in prayer. For instance, answering a question by Thomas—"Wherein doth communion and fellowship with God consist?"—Francis replies in part:

> In a nearness to God that is inexpressible, thro the Mediator, and in the enjoyment of God's favour and perfections, yielding nourishing satisfactions in God, as the souls full, everlasting portion and felicity. This enjoyment overwhelms the soul with wonder, glory, joy and triumph: it enflames it with vehement love to God and ardent wishes after his blissful presence in the heavenly world.[21]

---

20. "Queries and Solutions," Vol. 2, Remarks on Queries 7–8.
21. "Queries and Solutions," Vol. 1, Query 55.

Yet, as Francis well knew, these foretastes of glory given to the believer in prayer are not a resting place in this world. Christ, not *the believer's* experience of communing with him in prayer, is ever to be the focus of prayer. Thus, Francis could pray—and this text well reveals the Christ-centered nature of historic Calvinistic spirituality—only a year before his death:

> O that every sacrifice I offer were consumed with the fire of ardent love to Jesus. Reading, praying, studying and preaching are to me very cold exercises, if not warmed with the love of Christ. This, this is the quintessence of holiness, of happiness, of heaven. While many professors desire to know that Christ loves them, may it ever be my desire to know that I love him, by feeling his love mortifying in me the love of self, animating my whole soul to serve him, and, if called by his providence, to suffer even death for his sake.[22]

Coda

The struggles of Francis with regard to prayer were, and are, not unique to him. Most of us know the struggle that Francis described. But how few of us are willing to confess it to a close friend. Here we see the way that an intimate friendship can be of great help in the Christian life: confessing our failings to our closest friends so that they can help us and pray for us. Friendship, then, is a key means to fulfill the command found in James 5:16: "Confess your trespasses to one another, and pray for one another, that you may be healed."

Finally, the time that Francis and Thomas took to read each other's letters and queries and then, with their quill pens and inkwells, craft their answers, speaks to the way that friendships like theirs take time. Little wonder that far too many Christian men do not have deep friendships

---

22. Benjamin Francis, letter to a friend, November 6, 1798, in Flint, "Brief Narrative of the Life and Death of the Rev. Benjamin Francis, A.M.," 58–59.

like that of Francis and Thomas. For our modern Western culture is a busy, busy world that as a rule is far more interested in receiving and possessing than sacrificing and giving. The nurture and development of deep, long-lasting, satisfying friendships takes time and sacrifice. But such friendships are worth the investment of time, for they bear fruit both within our temporal and in the eternal world to come. As John Sutcliff rightly noted—sentiments to which Francis and Thomas would have wholeheartedly agreed: "Souls joined together with this heavenly cement [of friendship] are eternally united. Such acquaintance and intercourse are begun here below, but are to ripen and be perfected in the heavenly world. There, distance of place or difference of sentiment will never interrupt the communion of saints."[23]

23. Sutcliff, Letter, May 22, 1783, in *Christian Watchman and Reflector* (March 2, 1854): 35. For more practical guidance on developing biblical friendships, see Michael A. G. Haykin and Joel R. Beeke, *How Should We Develop Biblical Friendship?* (Reformation Heritage Books, 2015).

CHAPTER TWELVE

The Redeemed Man Witnessing to Unbelievers

David Strain

SPEAKING TO OTHERS about Jesus is becoming increasingly challenging. We live in a post-Christian society. The exclusive claims of Christ and the absolute demands of the moral law run counter to the norms and values of our cultural moment. To speak about Christ to a non-Christian friend is potentially to risk much. And yet, in view of this post-Christian world, and the countless numbers of unconverted men and women, boys and girls, facing a lost eternity, it has never been more urgent that Christian men face honestly the scriptural imperative to bear witness for Christ and learn to open their mouths to speak—humbly, lovingly, and courageously—for their Savior.

The Duty to Bear Witness

When Jesus said to the disciples, "You shall be witnesses to Me" (Acts 1:8), He was sending the church on His mission into the world. In particular, it was a task given to the apostles who were, quite literally, eyewitnesses of Christ's resurrection. They were sent by their risen Lord, as His authorized and inspired spokesmen, to interpret the meaning and significance of His first coming. There are no more apostles today. Yet still the duty to bear witness to Jesus Christ continues, for, while none of us have ever seen Christ with our eyes, we love Him and receive the end of our faith—the salvation of our souls (1 Peter 1:8).

We are united to Christ by faith, filled with His Spirit, and recipients of the benefits of His redeeming blood. He is ours, and we are His. And so, like the woman at the well, a redeemed man should actually find it difficult to refrain from telling his friends and neighbors, "Come, see a Man who told me all things that I ever did" (John 4:29). Like Peter and John before the Sanhedrin, we admit that "we cannot but speak the things which we have seen and heard" (Acts 4:20). Knowing Christ and keeping Him to ourselves is a contradiction in terms.

The duty of the redeemed man to bear witness to Christ is clear from a number of Scripture passages. In the context of the Sermon on the Mount, in Matthew 5:13–16, Jesus gave two pictures of the witnessing obligations of the ordinary Christian.

First, in verse 13, he compared His people to salt: "You are the salt of the earth; but if the salt loses its flavor, how shall it be seasoned? It is then good for nothing but to be thrown out and trampled underfoot by men." In the beatitudes which precede these verses, Jesus spoke in general terms of any person who meets certain qualifications: "Blessed are *they* who . . . ," meaning, "*These kinds* of people are the blessed ones. . . . " But beginning in verse 11, speaking about persecution, and continuing on here, Jesus gets more specific. He changes the pronoun. "Blessed are *you*," He says, speaking directly and exclusively now to His disciples. And this form of address continues on in verse 13, "*You* are the salt of the earth," that is, "you reviled and persecuted ones for righteousness" sake, *you* are the salt of the earth." Jesus is speaking to His own followers, for whom life in His service must involve both witness and suffering for Christ's sake.

So, what does it mean to be the salt of the earth? The clue comes in the initially puzzling statement that follows: "but if the salt loses its flavor, how shall it be seasoned? It is then good for nothing but to be thrown out and trampled underfoot by men." We know that, strictly speaking, sodium chloride cannot lose its flavor. But in Jesus's day, typically, "salt" was an impure mixture of minerals from which the sodium chloride could slowly be leached away over time. In such cases all that would be left was a lump of tasteless mineral of no use to anyone. The emphasis in the passage, therefore, is on the importance of retaining the distinctive flavor—the unique saltiness—of a Christian's whole-life devotion to Jesus Christ. As one commentator has put it, Christians "give a tang to life like salt to a dish of food."[1] It is the calling of a redeemed man to be *distinctive*. Perhaps especially in focus here, he is to be distinctive in his *lifestyle* of unmistakable trust in and love for the Lord Jesus Christ. Long before he says anything, who he is, his God-given, grace-wrought saltiness flavors all he does. This is the expectation of Jesus Christ for all His disciples.

And the second metaphor builds on this expectation. In verses 14–16 Jesus said, "You are the light of the world. A city that is set on a hill cannot be hidden. Nor do they light a lamp and put it under a basket, but on a lampstand, and it gives light to all who are in the house. Let your light so shine before men, that they may see your good works and glorify your Father in heaven." In other words, "Not only are you to be like salt—distinctively Mine—you are to be the light of the world. That is, your witness must be *unavoidable*."

The focus falls clearly on the *character* of light, and the *design* of the One who makes the light shine. A hilltop city at night cannot be hidden. Its light shines for all to see (v. 14). That is its *character*. In the same way, authentic Christians stand out. They are citizens of another world. The light of life shines in them amidst the darkness and spiritual death of the world all around. Likewise, Jesus says, if you light a lamp, you'd never cover it with a basket so that the house stayed dark. That would be absurd. No, you put the lamp up high on its stand, to give light for everyone in the house

---

1. Leon Morris, *The Gospel according to Matthew*, The Pillar New Testament Commentary (Eerdmans, 1992), 104.

that night (v. 15). The *purpose* of the light is the key thing. And its purpose is to be *seen*. If Christians are the light of the world, God's design in setting the lamps of our lives burning brightly is that everyone will see the truth clearly because of us. And so, Jesus applies His message in verse 16: "Let your light so shine before men, that they may see your good works and glorify your Father in heaven."

The point is inescapable: to be a faithful follower of Jesus Christ requires that the light of gospel truth shines brightly from our lives and from our lips. By His saving grace, God made His light to shine in your heart to "give [you] the light of the knowledge of the glory of God in the face of Jesus Christ" (2 Cor. 4:6). His design in lighting that lamp was, in part, that others might see it.

Let's ask ourselves, what is there of the distinctive saltiness of Christian discipleship about our lives? Jesus's warning is that salt that loses its saltiness—a so-called Christian without any distinctive flavor of Christ about him—is a worthless thing, in grave danger of divine condemnation. So, let's examine our lives and ask whether our light burns brightly enough, that all may see the truth of the gospel in our testimony. That was the purpose of God when He first lit His candle in your life. He intended that you would be His witness in a dark world. In Jesus's view, a Christian man who hides his light under a basket is an absurdity. We make the gospel a laughingstock when we who profess to believe it and love it and live for it are so afraid of a hostile world that we won't let anyone ever *hear* it from our lips or *see* its power at work in our lives!

Prerequisites for an Effective Witness

If bearing witness to Christ and His gospel is the redeemed man's duty, what are the necessary prerequisites that must be met for that witness to be effective? Many things might legitimately be said in this connection. I will restrict myself to four.

The first prerequisite for effective witness is *gospel clarity*. I will not say much about this, not because it is unimportant, but because it consists of objective knowledge that is relatively easy to obtain. We can and should learn the facts of the Christian gospel. Memorize some key verses of Scripture that summarize the bad news about human sin and the good news about God's provision for sinners in the obedience and blood of Christ.[2] Get a simple outline of the gospel in your mind so that you will be ready to share it whenever opportunity arises. So often our witness fails, not for a lack of willingness but for a lack of gospel clarity.

The second prerequisite for effective witness is *godly character*. The apostle Peter urges Christians to "sanctify the Lord God in your hearts, and always be ready to give a defense to everyone who asks you a reason for the hope that is in you, with meekness and fear; having a good conscience, that when they defame you as evildoers, those who revile your good conduct in Christ may be ashamed" (1 Peter 3:15–16). Notice the combination of readiness to speak for Christ ("always be ready to give a defense"), and godly character ("meekness and fear . . . a good conscience . . . your good conduct"). The life and the message must match. This, Peter says, is how we shall awaken the conscience of the unconverted. They may defame you and revile your good conduct, but your unimpeachable character will smite their consciences, and, we pray, will make them willing to reconsider the message of good news for guilty sinners that they have heard from us. Do your words and your works match? Does your life commend your message?

The apostle Paul's words to Titus about the conduct of slaves on this point use a helpful expression. We are to "adorn the gospel of God our Savior in all things" (Titus 2:10). The verb "to adorn" means to beautify something by decoration. But there's a striking difference between, say, the way Christmas lights adorn a plain green fir tree, and the way a

---

2. For example, Matt. 11:28–30; Acts 4:12; Rom. 3:23–25; 2 Cor. 5:21; Titus 3:3–7.

redeemed life adorns the doctrine of God our Savior. Our cosmetic decorations are meant to take something drab and ordinary, and make it more beautiful than it really is. That's not how we adorn the Word. The life of a redeemed sinner does not adorn the doctrine of God our Savior by adding anything to His beauty—as if God were some dreary, everyday object in need of the extra sparkle only we can provide! No, we adorn the doctrine of God by showing how unalterably and inexpressibly glorious He already is, by the open display in our lives and conversation of the power of the gospel that has saved us and made us new creatures in Christ. In other words, we adorn the doctrine of God our Savior by our godly character. If we would bear effective witness to God our Savior, our lives must adorn—not detract from—the truth we profess and proclaim.

Does your life show something of the beauty of God who saves sinners? Or would no one ever guess that you profess to follow Jesus from the way you live among them every day? Too often, ashamed of our moral failures and spiritual inconsistency, we refrain from sharing the gospel. We don't want our hypocrisy to be exposed, and so we hide our faith from view. But this is not the answer. Instead, repent of your lukewarm devotion to Jesus Christ. Turn from your mediocrity. Confess and forsake your hypocrisy. Humble yourself and speak up for Jesus. Admit to your unconverted friends that you are indeed a wretched sinner, filled with many inconsistencies, but you grieve over them and flee to the only One who can deal with them, pardon them, and remove them. And you urge them to join you in doing the same.

A third prerequisite necessary to bear effective witness is *zeal for the salvation of the lost*. What will drive us to open our mouths and take what sometimes feels like a terrible risk, and speak a word for Jesus Christ? We can do all the evangelism training, memorize gospel outlines, read book after book, and listen to sermon after sermon reinforcing the point that sharing the gospel is our duty, but until our hearts begin to melt with love and concern for the plight of our unconverted friends and neighbors, we will never get past our insecurity and speak up. Rico Tice tells the story of sharing with one of his friends on the rugby team a recording of an evangelistic sermon he had preached while at university:

> I remember that in the sermon, I simply and starkly said that either we pay for our sin in hell, or the Lamb pays for us on the cross. This friend, called Ed, played my sermon one night to his housemates who were in the same rugby team as us; and one of them, Dave, got very upset. He said, "If that's what Rico believes, the fact he's said nothing of it to me in months means he's not really my friend." So, Ed rang me up and said, "Rico, you need to speak to Dave; he's upset that you've never talked to him 'til now about what's in the sermon." And Dave was right. If I'd really loved him, I'd have warned him about hell, shown him the cross, and invited him to trust Jesus.[3]

Love constrains us to speak up. "The love of Christ compels us" (2 Cor. 5:14) ought to be our explanation for why we feel we must share the gospel with others.

Consider the example of the apostle Paul. He told his readers in Rome, "I have great sorrow and continual grief in my heart. For I could wish that I myself were accursed from Christ for my brethren, my countrymen according to the flesh" (Rom. 9:2–3). Paul loved his unconverted Jewish friends so intensely that he felt unceasing grief over their lost condition. He went so far as to suggest that he could almost wish to be severed from his union with Christ, if it might mean that they could be saved. This isn't melodrama or exaggeration.[4] It is the echo of the love of

---

3. Rico Tice, *Honest Evangelism: How to Talk about Jesus Even When It's Tough* (Good Book Company, 2015), 39.
4. Note that Paul begins the verse insisting on his sincerity as he makes his remarkable statement of sacrificial love: "I tell the truth in Christ, I am not lying, my conscience also bearing me witness in the Holy Spirit" (Rom. 9:1).

Jesus Christ for sinners in Paul's own heart and life. Jesus is the "Son of God who loved me and gave Himself for me" (Gal. 2:20). Jesus loved us and endured the hell of the cross that we might live. Surely, in the heart of every redeemed man, there ought to be something of an echo of the Savior's love for us, moving us to be willing to sacrifice self for the eternal good of others. Most of us are not likely to be called upon to give our lives for the gospel. Nor is there any possibility of being severed from Christ Himself. But can't we give up our comfort, risk a little embarrassment, step out of our comfort zone once in a while to tell people whom we profess to love about their great danger without Christ, and share his free invitation to them to find mercy in Him?

A fourth prerequisite for effective witness is *an unswerving confidence in the sovereignty of God in salvation*. After Jesus concluded His preaching tour of the Galilean towns of Bethsaida and Capernaum and Chorazin, He denounced these towns for their unbelief, comparing them unfavorably to Sodom and Gomorrah (Matt. 11:20–24). Remarkably, many in these towns failed to respond to His ministry. This reminds us that faithfulness does not always result in fruitfulness, not even when it is the incarnate Son of God who is preaching. The verses that follow then give us Jesus' personal response to the unbelief that confronted Him. As such they provide a remarkable resource for us as we contemplate the difficulties with which our own witness to the truth is often met.

In face of the relative ineffectiveness of His preaching ministry in these towns, Jesus turns to prayer. And then, strengthened by His communion with God, He immediately returns to proclaiming the good news of the gospel, saying, "Come to Me, all you who labor and are heavy laden, and I will give you rest. Take My yoke upon you and learn from Me, for I am gentle and lowly in heart, and you will find rest for your souls. For My yoke is easy and My burden is light" (Matt. 11:28–30).

It is a stunning moment. The people have not come thus far, though the incarnate Son of God Himself has pled with them to turn to Him. And yet, here He stands once more, calling the lost and recalcitrant people of Galilee to take from Him the freely offered rest they all so desperately need. What is it that bolstered and strengthened His resolve, after such a negative reaction to His ministry? Why not wash His hands of them, brush the dust from His feet, and move on to a more receptive audience? What encouraged our Lord to persist in His evangelism? It can only have been the truths He declared in His prayer of verses 25–27:

> I thank You, Father, Lord of heaven and earth, that You have hidden these things from the wise and prudent and have revealed them to babes. Even so, Father, for so it seemed good in Your sight. All things have been delivered to Me by My Father, and no one knows the Son except the Father. Nor does anyone know the Father except the Son, and the one to whom the Son wills to reveal Him.

Jesus's explanation for the minimal response of Bethsaida and Chorazin and Capernaum to His message was not to conclude that He had failed to apply the proper evangelistic technique in "sealing the deal" as He dealt with sinners. No, the reason Jesus's ministry met with limited success on this preaching tour of Galilee, according to Jesus, must be looked for in the sovereign design and electing purpose of Almighty God who has "hidden these things from the wise and prudent and have revealed them to babes . . . for so it seemed good" in His sight. Jesus rehearses the doctrines of election and irresistible grace and effectual calling in His prayer, and then, fortified by these great truths, He gets right back to preaching His message to the very people who have thus far thumbed their noses at Him. The sovereignty of God strengthened and propelled Jesus's evangelism, and it can do the same for ours!

Or consider the example of Paul. In Romans 9 we have the doctrine of election clearly outlined for us as the great explanation for the general rejection of the gospel by the majority of the Jewish people. Paul writes,

For He says to Moses, "I will have mercy on whomever I will have mercy, and I will have compassion on whomever I will have compassion." So then it is not of him who wills, nor of him who runs, but of God who shows mercy. For the Scripture says to the Pharaoh, "For this very purpose I have raised you up, that I may show My power in you, and that My name may be declared in all the earth." Therefore He has mercy on whom He wills, and whom He wills He hardens. (Rom. 9:15–18)

Here is a most robust declaration of election and reprobation. But far from the doctrines of grace hindering evangelistic zeal, as many say they must surely do, instead we hear Paul in the opening verses of the very next chapter praying for the conversion of the lost: "Brothers, my heart's desire and prayer to God for them is that they may be saved" (Rom. 10:1).

And in the verses that follow that, he provides the clearest statement of the need for evangelists in the New Testament:

"Whoever calls on the name of the Lord shall be saved." How then shall they call on Him in whom they have not believed? And how shall they believe in Him of whom they have not heard? And how shall they hear without a preacher? And how shall they preach unless they are sent? As it is written: "How beautiful are the feet of those who preach the gospel of peace, who bring glad tidings of good things!" But they have not all obeyed the gospel. For Isaiah says, "Lord, who has believed our report?" So then faith comes by hearing, and hearing by the word of God. (Rom. 10:13–17)

So, clearly, for our Lord Jesus and His apostle, the absolute sovereignty of God in the salvation of sinners is not a hindrance, or a contradiction, but actually the very foundation of prayer for the conversion of the lost and the best encouragement for every evangelist who dares open his mouth to speak the gospel to others. "God has mercy on whom He wills, and whom He wills he hardens. . . . My heart's desire and prayer to God for them is that they might be saved. . . . Faith comes by hearing, and hearing by the word of God." So far as Paul is concerned, these truths hold no contradiction. Instead, the first (God's sovereignty) is the bedrock of Christian confidence as we practice the other two.

You can pray for your unconverted friends' salvation *only* because you trust the God who has the power to save. He alone calls sinners from death to life. Salvation is in His alone to give. Why pray to a god who saves no one but must merely wait, hoping that some sinner will turn to him by his own volition? For all we know—for all such a god himself can know—all his designs may be defeated entirely by the unforeseen free choice of sinners to reject him. If that were the case, we could have certainty about none of Christ's promises to build His church, nor expect with any degree of confidence that John's vision would be fulfilled that a vast company of the redeemed from every tribe and language and nation will be gathered around the throne of God and of the Lamb. What if no one believes? What if only a few turn to Christ? A god who is not sovereign, cannot guarantee the fulfilment of his own promises. Who would pray to such a god? No! Grasp the sovereignty of the true God and pray for Him to bring your friends and loved ones into His kingdom! Pray in the confidence that the One you address is mighty to save, and at His voice, many a Lazarus will step alive again from his tomb.

Grasp the sovereignty of God in salvation, and, like Jesus and Paul, you will lift all the burden of trying to "close the sale" from your shoulders. If, as some suggest, conversion is primarily the work of man, then leading men to salvation is in large part the responsibility of those who evangelize. But if "salvation belongs to the LORD" (Ps. 3:8), it is not our task to save people, change their minds, or manipulate a decision for Jesus from them. It is our task, simply, faithfully, clearly, and lovingly to tell them the gospel. What an awful burden to bear to believe that the conversion of your wife, children, colleagues, or friends depends on your skill in persuading them to believe! The fear that our failure to do enough, to say it just right, to find the best combination of arguments and appeals to finally get through, must haunt those who believe they bear this responsibility in evangelism.

But a redeemed man need not be haunted by any such fear. He knows that God will surely save all His people. Jesus said, "All that the Father gives Me will come to Me, and the one who comes to Me I will by no means cast out" (John 6:37). None of them will be lost. All the elect of God, all for whom Jesus died, will respond to the gospel, believe, and be saved. The mission of the gospel in the world cannot fail. So, grasp firmly the sovereignty of God (Rom. 9:15-18), pray for sinners to come to the Savior (10:1), rise from your knees to tell them that there is salvation for them in Jesus Christ alone, and plead with them boldly to come to him (10:9-13). Your prayers and your proclamation are the means your sovereign God will use, in His time and as He chooses, to fulfil His purpose to save sinners.

The Practice of Bearing Witness

What steps can we take, then, to engage in the work of bearing faithful witness to Jesus Christ? Let me suggest five.

First, *pray*. Prayerfully consider the network of existing family, colleagues, neighbors, and friends in which God in His providence has placed you. Almost certainly, among those with whom you already have a relationship there will be unconverted people. Make a list of those names and commit to praying for their conversion. As you pray, ask God for opportunities, wisely and winsomely, to speak to them about eternal matters.

Second, *practice hospitality*. As circumstances permit, open your home to those with whom you have a relationship who do not yet know Jesus. If you are married, discuss and plan with your wife ways to do this. Invite unconverted visitors and inquirers from your church into your home for a meal. If you can, invite other faithful church members who might share common ground with your guests. Exposing non-Christians to the preaching of the gospel in church and then showing them afterwards the joy and mutual love of vibrant gospel-community in the context of a Christian home can be a powerful tool in provoking the unconverted to consider seriously the truth of the message they have heard.

Third, *build genuine friendships*. Ask lots of open questions. Inquire after people's households and families. Ask about their likes and loves. Ask about their vocations and avocations. Build on mutual interests and seek to establish genuine friendships.

When it comes to what has been called "friendship evangelism" two common mistakes should be avoided. Sometimes those who use this phrase mean something like "creating a friendship with the sole aim of sharing the gospel." But this is not a real friendship. When friendships are forged by one party in the relationship only as a means to an end, it cannot be considered the genuine article. And anyone who discovered that we were only interested in being his or her friend in order to persuade them to become Christians would likely be deeply and quite rightly offended.

But sometimes proponents of "friendship evangelism" fall into the opposite error. They have built a deep and genuine friendship with a non-Christian. That is good, so far as it goes. But they have no real intention of ever actually sharing the gospel message, for fear that it will cause offense. But by calling such relationships a kind of "friendship evangelism" they baptize a friendship that has really been built upon a foundation of worldly priorities, and are excusing their lack of gospel communication by suggesting that, somehow, through the unspoken lifestyle of love that they show, their unconverted friend will be provoked to believe in a Jesus (a Jesus, mind you, about whom we cannot bring ourselves to actually speak!). In other words, much of the difficulty with what many call "friendship evangelism" is that it fails to involve either real friendship or true evangelism. Instead, let us seek to build honest, well-intentioned friendships with non-Christians in whose lives and wellbeing we are genuinely interested and for whom we pray and care deeply. And, precisely because we *do* care deeply for them, let us take every opportunity lovingly to point them to Jesus Christ.

Fourth, *speak naturally about what matters most of all to you*. We need to work hard at speaking naturally and humbly about our trust in Jesus in the course of everyday conversations. Everyone you know will eagerly tell you all about the people, places, and pastimes they care about without embarrassment or a moment's worry. Work, sports, children or grandchildren, politics, and the arts fill our conversations daily. Most people never stop to consider if you'd like to talk about their favorite subject before launching enthusiastically into a conversation on the topic. Yet Christians clam up when it comes to mentioning the one *Person* they claim love more than any other (the Lord Jesus Christ), the one *place* where lives are supernaturally transformed every week (the local church), and the one *pastime* that fits us for eternity (corporate worship, and private prayer and the reading of God's holy Word).

We must learn to move seamlessly and cheerfully from conversations about all the mundane details of our weekends, shared in common with our non-Christian friends, to the subjects of the church and the gospel and our Savior, and back again once more to every-day details, without worrying what our conversation partners think of us as we do it. They may be most animated about their grandchildren or their sports teams. Let us be most animated about what the Lord taught us from His Word on Sunday, or about the missionary report we heard recently, or about the young woman who professed her faith and was baptized. We want our unconverted friends to see that Jesus Christ, and His expanding kingdom, is what matters most to our lives. We want them to see that, while we have so much in common with them, the Lord Jesus is the one thing we have that they do not have, and He makes all the difference.

Fifth, *share gospel resources*. Have a sermon-link ready to text or email to someone from your cellphone. Have a gospel tract or booklet on hand that you can share. Better still, invite them to come to Sunday worship, or to a church-sponsored evangelistic event during the week.

You may feel tongue-tied and self-conscious about trying to articulate the gospel to your friend. I'd encourage you to try nevertheless. You will find, to your surprise, that God often uses the stumbling and nervous efforts of ordinary, prayerful disciples to disarm and confront the intellectual pride of the unconverted. But, even if you feel you can't say much for Jesus, you can still give away a good book, or send a link of an audio sermon, or invite your friend to come church with you to hear the gospel. In fact, it is typically a combination of all of these (conversations over time, good literature, sharing an online sermon from your pastor, and finally an invitation to church to hear him in person), that will be required before a person begins to consider the claims of Christ in earnest.

In the end, it will not be clever techniques or sophisticated arguments that will win the lost or make your witness effective. It will be faithfulness to Jesus, prayer for opportunities, courage to take those opportunities, and trying, with many weaknesses, to speak of Christ in a way that commends Him to the lost as their only hope for time and eternity. You do not need to be a great evangelist to be an effective witness. You need only be a faithful follower of Jesus Christ who longs to see his friends come to know Jesus too.

PART 3

A Godly Man's Work

CHAPTER THIRTEEN

The Redeemed Man Viewing Work Rightly

Richard D. Phillips

TWO MEN MEET, and the conversation almost inevitably goes something like this. "Hi, my name is Tom Williams, what's your name." "Nice to meet you, Tom. I'm Bill Davis." "What do you do, Bill?" "I'm a mechanic. What do you do, Tom?" "I'm a salesman." Family name and occupation: in our society, these are the defining factors of a man's life.

Christians will often be quick to lament the way a man's vocation conveys such a large portion of his identity: our relationship to God undoubtedly should rank higher than any other consideration. Moreover, many men engage in an idolatry of their work: the god to which they bow rules over them from nine to five and beyond. And yet it is not only Western culture that defines a man by his work: the Bible presents a man's vocation as an important part of who he is and what he does. Yes, Christian men must not embrace their work as though it were God. But at the same time the Bible teaches men to embrace their work unto the Lord. In a generation when increasingly few men embrace their vocations with ambition and commitment, the redeemed man receives his work as both from God and for God. The Christian takes Paul's view toward his labor: "And whatever you do in word or deed, do all in the name of the Lord Jesus, giving thanks to God the Father through Him" (Col. 3:17).

Consider the scorn that Scripture heaps on a lazy man: "If anyone will not work," Paul writes, "neither shall he eat" (2 Thess. 3:10). Christianity does not say, "We'll provide for his needs whether he works or not." Instead, the Bible expects God's people to work, and especially for men to provide for their families. Men have a duty to work! Moreover, men feel good when they work hard, and a life of good works brings pleasure to the Lord.

The Goodness of Work

One distinctive of the biblical view of vocation is that Christians see our work as good. Working is not merely an evil that is necessary for gaining money or other benefits—something we do in order to reach the point where we no longer have to work. Instead, Scripture presents a man's work as given to him by the Lord. Just as we tend to do in social interactions, practically the first thing that Genesis says about the first man Adam was the work that God gave him to do: "Then the LORD God took the man and put him in the garden of Eden to tend and keep it" (Gen. 2:15). The word translated as "tend"—often rendered as "work"—means far more than mere labor.[1] But it certainly does not mean less than earnest labor!

In short, work is good since it occurs not as a result of man's sin or God's curse in the fall of man, but as an ordinance of God's creation. When God created and "saw that it was good" (Gen. 1:25), one of the things He commended and blessed was man's work. Bruce Waltke rightly says, "Work is a gift of God, not a punishment for sin. Even before the Fall humanity has duties to perform."[2] In God's eyes, it is good for men to

---

1. For an elaboration of the pattern set down in Genesis 2:15, see my book, *The Masculine Mandate: God's Plan for Men* (Reformation Trust, 2010).
2. Bruce Waltke, *Genesis: A Commentary* (Zondervan, 2001), 87.

work and work hard. From this it follows, wrote John Calvin, "that men were created to employ themselves in some work, and not to lie down in inactivity and idleness."[3]

A man in our church recently went through a series of cancer surgeries that left him hospitalized for several months. His treatment was successful, and he has slowly regained his health. What a great moment it was for him and an answer to our prayers when he was able to go back to work for the first time. "I have been so longing to be productive," he told me. This relief at being able to work once again reflects the Bible's endorsement of men laboring in their vocation.

One proof of the goodness of work is that we will have vocations to fulfill even in eternity. This is how Jesus presented the subject in His parables of the talents and the minas. Our Lord told how a master went away and entrusted a mina (about six months wages) to each worker. When the lord returned, he demanded an accounting. One of his servants presented a profit of ten more minas, to which the master replied, "Well done, good servant; because you were faithful in a very little, have authority over ten cities" (Luke 19:17). Another servant had made five minas, and he was rewarded with authority over five cities (v. 19). We see the same thing in the parable of the talents, in which the faithful servant who earned five talents more was made "ruler over many things" (Matt. 25:21). We do not know what kind of work these rewards of work will entail (except there is a clear note on authority), only that they will involve partnership with Jesus. When Jesus exclaimed, "Enter into the joy of your lord" (Matt. 25:21), He was referring in part to the work of eternal glory.

In light of the Bible's positive take on good work, Christians should raise their children to take satisfaction in a job well done. Our sons and daughters should be taught to work hard and put their heart into their

---

3. John Calvin, *Genesis* (1874; repr., Banner of Truth, 1992), 125.

labor.[4] What Paul declared to Christian slaves should be emulated by every follower of Jesus: we must enthusiastically embrace our work, "not with eyeservice, as men-pleasers, but in sincerity of heart, fearing God" (Col. 3:22). To be sure, Christians should have balance in their lives. We not only work, but we worship together with God's people, and we invest ourselves in important relationships (both of which are high forms of work!). But we remember that work is both good and profitable, as Proverbs 10:4 observes: "He who has a slack hand becomes poor, but the hand of the diligent makes rich."

Why Work Is Hard

If work is so good, then why are our jobs so often difficult, boring, or even painful? The answer to this question—as with all similar questions of human suffering—is mankind's fall into sin. After Adam fell through transgression, it was still good for man to work. But notice how God placed His curse precisely on the calling that so gripped Adam's heart—his work. Because Adam violated God's command and ate from the forbidden tree, the Lord declared a curse on the ground for his sake:

> In toil you shall eat of it all the days of your life. Both thorns and thistles it shall bring forth for you, and you shall eat the herb of the field. In the sweat of your face you shall eat bread till you return to the ground, for out of it you were taken; for dust you are, and to dust you shall return. (Gen. 3:17–19)

There is much to notice in this vital passage that explains so much of the hardship of life, not least of which is death as punishment for transgression. But notice that while Adam will still work, now his work will be difficult and painful.

4. See Mary Beeke, *Teach Them to Work: Building a Positive Work Ethics in Our Children* (Reformation Heritage Books, 2021).

It is because of sin that work so often fails to provide for our material needs and demands arduous toil that leaves us empty. Yet work still *works*, as Proverbs 12:27 reminds us: "The lazy man does not roast what he took in hunting, but diligence is man's precious possession." This commendation of work in our fallen state notes how challenging it can be for a man to find balance in life. He may desire to be home with his family for dinner, but his job sometimes will not allow it. After the fall, Adam and his sons have to hustle in the workplace, or they will fall behind.

Yet even in the dust-strewn world in which a yard is weeded but the weeds soon come back, men still can find great satisfaction in their work. We see this fact in the work that we call hobbies. After all, what do men do after their daily work is completed? Some relax by working in the garden—which is, of course, work. Or perhaps you are an avid fan of your college football team? Then you are likely performing complex mathematics to analyze your team's performance, and you work hard at knowing all the offensive and defensive schemes and learning the strengths and weaknesses of each player. Whatever your hobby is—hunting, fishing, beekeeping, stamp collecting—what you are enjoying is the blessing of work, which God created good!

Given the importance of a man's work, the demands of our jobs, and the challenge of maintaining life balance, Christian men should pray about their vocational labors. We should ask for strength to work hard and well and for grace to honor the Lord in our labor. We must pray for God's help in providing for our family's needs. And we must ask the Lord to bless our work in the spirit of Psalm 90:16–17:

> Let Your work appear to Your servants,
> And Your glory to their children.
> And let the beauty of the LORD our God be upon us,
> And establish the work of our hands for us;
> Yes, establish the work of our hands.

Thinking About Your Vocation

While work was created good, not all work is equal. Worldly people assess the value of a job by the money it provides or the prestige it offers. But Christians will think differently. Many young men therefore feel anxiety when choosing a vocational career, just as older men feel in assessing their careers. Let me provide some counsel on what makes for a good vocation for a Christian man.

The first and most important question is, *does this work glorify God?* In the medieval times, Christians thought that only the work of the clergy was truly honoring to the Lord. The Protestant Reformation countered this error by noting that many kinds of vocations honor the Lord as His people follow His calling in their work. But since not all work glorifies God, Christians should be discerning in this respect above all others.

The clearest way that we can assess if our vocation is God-honoring is to ensure that it does not involve violating the Ten Commandments. If a job calls for us to be deceitful to customers or involves provocations to malice, lust, or dishonesty, then a Christian should get out of such work. On many occasions as a pastor, I have had a man at church come to me with a vocational conundrum. "Pastor, I'm in a difficult situation. My boss wants me to lie." This, of course, is not a conundrum at all! The ninth commandment bars God's people from giving false testimony, and therefore, no believer should be willing to engage in sinful work practices. The same might be said of the conscious exploitation of workers, grossly polluting the environment, or selling defective products. Moreover, we must remember the fourth commandment, which requires us to keep the Sabbath holy. God has ordained one day in seven as a day of rest and spiritual refreshment. Therefore, a vocation that habitually keeps a Christian from church does not honor the Lord. Another diagnostic as to whether our vocation is God-honoring asks if it brings us into wholesome or bad associations. Does the work corrupt or build up my character?

A second way for Christians to assess their vocation is, *does this work do good to people?* All kinds of jobs perform useful services or offer valuable goods. A faithful trash collector provides a meaningful service. Farmers who grow food, shopkeepers who sell useful products, real estate agents who help people purchase or sell a home, nurses who care for the sick, and teachers who mold children's minds and hearts—to mention only a few kinds of jobs—do an enormous amount of good to people.

The point is that Christians should seek to make their living through work that benefits people. Jesus taught that along with loving the Lord our God, "You shall love your neighbor as yourself" (Matt. 22:39). Some occupations provide a good financial return but do not accomplish anything of value. Whether it is skimming profits off the stock market or marketing products that are worthless, work that produces nothing of value is not a suitable vocation for God's servant. A Christian might ask, "Would I be embarrassed if my pastor visited my workplace and saw what I do?" If the answer is "Yes," then the vocation is probably not a good one.

A third diagnostic considers, *is this work for which my talents and interests are suitable?* Parents should keep this criterion in mind when guiding their children toward careers. My older son is an attorney, and before he entered law school, we prayerfully considered this vocational pursuit. Did he have an aptitude for this kind of work and would he find it enjoyable? Has he had previous success in using the requisite skills? When we realized that he possessed a studious attitude, was mentally agile and well-spoken, and then also considered the enormous good that a Christian attorney can achieve, we affirmed this choice. My younger son was always more scientifically oriented, loving mathematics and especially chemistry. It was not a difficult choice for him to pursue a career as a research scientist.

Perhaps you are completely different from my sons. Perhaps you find school a painful chore and are happiest when outdoors. The good news is that there are vocations available for you! You may end up changing careers, as so many men do today in their later twenties or thirties. It is not always easy to discover the kind of work you will enjoy and succeed in, and Christians should seek God's help through prayer in finding a suitable vocation.

A fourth criterion is one that many people think of first: *does this job enable me to provide for myself and my family?* Christian men should not think first of the paycheck, remembering how Jesus taught us, "You cannot serve God and mammon" (Matt. 6:24). Nonetheless, a man with a wife and children needs to provide for their material needs, not to mention their education. He also needs to contribute financially to the work of the local church. With these realities in mind, a job that pays well is better in general than a job that pays little. This same consideration should motivate men to advance in their careers. What a high and blessed calling it is for a man to provide the money that feeds, clothes, and shelters his family, along with resourcing the preaching of Christ's gospel!

A fifth and final consideration in choosing a vocation asks, *does this job enable me to lead a balanced life?* As we noticed, work in a fallen world will often be demanding and will strain our other priorities. Almost every job has its days when other priorities have to take a back seat. Yet Christian men must realize that we have a number of vocations in which we are called to be faithful. Is there a wedding ring on your finger? Then you have the vocation (divine calling) of husband. Are there children in your house? Then you have the vocation of father. As a Christian, you are called to church membership, and this also is an essential vocation. The challenge, then, is to be faithful not merely in one vocation to the exclusion of the others, but to be faithful in all our callings from the Lord. A Christian man therefore seeks a work vocation that not only meets the previous criteria but also enables him to be faithful as a husband, father, and church member—not to mention as a friend, neighbor, and citizen.

In most cases, the real issue is not what job we pursue but whether we have a biblically wise set of priorities that seeks a balanced life of godly service and achievement. Very few of us will look back happily over a life of work success and wealth if we did not raise our children faithfully or if our marriage failed. So, we ask ourselves, which is more important: that I get the big promotion or that I regularly worship with God's people? Which will be more significant: the size of my retirement account or my family relationships? Of course, most men need to gain promotions and also must plan for retirement. But a biblically faithful approach to life will prayerfully pursue balance, not making an idol of career success in such a way that places our family and church on the altar of this false worship.

By Jesus's reckoning, our Lord delights to see His people's faith in action through their work. A good vocation is therefore one in which a believer can live openly as a follower of Christ, speak freely about God's Word, and tell others the good news of our Savior.

An Audience of One

In Colossians 3:17, Paul reminds us that the ultimate recipient of our labor is God Himself: "Whatever you do in word or deed, do all in the name of the Lord Jesus, giving thanks to God the Father through Him." One passage that provides Jesus's assessment of His peoples' lives is found in Matthew 25:34–36, where Jesus tells us in advance of the praise that He will give to His faithful people after He returns. These verses, therefore, show us how our Lord assigns value to a Christian's achievements—a set of values that upends the way that most of us think about our life and work. We tend to think of success in terms of work achievements, money, or positions. But listen to what Jesus will say in praise of His faithful people:

> Come, you blessed of My Father, inherit the kingdom prepared for you from the foundation of the world: for I was hungry and you gave Me food; I was thirsty and you gave Me drink; I was a

stranger and you took Me in; I was naked and you clothed Me; I was sick and you visited Me; I was in prison and you came to Me.

Do you notice where Jesus's gives His attention when viewing our labors? In His view, a successful life is one that provides loving care and support to others in need. According to Jesus's teaching, what He values about my life is not so much how many books I have written, the work I do in pastoring the church, my labor in preaching sermons, and the like, but the daily integrity and grace that I exhibit in my treatment of people. This is not to say that Jesus does not care for my "regular" work or yours. Yet He reminds us that every Christian possesses a vocational calling to love and mercy.

I have been helped by an illustration of an accomplished young pianist who was making his concert debut on a famous stage. He played brilliantly and to thunderous applause. When he departed, the stage manager urged him to go out for his encore, but surprisingly the young pianist refused. The older man pointed to all the people standing on their feet cheering. "They love you! Go take your encore!" he pleaded. But the pianist pointed around the curtain to a solitary old man in the balcony who was neither standing nor cheering. He answered, "When that man stands and cheers, I will take my encore." The stage manager spluttered, "What is it about that one man that makes you care so much about his opinion?" The pianist answered, "That man is my piano teacher."

The point of the illustration is that in our vocations Christians ultimately serve an audience of One. Paul thus urged, "Whatever you do, do it heartily, as to the Lord and not to men" (Col. 3:23). The good news is that our Lord is not a harsh, disapproving Master like the piano teacher in the illustration. Like parents rising to cheer a boy who makes a base hit in baseball, our loving heavenly Father is gracious and loving in His appraisal of our work. The point for us is that we labor in our vocations to serve and please Him. And if the world frowns upon us or ignores our labor completely, if God is pleased, then we are richly rewarded. Conversely, though the world cheer and shower us with riches, if God is offended, our labor is for nothing.

Let us therefore measure our success in work according to God's standards given in His Word. Our labor should be that of faith, offered up for the glory of God and the well-being of our neighbor. And when our work has been done in God's name through faith, then like ourselves it will be cleansed of every impurity through the blood of Christ and found acceptable in God's sight. What joy it will be on that great day to come when our life's work is presented to the Lord! Everything sinful will be cleansed by Christ's redeeming blood. But what will remain? The answer is that everything we have done through faith, in love, and to God's praise—all by His grace—will crown the labor of our lives. And with great joy we will place our crowns at the feet of Jesus Christ, who has led us through life as our Good Shepherd and whose pleasure is the greatest reward for which we ever could work.

CHAPTER FOURTEEN

The Redeemed Man Laboring at His Work

Daniel Doriani

THE WORKING LIFE of a Christian has both certainties and mysteries.[1] The faithful disciple knows God has given him gifts and will direct his steps. He will dedicate his skills and energies to love his neighbor and glorify his Lord. We hope that man also knows God's will thoroughly enough to follow his basic precepts and show wisdom as he works. But mysteries abound for workers, young and old. It is often difficult to see *how* we should seek to use our gifts, training, and providential opportunities. After a short summary of my work life, this essay will name five principles that guide the work of disciples. Then we will consider ways to find God's calling. We will assess the negative and positive aspects of ambition.

I knew I would be a teacher at age twelve. Before long I guessed "college professor." Yes, but that lasted for five years. Soon I was a seminary professor, then dean of the faculty. I began to preach, sometimes for a year or more, at local churches. That led to eleven years as lead pastor of a large church. Years later, I returned to academia and began writing furiously,

---

1. Portions of this chapter are adapted from Daniel M. Doriani, *Work: Its Purpose, Dignity, and Transformation* (P&R, 2019). Used with permission from P&R Publishing, Phillipsburg, N.J., www.prpbooks.com.

with six books in seven years. After that, I began serving large churches as a part-time interim and that eventually led to my current call, temporarily leading a megachurch far from home. Looking back, it's clear that teaching has been a constant; whatever my position, teaching has been the core ability and task, but I never anticipated the leadership roles that I've inhabited for thirty years.

Biblical Principles for a Godly Man's Work

The Holy Scriptures contain many principles to direct God's people in their labor. Here are five precepts of particular importance to guide a redeemed man in his work.

First, *a godly man works gladly, since work is good, even if the fall makes it frustrating.*[2] God created humans in His image; we work because He works. He created the universe and sustains it daily; therefore, we tend and sustain the world (Gen. 1:1–31; Isa. 45:18, Col. 1:16–17). Since the fall, work is difficult, but *in itself,* work is good, so that we can do all honest work heartily, offering it to the Lord (Col. 3:22–23). When God designed the world, he fashioned it to work best when humans develop and protect it (Gen. 2:15). We long to be creative at work because the Creator made us in His image. We like to solve problems and complete tasks because God solves problems and completes tasks that He set for Himself.

Many believers adopt the secular notion that work is nothing but a curse, or at best a necessary evil. They hope to work as little as possible and try to foist labor onto animals, fools, or machines. It is true that God cursed the ground after humanity rebelled, so that work *became* toilsome and frustrating (Gen. 3:17; Rom. 8:18–23). Even the best jobs have miseries. Even if we work hard and get the best training, our work can be

---

2. For more on the goodness of work before and after the fall of man, see the previous chapter (ch. 12).

more grinding than fulfilling or meaningful. Everyone has to "take out the garbage"—that is, to complete tasks that will always seem unpleasant. Nonetheless, our drive to fix things, make plans, and fulfill them reflects the God who planned and accomplished our redemption. The joy we feel when we finish a project mirrors the joy of Jesus when He completed the task of redemption (John 19:30; Heb. 12:2). Our work is meaningful and challenging because God planned it that way.

Second, *a godly man works six days, then rests, as God did.* God said, "Six days you shall labor and do all your work, but the seventh day is a Sabbath.... In it you shall do no work" (Ex. 20:9–10). The principle of work and rest corrects both workaholics and sluggards. God says, "Work!" He also says, "Stop working." There is more to God than the product of His work, and we rest because we need time to see that there is more to us than our accomplishments. God has an interior life. He worked, then paused and reflected and said, "What I made is good." We rest and play and meditate for the same reason.

Secular people think the ideal worker is like a machine. Machines do the same thing, hour after hour, without complaint, and good workers will supposedly endure anything if the pay is sufficient. But people need to stop, rest, and reflect, as God did.

Third, *the godly man honors both manual labor and mental labor.* God respects both manual and mental skills and toil. Secular people typically think manual labor is inferior, even demeaning, and avoid it if possible. But Jesus worked with His hands. Jesus was an artisan, and that dignifies manual labor. Paul also commended manual labor, although Roman society typically scorned it (Eph. 4:28). By teaching, Jesus and Paul also honored mental labor. All labor has dignity, whether farming, driving, welding, riveting, teaching, healing, or investing. It's dangerous to let society set the value of our work. After all, Western societies pay their best athletes a thousand times more than they pay their best elementary school teachers.

Millions are detached from their own work. They hardly care what they do as long as it pays well—or at least provides food, clothing, and shelter. They imagine that their work has no connection to their inner self. It doesn't matter whether they sell tires or manage dental offices. But our work does shape us; that is why the Bible identifies people by their occupation. Thus, Lydia was "a seller of purple" garments (Acts 16:14), Alexander was "the coppersmith" (2 Tim. 4:14), and Pilate was "the governor" (Matt. 27:2). Scripture also mentions fishermen, carpenters, shepherds, and soldiers because occupations shape us. Drivers pay more attention to weather, and physicians and counselors perceive tiny clues about their neighbor's physical and emotional health. God *primarily* establishes our identity by making us in His image. But our work does too; a man can say, "I am an engineer."

Fourth, *a godly man's work may or may not be his vocation*. For this point, we must establish definitions and distinctions. Let's accept David Miller's definition of work as a "sustained exercise of strength and skill that overcomes obstacles to produce or accomplish something."[3] That is, work is intensive and skilled labor that achieves goals. Miller wisely said nothing about payment. Yes, a "job" typically implies payment for a task, but work is broader than employment, as parents and dedicated volunteers know. We can work without having a job.

Also, let's recognize that we can have a job or occupation without a vocation. A job can even be important, but not necessarily a calling. A job pays the bills; a vocation fits our skills, interests, talents, even passions. A college student may wash dishes every summer, but it probably isn't a vocation. By contrast, a summer internship may be the start of a vocation. Frederick Buechner stated the ideal: "God calls you to the kind of work that you need most to do, and the world most needs to have done.... God

---

3. David Miller, *God at Work: The History and Promise of the Faith at Work Movement* (Oxford University Press, 2007), 19.

calls you [to] the place where your deep gladness and the world's deep hunger meet."[4]

Only a few people can say, "I always knew what I would do as an adult and I have done it." Most of us have a rough idea of our calling and discover it more fully as time passes. We need to try one job, then another, and slowly discover our vocation as we reflect on our labors. We should also listen to wise people who know the world and care enough to *see* us and help us discern our place in society.

Biblical history verifies this: Jesus worked with wood and stone, and Paul made tents. Both supported themselves through their labor, but both had other callings from God. Joseph and Moses were also heroes of the faith whom God moved from herding animals to political leadership. Likewise, Amos tended herds and fig trees in Tekoa, south of Jerusalem, until the Lord called him to prophesy against the idolatrous worship center in Bethel (Amos 7:10–15). He moved less than thirty miles, but he shifted from safety in central Judah to danger in the north, for he denounced the idolatry of northern Israel in the very city of the king. This list establishes that God can assigns people to new tasks in new places.

The apostle Paul explicitly states that disciples are free to move in his first epistle to the Corinthians. Writing in a Roman society that had millions of slaves, Paul asked, "Were you called [to faith] while a slave? Do not be concerned about it." Then he quickly adds, "But if you can be made free, rather use it" (1 Cor. 7:21). So, God assigns places and roles to His people but He also permits us to move to a new situation.

Fifth, *God calls everyone to full-time service*. Through honest labor, anyone can become God's hands, meeting the needs of family, friends, and neighbors near and far. For centuries, certain Christian leaders asserted that church work—perhaps also education and medicine—is "sacred" work, while other tasks are secular, worldly, inferior. To be sure, work is

---

4. Frederick Buechner, *Wishful Thinking: A Theological ABC* (Harper & Row, 1973), 95.

inferior if it fails to do good to any neighbor. One thinks of the gambling industry or the manufacture and sale of shoddy merchandise. Believers should avoid such work because there is no love of neighbor in it. But faithful farmers, manufacturers, engineers, teachers, homemakers, drivers, and pastors have the same ability to "do all to the glory of God" (1 Cor. 10:31). Every Christian can pray "Thy kingdom come" as they perform honest, helpful tasks. All can say, "Lord, bless and govern your world through me today." This holds for all legitimate work, including professions that exist because of sin. Soldiers, police officers, medical workers, and undertakers mitigate, even reverse some of the effects of sin. Those are good callings, too, and they faintly echo the work of Jesus, the Redeemer.

When people pray for their daily bread, God grants it through farmers who go to fields, bakers who rise in the morning to tend ovens, and drivers who transport bread to stores. We pray for clothing and shelter, and He sends shepherds and construction workers. We pray for safety, and He raises up engineers and mechanics. Much of this service goes unseen (Matt. 25:31–46), so that we are the stage crew behind the actors, the business managers supporting the play. This is another echo of God's work, since the Spirit's work is often unseen.

Ambitions and Callings

There is a role for ambition in a godly man's work. Our nations and our churches suffer from a chronic lack of godly leaders. We need men who will take God's call instead of fleeing it, men who hope to make the most of their gifts for the kingdom.

Like anger, ambition tends to be sinful. In Genesis 11, people toiled to build a tower to make a name for themselves. Nebuchadnezzar boasted, "Is not this great Babylon, that I have built for a royal dwelling . . . for the honor of my majesty?" (Dan. 4:30). Rabbis hoped to be revered as a spiritual "father" (Matt. 23:8–10). Others hoard wealth for themselves, so they can eat, drink, and be merry (Luke 12:13–21).

Ambition is often godless. Atheists may place their hope in political ambitions. For them, political struggles "are not simply fights over health care, tax credits, and farm subsidies." They include "the search for meaning."[5] Atheists look to fill the vacuum created by God's absence. If there is no god, the hope for justice, prosperity, or peace falls on humanity, and that notion breeds unhealthy ambition. It is even more common for men to seek a name or identity for themselves by obtaining wealth, power, or a reputation. The Lord primarily establishes human identity by making humanity in His image and adopting believers into His family, but sinners often look to work for meaning and security.

So then, "ambition" is often a negative concept in Christian circles. It's seen as a companion of pride, which is one of the seven deadly sins. Paul does say, "Let nothing be done through selfish ambition or conceit, but in lowliness of mind let each esteem others better than himself" (Phil. 2:3). *Selfish* ambition, which concentrates on "*my* name and career" is destructive. James says, "Where envy and self-seeking exist, confusion and every evil thing are there" (James 3:16). So, Scripture condemns selfish ambition.

But Scripture does not condemn all ambition; it affirms the ambition, desire, or drive to serve in a wider, possibly more dangerous, sphere. Paul declared, "I make it my aim to preach the gospel" where Christ was not known (Rom. 15:20). He wanted to plant churches throughout the Roman Empire. The Greek verb for setting one's aim on something or having ambition is *philotimeomai*. Paul uses it again when he says "we make it our aim" or ambition to please God and quietly live a godly life (2 Cor. 5:9; 1 Thess. 4:11). Paul also says, "If a man desires the position of a bishop

5. Ta-Nehisi Coates, *We Were Eight Years in Power: An American Tragedy* (One World, 2017), 110–11.

[elder], he desires a good work" (1 Tim. 3:1). While people like Moses and Jeremiah were reluctant to take up hard callings, David, Solomon, Nehemiah, Elisha, and Paul showed a godly passion to lead in God's causes. It is right to aspire to tasks that match our abilities.

Furthermore, Jesus had a zeal for His redemptive work that resembles ambition. One day, when Jesus was wearied by His labors, the disciples brought Him food, and He said, "My food is to do the will of Him who sent me, and to finish His work" (John 4:34). His work would weary Him, but His desire to complete it strengthened Him. Then, on the cross, just before He died, Jesus exulted, "It is finished," for He had completed the work the Father gave Him (John 19:30). When we fulfill godly ambitions, we follow Jesus. He expects us to avoid quests for wealth or glory while fulfilling our tasks.

Jesus said talent and skill bring responsibilities: "For everyone to whom much is given, from him much will be required" (Luke 12:48). If God gives much *to us*, he expects much *from us*. Our native capacities, mentors, and experiences are gifts, and God expects a return on His investment. The gifts are both ours and His. Jesus says He will ask us to give an account of the way we use them (Matt. 25:14–30, Luke 19:11–27). Speaking of gifts, Paul says, "let us use them" (Rom. 12:6). Anyone who has the energy and ability to lead should do so with zeal (v. 8). The world needs godly leaders. Let us therefore encourage each other to develop our gifts for service for God and man.

The doctrines of sin, depravity, and salvation constantly demand humility. Above all, the godly man knows Jesus is the Savior, and he is not. Yet there is a proper ambition to use our gifts well, to excel, to change our corner of the world. False humility can stifle that. Yes, ambition can feed a lust for fame, glory, or domination. But "the opposite of ambition is not humility; it is sloth, passivity, timidity, and complacency."[6]

---

6. James K. A. Smith, *On the Road with Augustine* (Brazos Press, 2019), 76–78.

Gifted men should have an ambition for work that makes a difference. CEOs have no additional capacity to please God or be godly. They have no additional *dignity* or worth, but they do have more *influence* than cleaning crews, because they make strategic decisions (for good or for ill). Without cleaning crews, a workplace quickly becomes miserable, but cleaners don't shape companies the way leaders do. If you sense that God gifted and trained you to lead, it is proper to desire—or have the ambition—to lead well, to change your corner of the world, whether small or large.

That said, *everyone* has the capacity to do good. Let no one say, "I just," as in, "I just chop salads," "I just approve loans," or "I just care for children." Parents care for a life that will go on forever, for weal or for woe. By God's grace, most of us can make a difference in our sphere. Moses, Ezra, and Daniel had strategic roles in the great affairs of kingdoms. Today, certain godly men have a position that gives them the ability to form teams and deploy resources for good causes. Agents of change face resistance. Efforts at reformation falter due to ignorance or opposition. Still, God's people persevere if they are confident that their cause is God's cause.

Healthy confidence and ambition seem helpful for many professions. Surgeons, lawyers, politicians, pro athletes, CEOs, professors, entertainers, entrepreneurs, politicians, and even pastors need confidence. They must believe they can contribute to their field or lead their people and organization. They need a sense of their skill, voice, and mission to lead well in the face of disapproval, opposition, foot-dragging, sabotage, and whisper campaigns.

Conclusion: Finding a Calling

Desires often help us to find a vocation well suited for us. Of course, this can be twisted into a selfish pursuit. A standard secular message today is, "Follow your heart. Seek your passion." We need an approach that is

God-centered and realistic in assessing our talents according to feedback we received from others.

However, desires still have a role in directing our vocational labors. Solomon said that if a man can "rejoice in his labor," it "is a gift of God" (Eccles. 5:19). Paul wants believers to enjoy using their gifts. People should show mercy "with cheerfulness" (Rom. 12:8). Motivation is a huge factor in accomplishing goals. For example, Israel quickly rebuilt the wall around Jerusalem after the exile, "for the people had a mind to work" (Neh. 4:6).

Ideally, a calling begins with interest and talent. But it must be confirmed by counsel from leaders. If, instead of hearing, "Thanks for your effort," we hear, "That was great. Could you join our team?" we should take it seriously. When godly ambition matches with talent, a godly man may have found a place where he can well serve God and his neighbor.

CHAPTER FIFTEEN

The Redeemed Man Serving in His Church

Kevin DeYoung

MY WIFE and I are blessed with nine children, five of whom are boys. As I write this chapter, my oldest son just turned twenty-one, and my next oldest son is heading off to college. So, when I think about this book, and my chapter in particular, I can't help but think of the young men in my own household. The thought in my mind is not just "What do I want men to know about serving in the church," but "What do I want *my* sons to know about serving in the church?"

Before talking about anything else, I want my sons (and every other man for that matter) to notice four words in the title of this chapter.

The first word is "redeemed." As Christian parents, we pray for more than morally decent, responsible, respectful, hard-working adult children. We must pray that our children would be genuine, born-again, blood-bought Christians. Every man reading this book must endeavor to know his own soul and be sure that he is, first and foremost, a redeemed man.

The second word is "church." It isn't enough for the Christian man to read his Bible and pray, or to be a part of a Bible study during the week, or to get involved in a campus ministry while in college, or to read good theology books, or to listen to good Christian podcasts, or to listen to good sermons while he's driving in the car. The redeemed man must be involved in a church. In one of the last books that he wrote before he died, John Stott said this about the importance of the church: "I trust that none of my readers is that grotesque anomaly, an unchurched Christian. The New Testament knows nothing of such a person. For the church lies at the very centre of the eternal purpose of God."[1] Stott was right. An unchurched Christian is a contradiction in terms.

The third word is "his." I understand that some people don't like putting a possessive pronoun before the word "church." The argument is that we shouldn't speak of "my" church, "their" church, or "pastor so-and-so's church" because the church belongs to Christ and not to us. While I appreciate the caution, it seems to me there is something healthy about referring to "my" church or speaking about the Christian man and "his" church. The possessive pronoun reminds us that the Christian isn't merely a member of the universal church; he must belong to a specific local church—a body of believers that meets in a specific place, at a specific time, under the leadership of specific men. The word "his" also underscores that we don't need more church hoppers. The mature man doesn't float from church to church, flitting in and out of different congregations as his mood (and his weekend schedule) dictates. God calls men to belong to a local church and to be in that church every Sunday unless providentially hindered (such as by illness, death, emergency) or unless necessary travel (such as family vacation or essential work commitments) means he will worship in a different church.

The fourth word is "serving." I almost missed this word myself. I started to write about the three words that I want my sons to notice, and then I came back and realized I had skipped what may be the most important word in the title. The goal is not simply to have redeemed men who join a good church and sit in the pew Sunday after Sunday. All of that is

1. John Stott, *The Living Church* (InterVarsity, 2007), 19.

foundational and indispensable. But the call of God is more than signing up and showing up. The call of God is to *serve* in the church. This call may mean serving in church office as an elder or deacon. This may mean, for an even smaller subset of men, serving as a pastor or staff member in the church. But those are just the most obvious ways to serve. Whether a man ever holds ecclesiastical office or not, he is still called to be a serving member of the church. He must be more than a consumer of fine preaching, quality programs, or excellent music. Certainly, his church involvement must consist of more than making good business connections, making himself look good in the eyes of others, or simply making his wife happy. The redeemed man is in his church in order to serve his church, because in serving the body of Christ he serves Christ Himself.

Set Apart to Serve

When I think about redeemed men serving in the church, my mind goes immediately to the many fine elders I have served with. I know too many pastors have horror stories of the immature, untaught, sometimes even unconverted men they have had to serve with on the session (the governing elder board). By God's grace, I don't have those stories. With very few exceptions, the men I've served with have been sincere, hard-working, and eager to do God's work in His ways.

I could talk about many such men, but I'll just mention one. I'll call him Tom, so as not to embarrass him if he ever reads this book. Tom was one of those pillars in the church, the kind of unflashy, but stalwart individuals that every church needs. For decades, he worked a blue-collar job—a tough, monotonous, on-your-feet-all-day kind of job that, in my opinion, sounded harder than being a pastor. Although he was often tired, I didn't hear him complain. He worked his normal job, and then gave hours and hours after that to the church. I'm pretty sure he didn't make a lot of money, but I know he gave consistently and generously. He showed up every Sunday morning and evening. He and his godly wife raised four children, all of whom are walking with the Lord. He liked to read history especially. He took seriously his responsibility to care for the members in his elder district. He volunteered for committees. He discipled younger men. He and his wife welcomed people in their home. He read his Bible every morning. And often, when he shook my hand after church, he'd look me in the eye and say, "I want you to know I pray for you every day."

Tom would be the first (and last) to tell you that he wasn't perfect. He'd list the gifts he didn't have in abundance. He'd tell you what he wasn't good at. He'd demur, without any false humility, that he wasn't sure he was qualified to be an elder. But he was a great elder. Better yet, he was (and is) a great Christian. And that's crucial, because there is no being a truly great elder or a great pastor or a great man in the church without first being a great Christian. "Be thou an example of the believers," Paul exhorted Timothy, "in word, in conversation, in charity, in spirit, in faith, in purity" (1 Tim. 4:12). That's a lot of ground to cover, but that's what my friend Tom was like, and that's what godly manhood looks like—to be exemplary in what we say with our mouths, where we go with our feet, what we do with our hands, what we believe in our heads, and what we do with our sexual thoughts and sexual parts. After more than twenty years in ministry, I still find 1 Timothy 4:12 challenging, convicting, and inspiring.

When the church in Jerusalem was struggling to minister to the widows in Acts 6, the answer was to find godly men to address the problem. The situation was volatile. Some women were being overlooked in the daily distribution, and the oversight looked like ethnic prejudice to boot (v. 1). The apostles knew they couldn't ignore the problem, but they also knew they were not the ones to directly fix the problem. Their God-given priorities were prayer and the ministry of the word (v. 4). The God-given solution was to find "seven men of honest report, full of the Holy Ghost and wisdom, whom we may appoint over this business" (v. 3). Not just any old warm bodies, but men they could trust, men who were good with people, men who were spiritual in the deepest sense of the word.

We know that women also served in the early church (Rom. 16:1), no doubt in integral and invaluable ways (see, for example, all the women mentioned in the rest of Romans 16). But the spiritual temperature of the church will always have a hard time rising higher than the spiritual temperature of the men in the church. That's not a statement of comparative worth between the sexes. It's a statement about reality—the way God made human beings and the way He made the church. Godly women flourish when they have godly men in the church to serve and to lead. It was a judgment upon ancient Israel when they had women to rule over them (Isa. 3:12), not because every man is apt to be a better ruler than every woman, but because it is a sign of spiritual declension when strong, wise, just, compassionate men—to govern and to rule—are nowhere to be found.

Older Men

The New Testament says more about what men should be like in the church than what men specifically should be doing in the church (other than possibly serving as officers). That makes sense because no amount of competence can make up for a lack of character. If we don't want to be "barren" or "unfruitful" in our knowledge of the Lord Jesus Christ, we must be growing in godliness (2 Peter 1:5–8). One of the few character texts addressed specifically to men is found in Titus 2. There Paul tells Titus what particularly he ought to tell the older men, the older women, the younger women, and the younger men. Let's look at the first and last of those categories.

In Titus 2:2, Paul admonishes "the aged men" to be marked by six qualities: sober, grave, temperate, sound in faith, in charity, in peace."

(1) *Sober* may have reference to alcohol, but the term means more than that. To be sober is to be balanced. The problem with alcohol isn't

alcohol per se; the problem is with imbalanced intake of alcohol. God is telling older men to be measured, even-keeled, and balanced. After walking with the Lord for many years, older men should be less inclined to get tipped over to one side or the other. They don't fly off the handle with anger. They hear both sides. They are consistent. Godly men are calm, clear-headed, not governed by the mob, not willing to give in to negative peer pressure. Older Christian men should be anchors.

(2) Older men should also be *grave*. This doesn't mean dour, grim, and joyless. Think of the word *gravitas*. It suggests someone who is dignified, serious about the right things, and worthy of respect. We live in a society where people are famous for being famous. The digital age promises instant notoriety, instant influence, and insta-everything. The church, on the other hand, needs men who know to love and for their wives for decade after decade, men who know how to raise godly children, men who prioritize substance over sizzle.

(3) Older men must also be *temperate*. We sometimes laugh at cranky old men, but irritability and rage are not fruits of the Spirit. To be temperate is to be self-controlled. Older men ought to have a measure of discipline in their lives—in prayer, in the word, in conversation, in what they eat, in what they watch, in how they spend their time.

(4) Older men are to be *sound in faith*. This does not mean that the older man has every question answered. But it does mean that his life is marked by a profound trust in God. The older man has been through the highs and lows of life. He should be able to look back and say,

Hitherto Thy love has blest me;
Thou hast brought me to this place;
And I know Thy hand will bring me
Safely home by Thy good grace.[2]

2. Robert Robinson, "Come, Thou Fount of Every Blessing," adapted by E. Margaret Clarkson (1986).

(5) Older men should also be *sound in charity*. I remember from a previous church an older man I sat next to in the choir. He was smart, well-educated, funny, and happy. He also had a number of quirks and not a few, um, senior moments. He was a godly man too. I knew that his wife had health problems because she never came to church. When I heard that she was in the hospital again, I asked what it was like to care for her as her health deteriorated. Without a word of complaint, he rattled off all he had to do for her, where he had to take her, and how he had to give her pills, change her clothes, and keep her washed. "Oh," I said, "It must be hard having to do that for. . . . " I didn't finish the sentence, because I didn't know how long he had been caring for his invalid wife. Then he filled in the blank: "Twenty-seven years." Here was a man sound in charity.

(6) Finally, older men are to be *sound in patience*. Oh, how the church needs saints who finish well. Anybody can be impressive at twenty five, but what about sixty five, seventy five, or eighty five? Too many Christians fizzle out. They press on at first but end up coasting. The Christian race takes endurance. If you are a seasoned saint reading this, don't put the controls on autopilot. Don't waste twenty years of your life in trivialities. Of course, we are bound to slow down. Spending time with grandkids is good. Hobbies can be pleasing to the Lord. If we live long enough, we will retire from a job, but we don't retire from the kingdom. Winston Churchill lived an amazingly full life, and then he became Prime Minister. The church needs Christian men who run the race all the way through the tape. After winning the gold medal in the 1924 Olympics, Eric Liddel was asked the secret of his success in the 400 meters. Liddel replied, "I run the first 200 meters as hard I can. Then, for the second 200 meters, with God's help, I run harder."[3]

---

3. Russell W. Ramsey, *God's Joyful Runner* (Bridge, 1987), 68.

Younger Men

After beginning his exhortations by singling out the older men, Paul finishes his instructions to Titus by mentioning the younger men. Somewhat surprisingly, Paul only has one command for the younger men: "be sober minded" (*sōphronein*, Titus 2:6). Verses 7 and 8 apply to the younger men too, but they are strictly speaking Paul's instructions for Titus as an example to younger men. There is only one direct command for the younger men, and it's not at all original. Closely related Greek words are used in verse 2 (*sōphrōn*, translated "temperate"), verse 5 (*sōphrōn*, "discreet"), and again in verse 12 (*sōphronōs*, "soberly"). So, is Paul going soft on the young men with this one meager command?

Not at all. Paul issued instructions that were not, by and large, exclusive to any one group, but addressed that group's particular challenge. Take the older men. They are into the second half of their lives, so God is concerned that they be dignified, worthy of respect, and finish well with patience and endurance. Older women, without kids in tow, might wander from house to house, talking more than they should. God is concerned that they not be slanderers, but examples and teachers for the younger women. On the other hand, the younger women, for their season of life, need exhortations regarding the family and the home. In each case, there is some overlap, but the commands are chosen to fit what that specific group needs to hear.

It seems likely, then, that Paul hits on this characteristic of godliness because it is the one that young men struggle with most, and perhaps the type of virtue that young men aspire to least.

Being sensible and disciplined is not what teenage boys and college-aged men are known for. Harnessed by the Spirit, young men can be bold, fearless, courageous, and accomplish great things. Ruled by their hormones and their not-yet-fully-formed brains, young men can push each other to be wild, foolish, and careless. The ungodly man will not just stumble into a less than sober minded life; he will look for it. Self-control, for young men, is often an area of vice not a virtue.

But it doesn't have to be that way. We mustn't think that the only kind of masculinity is toxic masculinity. God made men to be strong, aggressive, risk-taking, protective, and self-sacrificing. If young men are to serve well in the church, they must show themselves to be sober minded sexually (channeling the sex drive into marriage), sober minded emotionally (putting to death fits of rage), sober minded socially (proving to be responsible, dependable, and reliable) and sober mind spiritually (pursuing Christian service and Christian maturity with the same passion that they pursue sports, career, hobbies, and adventure). Throughout church history, young men have been catalysts for missionary movements, for reforming the church, for bettering their homes, and for reaching their neighbors with the gospel. A zealous young Christian man with wisdom, discernment, and self-control is a holy weapon in the hand of God.

The Manly Virtue of Magnanimity

We learn another character quality crucial for serving the church from John Witherspoon, who was the president of Princeton (then called the College of New Jersey) from 1768, when he arrived from his native Scotland after a career in pastoral ministry, until he died in 1794. Twice during his presidency—in 1775 and again in 1787—Witherspoon preached a message before commencement on a theme we don't hear a lot about today. "My single purpose from these words at this time," he told his all-male students, "is to explain and recommend magnanimity as a Christian virtue."[4]

4. John Witherspoon, "Christian Magnanimity" in *The Selected Writings of John Witherspoon,* ed. Thomas Miller (Southern Illinois University Press, 1990), 117. The last section of this chapter is based on my article "The Manly Virtue of Magnanimity" which first appeared on February 22, 2022, in *World Opinions,* https://wng.org/opinions/the-manly-virtue-of-magnanimity-1645529342. Used with permission.

The heading above calls magnanimity a "manly virtue." By that, I don't mean that magnanimity is unique to men or that women are not also called to this trait. But I do think magnanimity is a virtue particularly befitting to manhood, and that manhood bereft of magnanimity is especially lamentable. When the apostle Paul enjoined the Corinthians to be strong, to stand firm in the faith, and to "quit you like men" (1 Cor. 16:13), he was calling men and women to courage, but he was also embracing the notion that fortitude in the face of opposition is what we associate with manliness.

According to Witherspoon, magnanimity entails five commitments: (1) "to attempt great and difficult things," (2) "to aspire after great and valuable possessions," (3) to face "dangers with resolution," (4) "to struggle against difficulties with perseverance," and (5) "to bear sufferings with fortitude and patience."[5] In short, the magnanimous Christian is eager to attempt great things and willing to endure great hardships.

Witherspoon took for granted that the world approves of magnanimity. His concern was that some might conclude that calling men (like his Princeton graduates) to strength and valor and ambition does not fit with the tenor of the gospel. Christians have often struggled to know how godliness and manliness mesh. But virtues, Witherspoon insisted, can never be inconsistent with each other. He noted that while the gospel would have us mourn for our sin and cultivate a humility of spirit, we are also "called to live and act for the glory of God and the good of others."[6]

Christianity is not opposed to ambition, but ambition will look different for the Christian. "Everyone must acknowledge," Witherspoon said, "that ostentation and love of praise, and whatever is contrary to the

---

5. Witherspoon, "Christian Magnanimity," in *Selected Writings*, 118. With respect to aspiring after possessions, Witherspoon commented, "His desires after present enjoyments are subjected to the will of God.... But the glorious object of the Christian's ambition is the inheritance incorruptible and undefiled, and that fadeth not away" (122).

6. Witherspoon, "Christian Magnanimity," in *Selected Writings*, 121.

self-denial of the gospel, tarnish the beauty of the greatest actions."[7] True greatness does not lie in self-promotion, endless bravado, and passing along our own praise.

Likewise, manliness does not mean we must be larger-than-life gunslingers and gladiators who swagger into town ready to kill or be killed. There is more than one way to be brave and many ways to be strong. Not everyone will be gifted with brains or brawn. Not everyone will have the opportunity for world-altering heroism. "But," Witherspoon noted, "that magnanimity which is the fruit of true religion, being indeed the product of divine grace, is a virtue of the heart and may be attained by persons of mean talents and narrow possessions and in the very lowest stations of human life."[8]

If magnanimity calls us to attempt great things, it also compels us to endure great suffering. Merriam-Webster defines magnanimity as "loftiness of spirit enabling one to bear trouble calmly, to disdain meanness and pettiness, and to display a noble generosity." Would that our leading Christian voices, and Christian men in particular, were models of this kind of magnanimity! While we all should disdain pettiness, there is something particularly discomfiting when a man feels the need to advertise the offenses against him and swing at every offender. The magnanimous person does not bear grudges, does not wallow in self-pity, does not demand penance, and does not stoop to settle every score.

In the end, the two parts of magnanimity are inseparable, for the great man is measured not only by what he does but by what he does not do. We would do well to be more like David pardoning Shimei than the sons of Zeruiah looking for the next enemy to execute. Bearing burdens, eschewing meanness, and setting an example of noble generosity is not just a saner and more effective way to live; it is the way of the cross. For

---

7. Witherspoon, "Christian Magnanimity," in *Selected Writings*, 124.
8. Witherspoon, "Christian Magnanimity," in *Selected Writings*, 124.

the manly virtue of magnanimity is the way of the One who accomplished great things by defeating His foes, even while crying out, "Father forgive them; for they know not what they do" (Luke 23:34).

The redeemed man who would serve in his church—no matter what specific tasks, offices, or responsibilities he signs up for—must be a man we can look up to. He may be ordinary in gifting, in resources, in abilities, and ordinary in a dozen other things, but he must be exemplary in virtue. The men in our churches need not make any apologies for being men, but they do need to keep their eyes on Jesus in order to see what true manhood looks like. We must press hard after the manly virtue of magnanimity, for such is the Savior we serve.

CHAPTER SIXTEEN

The Redeemed Man Managing His Resources

Jim Newheiser

THE APOSTLE PAUL says, "Charge them that are rich in this world, that they be not highminded, nor trust in uncertain riches, but in the living God, who giveth us richly all thing to enjoy; that they do good, that they be rich in good works, ready to distribute, willing to communicate; laying up in store for themselves a good foundation against the time to come, that they may lay hold on eternal life" (1 Tim. 6:17–19).[1]

A redeemed man recognizes that his greatest purpose in life is to serve, please, and glorify God (2 Cor. 5:9; 1 Cor. 10:31). He acknowledges that God is the owner and source of all wealth (Deut. 8:18; Pss. 24:1; 50:10). Wealth can take many forms—cash, real estate, equities, precious metals, and so on—the value of which is set by what someone else is willing to give you for it. The redeemed man seeks to have wise perspective on wealth as he seeks to wisely steward the resources God has entrusted to him.

---

1. Portions of this chapter are adapted from Jim Newheiser, *Money, Debt, and Finances: Critical Questions and Answers* (P&R, 2021). Used with permission from P&R Publishing, www.prpbooks.com.

Wealth Is Acquired Through Wisdom

Scripture teaches that wealth is built through hard work (Prov. 10:4) and skill (22:29) as one produces services and goods which benefit others. Those who are wise patiently build wealth over time and stay away from get-rich-quick schemes (28:20, 22), which seek to circumvent God's design for prosperity. They avoid personal debt (22:7) and refuse to foolishly cosign for the debts of others (6:1–5; 22:26–27). (While debt may be necessary for huge expenses such as purchasing a home, I advise that one save for most major purchases—instead of borrowing—and that we should never owe more than the amount for which we could quickly sell the item.) It is also wise for people to carefully plan their spending by using a budget (21:5). They avoid extravagance and learn to be content with the basics (v. 17; 1 Tim. 6:6–8).

The wise refuse to compromise their integrity to get ahead financially (Prov. 10:2; 13:11; 20:17). Nor do they sacrifice their relationships with God, their families, or the church in the quest for riches. Those who are wise rest from their labors on the Lord's Day, trusting that just as God provided sufficient manna for the children of Israel on the sixth day, He will provide for those who worship and rest on Sunday. He sincerely believes God's greatest blessing come through cheerful obedience.

Wealth Can Be a Blessing

Wealth is often portrayed as a blessing from God to those who are faithful. Prosperity was a reward for obedience under the old covenant (Deut. 28:1–12). God graciously blessed the patriarchs and faithful kings with riches (Gen. 24:35; 30:43; 1 Kings 10:23). Proverbs instructs the young man how he can wisely acquire and steward his wealth.

Wealth can be a blessing because it is the means by which you may fulfill your responsibilities to care for your family (1 Tim. 5:8) and avoid being a burden upon others (2 Thess. 3:8). Wealth can offer protection in times of calamity: "The rich man's wealth is his strong city: the destruction of the poor is their poverty" (Prov. 10:15). Those who save during their "fat cow" years can ride out hard economic times (cf. Genesis 41). Those who are poor cannot pay for unexpected car repairs or medical bills without going into debt. Proverbs tells us that wealth may aid one socially, as the rich have many friends—though some of those friends may not be worth having (Prov. 14:20; 19:4).

Perhaps the greatest blessing of wealth is that those who have financial resources are able to be "rich in good works" (1 Tim. 6:18). Churches, seminaries, and missionary activities are not financed primarily by people scraping by on a minimum wage (though we can be thankful for the faithful stewardship of those with less wealth and income). God moves in the hearts of productive people to use their wealth to finance great projects. I have been in full-time ministry for over thirty-five years. I have served churches which built buildings, planted daughter churches, and sent out missionaries through the humble generosity of a few. I now work for a seminary at which our primary source of income is donors who are committed to the future of the church. Productive people have made the ministries in which I have been involved possible.

Wealth Can Be Very Dangerous

There are many warnings in the Bible about the hazards of wealth. Some misquote Scripture claiming that money itself is the root of all evil. Actually, Paul warns about the love of money: "For the love of money is the root of all evil: which while some coveted after, they have erred from the faith and pierced themselves through with many sorrows" (1 Tim. 6:10). Several verses later Paul warns the rich "that they not be highminded" nor trust in the uncertainty of riches (v. 17).

It is all too easy to make money an idol (Col. 3:5). We make money an idol when we put our trust in our wealth rather than God, as illustrated by the parable of the rich fool whose barns full of grain did not prepare him for death (Luke 12:16–21). We also make wealth an idol when we value our possessions more than we value God, as illustrated by Jesus's encounter with the rich young ruler who was unwilling to give up his wealth to follow the Lord (Matt. 19:16–22). Jesus observes, "It is easier for a camel to go through the eye of a needle, than for a rich man to enter into the kingdom of God" (v. 24). He also offers hope that what is impossible with men is possible with God (v. 26). Hope is also offered in 1 Corinthians 1:26 where Paul, writing of God's calling people to salvation, does not say "not *any* mighty or noble," but instead, "not many," inferring that God chooses some among the world's elite.

The parable of the soils also warns that some who initially respond to the gospel fall away because their faith is choked out by the "deceitfulness of riches" (Matt. 13:22). Those who love money more than God will be tempted to sinfully acquire money through fraud (Prov. 11:1) or through the folly of gambling or greedy get-rich-quick schemes (28:19). Scripture reminds us that there are many things in life more valuable than money (15:17; 16:8, 16). Those who make wealth an idol incur God's judgment, which includes the destruction of sinfully gained riches (13:11; 20:17; 22:16).

Many people pray that they will have more money. Have you ever prayed that you wouldn't have too much? Such a prayer is in Proverbs 30:8–9, "Remove far from me vanity and lies: give me neither poverty nor riches; feed me with food convenient for me: lest I be full, and deny thee, and say, who is the LORD? Or lest I be poor, and steal, and take the name of my God in vain."

Wealth Can Be an Instrument of Your Sanctification

God's people often go through financially lean times. Such trials, while not enjoyable in the moment, can be for our spiritual good (Heb. 12:11; James 1:2–5). Financial trials may expose our misplaced trust in riches and drive us to our knees so that we will trust God to meet our needs. Praying, "Give us this day our daily bread" (Matt. 6:11), is much more meaningful when we are not sure how we will pay the rent. Money troubles can also expose our love of money and should hopefully loosen our grip on our possessions which can never satisfy. Instead, we learn to cling to the Lord who feeds and fills us (Isa. 55:1–2). Experiencing God's deliverance through economic difficulties helps build our faith to endure future trials.

Wealth Brings Great Responsibility and Freedom

Imagine that tomorrow you learn that you have suddenly and unexpectedly inherited three million dollars. Now what should you do? There are three things one could do with wealth. You could spend money improving your lifestyle. You could save money for the future (perhaps after paying off any debts). And you could give money away to the Lord's work and to those in need. When Paul addresses the rich in 1 Timothy 6:17–19 he mentions all three categories.

First, Paul reminds us that God has given us "richly all things to enjoy" (1 Tim. 6:17). If you have been renting an apartment, you may use your new wealth to buy a house. If you have been driving a beat-up old car with high mileage, you may choose to buy a nicer, newer vehicle. If you have been living on a diet of ramen, rice, and beans, you can now afford to eat fresh produce and meat. You may dine out more often. Biblical Christians are not called to be ascetics. God has given us earthly blessings to be enjoyed with thanksgiving to His glory (4:3–5).

Second, it is also reasonable that you may save some of the wealth God has entrusted to you. Paul does not tell the rich to repent of being wealthy, ordering them to give away their resources to embark on a life of poverty.[2] The wise ant (Prov. 6:8; 30:25) and Joseph (Gen. 41:25–36)

---

2. Jesus's encounter with the rich young ruler was a unique situation illustrating the nature of the call to discipleship (Luke 18:18–27), but this event does not imply that every Christian is called to do exactly the same thing.

both exemplify the wisdom of saving resources during times of prosperity to be prepared for seasons of want. There is wisdom in saving for a time when you may no longer have income from employment. I am not an advocate of retirement, per se. I believe that God made us to work six days a week, and that we should be as productive as possible all the days the Lord gives us (Ps. 90:10, 12, 17). But a time may come when you are physically or mentally no longer able to work for a living. Some save so that they can spend their later years as financially self-sufficient missionaries or church workers. Many save for their children's education, future major purchases, or to be prepared for unplanned major expenses.

Thirdly, you should also use your wealth to do good for God's kingdom. Often in Scripture we are called to give generously and gladly (2 Cor. 9:6–7) according to the measure God has prospered us (Prov. 3:9; 1 Cor. 16:2) and out of gratitude (2 Cor. 8:9). Generous giving is an act of faith, trusting that God will meet our future needs and believing that we will be richly blessed through our generosity (1 Tim. 6:19). Some, however, misunderstand the nature of the blessing God offers. Giving to God's work is not an investment scheme by which you can expect to multiply your money. Earthly wealth is temporary and fleeting (2 Peter 3:10–11). The treasure we seek is in heaven (Matt. 6:19–20). It is a privilege to participate in the Lord's work (2 Cor. 9:15).

Now that we have identified these three legitimate possible uses of wealth, how do you decide what resources you should devote to each category? In some ways it would be easier if the Bible had a formula that specifies the percentage that you should give, save, and spend. How nice a lifestyle may you lead? How much is too much to save? Scripture gives us great freedom and responsibility to allocate our resources to the glory of God. We will always feel some tension in light of the needs all around us. We need to be careful not to judge brothers who make different choices. Some advocate that we give God ten percent, and then we can do whatever we want with the rest. While the tithe can be a helpful guideline, I would argue that those to whom God has entrusted great wealth have greater responsibility to be generous. Some make it a goal to joyfully give away more and more over the years. We are to spend, save, and give all to the glory of God (1 Cor. 10:31).

Practical Wisdom Regarding Wealth Management

Having offered some biblical principles regarding wealth, I now proceed to give practical directions in how to handle one's financial resources.

Prepare for the Future

The book of Proverbs teaches that the wise think long term.

Several years ago, I gave a million-dollars-worth of counsel in less than five minutes. I was staying with a friend and his dear family. I would be awakened in the morning by his five young sons playfully pouncing on my bed. On the way to the airport, I asked my friend if he had life insurance and a will. He told me that he had meant to do that, but he was busy, and money was tight. I encouraged him to make provision for his family so that if something were to happen to him, his wife would not be burdened financially while trying to finish raising their five boys. I told him that at his age he could get a substantial amount of life insurance at a very reasonable cost. Several months later I heard that my friend had been diagnosed with a rare and lethal form of cancer. Shortly after he passed away, we received a personal note from his young widow thanking me for encouraging him to get life insurance. She told me that he took my advice before he became ill, and that insurance would be the provision for her and their sons. I recommend that a man who is the primary breadwinner purchase at least a million dollars of term life insurance with a level premium for as many years as you may need it. (In my friend's case, at least fifteen years—which is when his sons would have reached adulthood).

Other forms of insurance can be purchased to provide protection against calamities such as major medical expenses, disability, and major property loss (Prov. 22:3). Don't purchase every kind of insurance offered. A general rule is not to spend money to insure against that which you could afford to pay.[3]

Another way to prepare for the future is to have a will. Those with minor children need a will so that they can designate who will care for surviving children if both parents pass away. A will also designates how your assets should be distributed upon your death (Prov. 13:22). Along with your will you should include information regarding insurance, investments, and passwords which would be needed if something happens to you.

A third way to prepare for the future is through savings. As I mentioned earlier, while many of us hope to work into old age, the time may come when you are unable to earn a living. It also is wise to have emergency savings for unanticipated major expenses such as medical bills or car repairs, and to save for future major purchases such as paying cash for an automobile or making the down payment for a house.

Invest Wisely

Bad investments have been causing financial harm for at least three thousand years. "There is a sore evil which I have seen under the sun, namely, riches kept for the owners thereof to their hurt. But those riches perish by evil travail: and he begetteth a son and there is nothing in his hand" (Eccl. 5:13–14). Other translations say that "those riches perish through bad business" (NKJV mg.), suggesting a bad investment. Many make foolish investment choices because of greed and impatience (1 Tim. 6:9). "A faithful man shall abound with blessings: but he that maketh haste to be rich shall not be innocent. . . . He that hasteth to be rich hath an evil eye,

---

3. For more detailed advice regarding insurance see Newheiser, *Money, Debt, and Finances*, 267–77.

and considereth not that poverty shall come upon him" (Prov. 28:20, 22). Wealth is patiently built through hard work over time (13:11). Unscrupulous investment advisors take advantage of the ignorance or greed of others. Some such advisors find their victims in the trusting environment of a local church.

How can you avoid making disastrous financial decisions?

First, *if it sounds too good to be true, it is.*

Second, *greater rewards can only be gained through taking more risks.* If someone says that they can give you an exceptionally high return without corresponding risk, run away! An investment advisor who claimed to be a committed Christian once invited me to participate in a complicated scheme in which he claimed that we could multiply the return on our money with zero risk. Sadly, several of his clients, including some from a Bible study in which he participated, lost a great deal of money. In addition, his investment company was sanctioned by government authorities.

Third, *different kinds of investments have different sorts of risks.* For example, long term bonds lose value in times of inflation and rising interest rates. Or a stock may drop because of the misfortune of the company in which you invested or because the market as a whole goes down.

Fourth, *learn how the person who is advising you is making his money.* Some fees and commissions are hidden. Some investment advisors steer their clients into products which give them the greatest commission, rather than acting in the best interest of the client. I counseled in a case in which a man who inherited a great deal of money trusted a man he met in church with his newfound wealth. The investment advisor lost a great deal of the money in a venture in which he had a conflict of interest. And the rest of the money was put into an annuity product which paid the advisor a fat commission but paid a poor return and charged exorbitant penalties to the client who wanted to withdraw his money during the first ten years. Don't invest until you fully understand the related fees and expenses. If you wanted your money back next week, how much would you have lost?

Fifth, *never invest in a financial product which you do not understand*. For example, if you don't understand how cryptocurrencies are created and valued, I recommend that you don't invest in them. I have seen many doctors and other high earners who have lost a great deal of money in complicated financial schemes (often for tax avoidance).

Sixth, *don't put all your eggs into one basket*. Instead, diversify. "In the morning sow thy seed, and in the evening withhold not thy hand: for thou knowest not whether shall prosper, either this or that, or whether they both shall be alike good" (Eccl. 11:6). When I worked in business, many of my coworkers put most of their savings into company stock. The problem was that if the company had major problems these employees might lose both their jobs and their savings. Mutual funds invest in the stock of many companies, thus spreading risk. As your savings grow, you may choose to diversify into other investments, such as savings accounts, rental property, precious metals, and bonds.[4]

Seventh, *beware of becoming involved financially with family and friends*. While all debt is dangerous, it is especially risky to engage in borrowing and lending with those close to us. Proverbs 22:7 warns, "The rich ruleth over the poor, and the borrower is servant to the lender." When debts are not repaid, both the lender and the borrower are tempted to bitterness. The lender is angry because the borrower is not meeting his obligation. The borrower often resents the lender because no one wants to be a servant (slave). Proverbs repeatedly warns against cosigning for the debts of others. Proverbs 22:26–27 is vivid: "Be not thou one of them that strike hands, or of them that are sureties for debts. If thou hast nothing to pay, why should he take away thy bed from under thee?" If you choose to engage in financial matters (including going into business) with family and friends, I strongly urge you to put detailed mutual expectations explicitly in writing.

---

4. For a more in-depth analysis of investment options see Newheiser, *Money, Debt, and Finances*, 227–59.

Include Your Wife in Your Family Finances

When the husband manages the family finances, he should involve his wife in decision making and keep her informed regarding their investments. By so doing a husband shows respect to his wife as his spiritual equal (1 Peter 3:7) and acknowledges that she may offer wisdom that will benefit the family finances (Prov. 31:11–12, 16). Sometimes it is the wife who is savvier in financial matters. A wise husband will gladly encourage her to use her gifts for the benefit of the family. She likewise would keep her husband informed and give him a major say in the management of their resources.

Conclusion

God's Word provides great wisdom in financial matters. I end with two reminders to help you to keep finances in proper perspective.

First, *make it your goal to be wise, not rich*. We live in a materialistic culture that makes an idol of wealth. While wealth may be of some benefit, it will never bring ultimate satisfaction (Eccl. 5:10; Isa. 55:1–2). God's wisdom is much more valuable: "For wisdom is better than rubies; and all the things that may be desired are not to be compared to it" (Prov. 8:11).

Second, *remember that Jesus paid your debt and made you rich*. Though Proverbs warns against taking on the debt of others, that is exactly what our Savior did for us—knowing the price He would have to pay. Paul says, "For ye know the grace of our Lord Jesus Christ, that, though he was rich, yet for your sakes he became poor, that ye through his poverty might be rich" (2 Cor. 8:9). Jesus not only paid our debt, but He also made us rich. We who have received such grace should be rich in good works.

CHAPTER SEVENTEEN

The Redeemed Man Enjoying His Recreations

Gerard Hemmings

SOME YEARS AGO, I had a recurring nightmare. My wife, our four children, and I were loaded up in the family car and on the road to somewhere. As we journeyed, the single-track road became steeper and steeper. I could not stop because the brakes would not hold. I could not turn around because the road was too narrow, and there were no exits. The only option was to keep going until, with the engine screaming and our car almost vertical, I would wake up.

Though it was only a dream, it was a window into my heart. I knew what the dream meant. Life was so demanding, and the schedule so punishing, that I found it almost impossible to stop. I was driven but not in control. I was too busy to rest. The only escape lane was illness or bereavement. And the worst of it was that I had brought my wife and children along for the ride!

Was this how I was to live? As a redeemed man, should I not be up and doing for Jesus? Should I not be presenting my body as a living sacrifice and using every waking hour God had given me to serve Him without restraints and without regrets? However, the danger of turning my life into a car crash was all too clear.

So, what does the Bible say about rest, refreshment, and recreation? Well, at first glance not much. There is Mark 6:30–32. The disciples had been so busy they had barely time to eat and so, Jesus said, it was time for a holiday: "Come aside by yourselves to a deserted place and rest a while" (v. 31).

- "Come aside" for a season of rest and recreation;
- "by yourselves" to escape from the usual pressures;
- "to a deserted place" for a change of scenery where they can unwind;
- "and rest a while" for a period of planned, purposeful recreation before they return to the fray.

So here were my verses. A time to enjoy recreation in the happy company of Jesus and friends. But they seemed only a few verses in an ocean of service. Furthermore, as the narrative makes clear, the disciple never got to rest!

So, are there just a handful of verses about the redeemed man enjoying his recreations? On this subject, do we have to leave the pages of Scripture? Let us go back to the beginning and to the first man. What is God's design for the redeemed man enjoying his recreations?

The Who of Recreation

Adam was made in the image of God (Gen. 1:26–27). He was the finite reflection of the infinite God. He was made in two stages. First, God formed his body: "And the LORD God formed man of the dust of the ground, and breathed into his nostrils the breath of life; and the man became a living being" (Gen. 2:7).

The Lord took the dust and, like an artisan working with his material, lovingly created a perfect body—but Adam is not yet alive. So, the Lord breathed into his nostrils the breath of life "and the man became a living being." It is almost as though God awakened Adam with a kiss, and as he opened his eyes, he was face to face with his Maker. Adam is therefore made of the dust of the earth and filled with the breath of heaven.

He is body and soul, a psychosomatic whole, an embodied spirit. All of which means that true recreation must involve body and soul. The two are inseparable. If we neglect the body, the soul will suffer; and if we neglect the soul, the body will suffer. We are an integrated whole, and so recreation is to be enjoyed by the whole man.

The Where of Recreation

Not only was Adam made of the dust but his relationship with the ground is repeatedly emphasized (Gen. 2:7, 9, 19; 3:17, 19, 23). All of which means that our well-being is intimately connected with the ground we walk on. Ask yourself, where do I find it easiest to relax and return refreshed? We read that "Isaac went out to meditate in the field in the evening" (Gen. 24:63). Our welfare is bound up with the land on which we live. But of course, we can say more. Adam's home was a garden planted by the Lord Himself: "The LORD God planted a garden eastward in Eden, and there He put the man whom He had formed. . . . Now a river went out of Eden to water the garden" (Gen. 2:8, 10).

Think of it. Every morning Adam awoke to the sunrise to find a garden filled with the golds, reds, and purples of the dawn. Stopping to listen he would hear the morning chorus of birdsong, the rustle of the leaves, and the murmuring of a mountain stream. Breathing in the air of the new day, he would smell the scent of the garden. Having feasted his senses on the wonder of it all, he would walk among the symmetry, beauty, and architecture of the trees that God had planted. In Hebrew *Eden* means delight. Adam's home was a healing, refreshing garden of delights.

True refreshment and recreation are so often found where our environment is delightful, where the whole man can find refreshment and renewal. How many of us have a special place which we seek out in times of stress and change? It may be a garden, a glade, a forest, a mountain, or a river. It will, though, have a flavor of Eden.

It is interesting that Adam's home was filled with trees. Trees are good for our well-being. When the emerald ash borer beetle devastated avenues of ash trees in the United States, a striking discovery was made. As the trees died, and the landscape changed, people's health and well-being also deteriorated. Indeed, folk began to die at a faster rate than before.[1] It is clear the Lord loves trees, which is why as His image bearers, we love them too, and why losing them somehow robs us of a part of who we are.

The With of Recreation

"The LORD God said, 'It is not good that man should be alone; I will make him a helper comparable to him'" (Gen. 2:18).

God is never alone. He is three persons: Father, Son and Holy Spirit. It is therefore not good that His image bearer should be alone. So, the Lord built Adam a woman, a lover, a companion, and a friend. She was like him and yet unlike him, and as his helper, shared this new world with him, so that together they could fulfil God's calling to be fruitful and multiply, and fill the earth and subdue it (Gen. 1:28).

Sometimes the best recreation for weary redeemed men is, in the words of one medical practitioner, to "chase your wife around the garden." Developing recreational activities with your wife, both spiritually and physically, can be a great blessing to your entire manhood.

If it is not good that man should be alone, that is surely a reminder that we are not to go it alone. We are social beings, and loneliness is corrosive. Recreation, even allowing for differences in temperament, opportunities,

---

1. Geoffrey H. Donovan, David T. Butry, Yvonne L. Michael, Jeffrey P. Prestemon, Andrew M. Liebhold, Demetrios Gatziolis, and Megan Y. Mao, "The Relationship Between Trees and Human Health: Evidence from the Spread of the Emerald Ash Borer," *American Journal of Preventative Medicine* 44, no. 2 (February 2013): 139–45.

and abilities, must mean at some point the embrace of friendship and the joy of camaraderie. Such things are not add-ons but are essential ingredients if we are to enjoy our recreation.

The When of Recreation

When God made the universe, He put clocks in the sky—sun, moon and stars to measure days, to announce the seasons, to control the tides and to mark the years (Gen. 1:14). God created time, and as creatures of time we are to follow the rhythms of work, rest, and play. Adam worked hard in the day, but in the cool of the evening he met with the Lord.

Adam was created on the sixth day, which means that his first full day was the sabbath, a day of rest (Gen. 2:1–3). It is striking that if a perfect man, in a perfect world, with a perfect marriage, and a perfect calling needed a weekly day of rest, how much more do redeemed men in a fallen world need to keep the sabbath day holy?

Of course, with Jesus's resurrection and the launch of God's new creation, the sabbath is now the first day of the week but if the bodies and souls of redeemed men are to be refreshed and renewed, they must keep to the weekly pattern established by God. We must be careful, however, not to hijack the Lord's Day for the pursuit of personal recreation. Nevertheless, the man who keeps Sunday special will be well positioned to keep a daily, weekly, monthly, and yearly rhythm of work and recreation.

The Walk of Recreation

One evening when the Lord came into the garden to meet with Adam, he was nowhere to be found. He had sinned. He had trampled underfoot the love of God. He was hiding and afraid, and of course the judgment of God fell upon our first parents. Having been made body and soul the process was put into reverse. Decay, dysfunction, and death would now mark rebellious Adam and his children, "for dust you are, and to dust you shall return" (Gen. 3:19).

We have all wronged God. We have lived as though the things that God has made are more real, substantial, and satisfying than the God who made them. We are idolaters at heart and have worshipped a whole pantheon of petty gods rather than the true and living God. So as redeemed men, if we are to truly enjoy our recreation and give glory of God, we must do so in fellowship with the God "who gives us richly all things to enjoy" (1 Tim. 6:17).

In John 21, the risen Lord Jesus met with His disciples, and Peter in particular, for the third time. Now back on home turf by the Sea of Galilee, Peter decided to go fishing, and the others accompanied him. Is Peter returning to work? On the contrary, it reads more like a distraction or even a night's recreation. After all, of the six disciples in the fishing boat, only two were actually fishermen. That night they caught nothing, and when, in the pale light of dawn, Jesus asked if they had caught any fish, "they answered Him, 'No'" (v. 5). These men were cold, wet, tired, and hungry. They had been up all night and caught nothing. But now at Jesus's word they landed a huge catch of fish. As they returned to the shore, Jesus welcomed them with a charcoal fire and the most cheering words hungry men can ever hear, "Come and eat breakfast" (v. 12). Effectively Jesus invited them to warm themselves and eat as much as they want. As they ate, the light returned to their eyes, and there may have been the noise of conversation and laughter. All this and Jesus too! Jesus understands men. They would never forget this breakfast with Jesus by the Sea of Galile. It did not simply warm their bodies; it did something more. It ministered healing and rest to the whole man. Furthermore, Peter, having breakfasted, is now ready to have that conversation with Jesus where he will be restored.

The word "recreation" is from the Latin *recreare*, which means to create again. So where did these redeemed men enjoy true re-creation? Was it on the boat without Jesus or on the shore with Jesus? Recreation, if it is to be enjoyed guilt free and to the glory of God, must be enjoyed in fellowship with Jesus. Recreation that robs us of our devotion to the Lord is, in the long run, self-destructive.

Masculinity and Recreation

Adam was to work hard, to provide for and protect his growing family, to train up the next generation, and ultimately to subdue the earth and have dominion over every living thing (Gen. 1:28). He therefore needed to be strong, driven, and competitive. He needed to take risks and rise to a challenge. He needed energy, ambition, and controlled aggression. And he needed to foster a team ethos, so that he and his descendants could work together to build the kingdom. Which of course is why, as men, we have testosterone.

This explains why in our recreation we seek to bring order, for example, in gardening or do-it-yourself projects. It explains why we seek to achieve personal bests in sport. It explains the desire for team sports where we learn self-mastery, controlled aggression, and to put our energies into the service of others.

Recreation is therefore good. It is an outworking of Genesis 1:28. We need to sweat, run, and wrestle. We need to refuse to give up, when everything inside says we should. We need to escape our phones and screens. Recreation is part of the redeemed man's training in godliness. Nothing mighty rests upon it because it is recreation, and yet it plays its part in producing mighty men of God.

Practical Reflections on Recreation

The last thing I wish to do is to cramp any man's style, so these reflections are not exhaustive but simply helpful pointers.

Temperament. Some men enjoy adrenaline-soaked contact sports.

Some men prefer the quietness of the art gallery and find refreshment in classical music. Some enjoy indoor, comfortable pastimes, whereas others seek the adventure of the outdoors. Some men thrive in social situations that other men would find exhausting. Equally, others need the solitude and respite of a country walk or fishing.

Stage of Life. High octane sports are thrilling when we are young but are simply beyond us after a certain age. The tapes of my youth are not the same as my Spotify choices of today. Mars has been eclipsed by Venus. We need to recognize this. One busy brother analyzed this change. He realized that he needed to slow down and so he took up photography to give himself unhurried time to think. Do I need to say more?

Connections. How connected am I? Men need the friendship of men. Jesus, the manliest man who ever lived, had three close friends: Peter, James, and John. In the Garden of Gethsemane, He needed their friendship as never before. "Then He said to them, 'My soul is exceedingly sorrowful, even to death. Stay here and watch with me'" (Matt. 26:38).

None of us is made to go it alone. David and Jonathan needed each other. Jonathan strengthened David's hand in God. So, in our busy, often stressful, lives, redeemed men need the friendship of one another, and so often we cultivate such friendships through shared recreational pursuits.

In this respect, we need to recognize the value of team sports and pastimes. Men need to belong to and to become a band of brothers. Through sports young men learn to rule over themselves, to control their aggression, to exercise courage, and to harmonize their gifts with the rest of the team. They learn to serve by putting the welfare of the team above their own. Such qualities prepare men for serving the Lord. Furthermore, the bar is raised. Young men rub shoulders with men godlier than themselves, all of which helps them to develop lives of heroic and principled obedience. Finally, team games and shared pastimes help us to connect with unbelieving friends with whom we can share the Friend of sinners.

When Did I Last Enjoy Some Recreation?

Some years ago, when taking a sabbatical, I began to crash and burn. When the adrenaline switched off, my body and spirit started to fall apart. I was rescued by a doctor friend who asked this simple question: "What do you enjoy doing?" I trotted out my answer to which he responded, "So, when was the last time you did those things?" I could not remember. It was so long ago. He continued, "Your enjoyment of those things has not gone away. They are part of your humanity. You simply need to reacquaint yourself with them." It was sage advice.

And so, I went fishing, painted, and swam. To my surprise, I found a renewal of body and spirit. I did not simply pray myself out of the hole in which I found myself, but under the Lord's tender care, I began to recover my humanity. Like a cushion that had been sat on for too long, I needed to return to my former symmetry.

All of which means that recreation needs to be purposeful, regular, and enjoyable. It is to be part of the rhythm of our lives. It not only gives us a break from our day job but gives us a hinterland of interests. After all, single-topic men are boring.

In all of this we need a healthy self-knowledge and perhaps an ability to head ourselves off at the pass before the pressures become overwhelming. We must find ways to overwrite the hard disc with zeros and ones. Dr. F. W. Boreham found his relaxation in cricket. He wrote,

> I have devoted so much time to the game for three reasons. (1) I love it. (2) I find it the most perfect holiday. If I go to the beach or the bush my mind runs on sermons and articles; if I go to cricket, I forget everything but runs and wickets. And (3) I have found it good to form a set of delightful friendships outside the circles

in which I habitually move. I review quite impenitently the hundreds of long and leisurely days that I have spent at cricket.[2]

The Danger of Going Without Recreation

What if we feel our callings and responsibilities are too significant to take time out for refreshment? What if we feel that for the redeemed man recreation is a luxury? What if we put a spiritual gloss on our recreation to make it sound worthy and minimize the need for real time out?

Consider the warning of Psalm 127: "Unless the LORD builds the house, they labor in vain who build it; unless the LORD guards the city, the watchman stays awake in vain. It is in vain for you to rise up early, to sit up late, to eat the bread of sorrows; for so He gives His beloved sleep" (vv. 1–2).

If the building in question is the temple and the city, Jerusalem, what could be more important? So, does the Lord expect His servants to work until they drop? On the contrary, He wants them to enjoy rest.

When building the house, those charged with its construction must work hard. Nevertheless, it is the Lord who builds the house. The outcome is in His hands, not theirs. Similarly, for the safety of the city, the watchman must stay awake; nevertheless, it is the Lord Himself who keeps the city safe.

Now the application of these verses for the Christian ministry is obvious, but we all have our callings, and it applies to them as well. Therefore, while the Lord expects us to be diligent and hardworking, the outcome of our service rests with Him and not us. The redeemed man who thinks it

---

2. F. W. Boreham, *My Pilgrimage: An Autobiography* (Epworth Press, 1940), 16–17. For our readers in the United States, cricket is a ball-and-bat sport that originated in England and is played in nations around the world.

all depends on him, will find his working day starts increasingly early and finishes increasingly late. He will be filled with anxious toil. He will be burning the candle at both ends, and the first thing to go will be any time for recreation. All of which means he will burn himself out. We are called to be living sacrifices. We are not called to self-destruction.

Do I have a savior complex, that somehow it all depends on me? If I do, my working day will lengthen to accomplish all that I set myself. I will micromanage. I will manipulate and control those around me until they too are sucked into the vortex of overwork. All of which means I rob myself and others of time for recreation. Those who enjoy their recreation will in the long term achieve so much more for the Lord. There is only one Savior, and it is not me! Recreation is an exercise in trust. It is trusting the Lord with our labors and believing that He gives to His beloved people the rest they need.

The alternative can be devastating. Imagine a man who has served God faithfully for twenty years. He is now middle-aged and is slowing down. He has not allowed himself to find regular refreshment in healthy rest and recreation. Now his heart is subtly turning. Comfort is becoming more important than challenge. He has been alone with little support. While he has been spending himself for the people of God, others have been at peace. Here is an isolated, weary, redeemed man who now feels that he is entitled to some well-deserved rest. And when Satan comes in the form of some Delilah who offers comfort and escape, he is ripe for a fall.

Have I reached that same vulnerable place? Have I eschewed times of rest and recreation in pursuit of my calling? Have I neglected body and soul, and now the dust of which I am made is catching up with me? Redeemed men need to enjoy their God-given recreation. It is not an add-on or an opt-out. On the contrary, it is vital to fighting the good fight, finishing the race, and keeping the faith.

Conclusion

Our Lord Jesus was the complete human being. He was in all points tempted as we are, yet without sin. He was therefore tempted to overwork and to laziness and so cannot but sympathize with us in all our struggles. In His punishing schedule, He made time to stand and stare at the birds as they wheeled and banked in the Galilean thermals. He took time to look at the lilies of the field and to enjoy their fragile beauty. He gave nicknames to some of His disciples with all the healthy friendships and camaraderie which that implies. He lived in perfect fellowship with the Father, trusting Him to richly provide Him with everything to enjoy. He was a wise steward of His body and soul, so that He could finish the work the Father had given Him to do. It is in the company of Jesus that we learn that there is no contradiction between enjoying our recreation and bringing glory to God.

CHAPTER EIGHTEEN

The Redeemed Man Governing as a Citizen

David C. Innes

IN A FALLEN world, God provides government for our good, beginning with civil peace, which starts with basic order and the rudiments of justice. This peace is no small good. It supplies the setting in which all other goods may be pursued—the materially, morally, and spiritually productive work of home and church, farm and shop. Without this civic service in a world of scarcity and rapacity, malice and perversity, life quickly descends into crude savagery, "filled with violence" (Gen. 6:11), becoming, as Thomas Hobbes described it, "solitary, poor, nasty, brutish, and short."[1]

But while basic civic order—protection against assault, theft, and invasion—is a good that even tyrants provide, the fullness of God's blessing through civil government is a richer and more comprehensive good. The apostle tells us that government is "God's minister" for our good (Rom. 13:4). Government has the power and authority to secure its people, not only in their bare lives but also in the fuller quality of those lives, that is, in their Christian piety, material prosperity, and moral flourishing.[2] In

---

1. Thomas Hobbes, *Leviathan* (Penguin, 1968), 186.
2. David C. Innes, *Christ and the Kingdoms of Men: Foundations of Political Life* (P&R, 2019), 45, III.

this way, when government—any government at any level—serves God faithfully, it secures a setting for people in which they can faithfully and more effectively pursue their various callings, developing and enjoying God's creation for His glory, and providing for themselves and their neighbors, even for their delight.

Accordingly, good government in the fulness of its faithful service is righteous and wise government. It serves in knowledgeable obedience to God and charitable service to the governed. Thus, only godly government can, strictly speaking, be good government. Is it wise? The book of Proverbs tells us that wisdom begins with the fear of God (Prov. 9:10). Is it righteous? "The fear of the LORD is to hate evil" (8:13).

Though without the fear of God and the wisdom of God there is no good government for our good, even the shrewd government of wicked men can provide the blessings of peace and the basic elements of justice. The unrighteous judge in Christ's parable, though he did not fear God or respect man, still gave justice to the persistent widow (Luke 18:4–5). In Proverbs, Wisdom says, "By me kings reign, and rulers decree justice. By me princes rule, and nobles, all the judges of the earth" (Prov. 8:15–16). They should reign by God's wisdom, and whatever wisdom they have comes from God.

So, must one be a Christian to serve God adequately as civil magistrate for the people's good? Has God not mercifully given wisdom sufficient for rule to the godly and the ungodly alike? Is the natural law not written on everyone's heart, the moral law accessible by reason, that is, by rational reflection on the world, oneself, and the ordinary course of life? Alas, if only it were so simple! Despite this universal natural testimony, the "ungodliness and unrighteousness of men" places the world under judgment (Rom. 1:18). Thus, because of men's deadness to God and deafness to God's voice in nature, positions of government are often occupied by thieves, boasters, and scoundrels. Power draws the power-hungry. Though God knows this, He elevates them for His service anyway. In the sinful state of the world, God by His common grace uses whatever government He provides to secure people in some measure of good or another, especially the redeemed for their service in the kingdom of God.

This is not to say that government service by those who are dead in sin and enemies of God is illegitimate. Legitimacy and the fully faithful government provision of "good" are separate, though related, questions. The apostles recognized the Roman and Jewish authorities as legitimately serving God in their offices even though they were ignorant of God. They were indeed God's ministers for good (Rom. 13:4), but unfaithful and treasonous. The pagan Roman government in particular not only allowed the moral abominations that were accepted at the time, but also suppressed God's church. Many American governments of our day—local, state and federal—celebrate maternal infanticide as a noble right, often even up to the point of birth. They often encourage sexual confusion, even in young children. The failure of these governments to punish evil and praise well-doing, as God would have them do, is traceable to their ignorance of God and even their conscious hatred of godliness.

Many people in government, though not all, whether autocratic or democratic, are "fools," according to a biblical understanding of wisdom. Regardless of what they profess with their lips, in their hearts they say, "There is no God" (Ps. 14:1). But just as most people, though fools, are responsible before God their Creator and Judge to be wise and not foolish, so too those in positions of civil authority. Thus, properly speaking, God established these positions of authority not for fools but for redeemed men whose Shepherd is the King of love (Ps. 23:1) and whose delight is in the law of the Lord (1:2). It is not only "lawful for Christians to accept and execute the office of a magistrate";[3] it is the proper place of a redeemed man to exercise rule, not only in his home and in the church, but also in his community and nation.

3. Westminster Confession of Faith (23.2), in *The Westminster Confession* (Free Presbyterian Publications, 1994), 100.

God's Calling for Men: The Creation Mandate

The redeemed man is the restored man, or one who is being restored to the untarnished image of God. So, for insight into the character and calling of man-as-redeemed, we must look to the opening chapters of Genesis. We are considering the excellencies of God's work of redemption in restoring human beings—specifically *men* in this case—to the fulness of their creational glory and more. "I have come that they may have life, and that they may have it more abundantly" (John 10:10). The specifically civic virtue of a redeemed man, the righteous ruler of whatever God has given him to order and develop, "a man in the full" one could say, must have reference back to Genesis 1–2, as that is where we see his human calling, his divine marching orders as God's image-bearing agent in the world. Any specifically civic calling would be a species of this.

God the Creator made everything from nothing and for His own purposes, for His own glory, to magnify His name. He sustains all things from moment to moment, from the sun in all its fearful brilliance to the smallest, most contemptible insect,[4] and even subatomic activity (Col. 1:17; Heb. 1:3). Rule is not something God just happens also to do among His many activities. It is inseparable from Him as Creator.

Man was made in the image of this God, to represent Him within the creation, to do God's work for His glory. As such, man was made to be righteous *like* God and to rule *for* God.[5] God blessed the first man and woman, and said to them, "Be fruitful and multiply; fill the earth and subdue it; have dominion over the fish of the sea, over the birds of the air, and over every living thing that moves on the earth" (Gen. 1:28). This enterprise of dominion over the earth is the creation mandate. It is God's

---

4. Here I echo Augustine of Hippo, *City of God*, 5.11, in *A Select Library of the Nicene and Post-Nicene Fathers of the Christian Church, First Series*, ed. Philip Schaff (Buffalo, NY, 1887), 2:93.
5. Innes, *Christ and the Kingdoms of Men*, 11.

command to all His human creation, but it is chiefly the task of men. Both men and women are made in God's image, but women have a supportive role as helpers who are suited to both the man and the task (Gen. 2:18–22). The lead role, the chief responsibility, falls to the man. Men rule. They should rule themselves in righteousness, then the earth, their families, and whatever community they form in elaborating God's glory, extending His kingdom, and loving their neighbors.

The role of women in this human calling is indispensable, specifically in marriage and family, which are central to fulfilling our obligation for dominion. An individual man or woman may advance this dominion apart from marriage, not only young men and women but also anyone who is called to an unmarried state for a more undistracted service to God.[6] But is a married woman not allowed, say for example, to write thoughtful, probing literature? Should she only support her husband in his own writing vocation? Of course she may! But as a married woman, her ministry of support to her husband and family would come first. This is not a loophole through which to drive the garbage truck of feminist interchangeability.

In creating the world, God brought it into being and ordered it. Accordingly, Adam cultivated and ordered in obedience to God's mandate. This included, with Eve's indispensable help, generating a family and governing his home in such a way as to raise his children for godly service. He begat and he ordered. Later we are told that Abraham governed his children, which is to say he ordered his home (Gen. 18:19). In the church, elders must have their households in order (1 Tim. 3:4). But just as tilling the earth was complicated by man's fall into sin, so too was ordering the home and cultivating successive generations. Thus, the tragic story of Cain and Abel follows swiftly upon the fall (Gen. 4:1–15).

In an unfallen world, as Adam's family grew, the children and their descendants would have spread out, obeying God's command to fill the

---

6. See chapter 6, "The Redeemed Man Living in Singleness."

earth, forming distinct nations in different regions shaped in their national characters by geography, climate, shared experience, and local traditions, but without conflict between them and with a common language and uniformly faithful worship. Adam would have been governor of the nations, being the deathless paterfamilias, insofar as that was necessary for the worldwide task of dominion. Christ, the last Adam, has had that office since His ascension (1 Cor. 15:45).

The Marks of a Man: Build, Serve, Protect

Men—all men—are made to govern. A man governs his vocational sphere, his home, and, by extension, his community. That dominion is the labor of ordering and building. Sin notwithstanding, he serves his neighbors through what he builds. But a man must also protect what he has ordered and built. Even before the fall, he was to protect the sanctity of the garden-temple. The marks of a man are that he builds, serves, and protects.

In this manly life, he follows the perfect man, Christ, who thus also builds, serves, and protects. Christ is building His universal church, His kingdom on earth. Christ "did not come to be served, but to serve, and to give His life a ransom for many" (Matt. 20:28; Mark 10:45). His sacrificial service to His church was "that He might sanctify" her, that is, beautify her with holiness (Eph. 5:25–26). As protector, Christ rules and defends His saints against the world, the flesh, and the devil (Matt. 28:18–20; 1 Cor. 15:25).[7]

Build

Man as builder was not only to maintain the garden as he received it from God but also to develop it, and eventually the whole world, into what it

7. See the Westminster Larger Catechism 45; and the Westminster Shorter Catechism 26; in *Westminster Confession of Faith*, 149–50, 293–94.

was capable of becoming—to unfold and elaborate the latent glory and wealth of the creation. A modern though incomplete way of stating this commission would be that he was to build wealth or, more broadly, to build value: family, goods, and services; farms, shops, and industries; towns, cities, and suburbs; commodious buildings—homes, halls, houses of business and pleasure—and highways of movement by water and by land to bring his good work to his descendants around the world, and in turn to bring their work back again. From his spreading family, he would form communities and cultures, the rituals and rhythms of beloved traditions, recreations, music, art and adornments, language and literature. But he would also conceive structures of understanding, empirical and theoretical accounts of the world, every branch of learning. And all of this, even apart from the fall, would require government—tribal elders, gifted administrators, and creative planners.

Serve

All efforts at building aim at God's pleasure and the well-being of one's neighbors, the glory of God and the common good.[8] Your building activity must support or edify your neighbor. It must supply his good and supply him with opportunity or equipment for doing good in his own ministry of building, serving, and protecting. If your creative labors in building do not conform to God's moral law, then you are not building but destroying, like the Destroyer himself (Rev. 9:11). For this reason, any good or service a man produces that poisons his neighbor's body, mind, or heart or that supplies an opportunity or setting that would, by its nature, incline him to sin or to ill-health is not building but destroying. If it is not serving, that is, giving glory to God and real gain to neighbor, then it is not building.

---

8. The fall complicated the relationship between the individual good and the common good we all share. Any requirement for sacrifice, especially death in battle, but also any self-denial for the sake of friend, family, or neighbor, illustrates this.

Protect

This third "mark of a man" is a postlapsarian elaboration of what it means to serve. But it bears separate mentioning and special emphasis. It is an order of service that demands distinct virtues for its execution. Serving is an elaboration of building. It is contained within the concept of "build," properly understood. We build with purpose in view. What we build has planned function, whether a plough, an organization, or a language. It "serves" a function, and it functions for some intended good.

So too, after the fall, "service" contains but is not reducible to the service of protection because with the fall came vulnerability and threat of harm. Thus came the need for men—who are the bigger, stronger sex and are charged with headship in the home—to protect their families and the fruit of their labors, their communities, and any stranger in need, not only from physical harm but also from moral and spiritual assault. But men are not alone in this. Homes constitute communities where men work together in defense of those communities, historically against ferocious, wild animals but also against wild neighbors and ferocious invaders. He protects his and his neighbors' liberty—physical, moral, and spiritual—against tyrants, oligarchs, and demagogues.

Protection is a large part of government's purpose after mankind's fall into sin, and it is an extension of each man's task in his family and community. But every man must also be vigilant to defend his family and community against encroachments by that government on their freedom to build wealth, culture, character, and the kingdom of God both locally and around the world. So, when he is not taking a hand in government directly, the redeemed man is supporting (as opportunity provides) godly men in government who understand their proper role as God's servants for our good.

The Civic Duty of a Man: The Christian Free Citizen

This work of protection requires leadership, even championship. Hence, the rise of kings. Kings, notice! Not queens. In the unrighteous line of Cain, kingship quickly became tyranny, the use of public authority not for public benefit but for private advantage, such as glory, wealth, revenge, and venting every lust. We see this in Cain's infamous descendant, Lamech (Gen. 4:19–24). But godly kings served their people with their people's consent. This does not mean they came to power by free and fair elections with universal suffrage, but only by the agreement of tribal elders who were understood as speaking for their people.[9] Even King David, though anointed by God for his office, was not fully established on Israel's throne until he had the express support of all the tribes of Israel (2 Sam. 5:1–3).

Though unfallen Adam would have been king over all the earth, his rule would not have been an absolute rule. Aside from the limitations imposed by distance, a universal absolute monarchy would deny or diminish the ruling responsibility—as well as ruling dignity and pleasure—of all other men. The multiplying generations of heads of household would not expect to be ruled as though they were children. As mature and fully capable men, they would govern their households and their wider affairs. As they spread out across the earth, forming themselves into distinct nations and, within those nations, into provinces and communities, they would govern themselves *as* communities. These would be communities of political self-government, as befits free people. Though there would be no sin in the world to restrain and punish, there would still be a need for government, just as there is much that occupies any government, even merely administrative government, that has no reference to sin and its restraint.

---

9. In the Bible, there are times when the phrase "all the children of Israel" cannot possibly refer to the whole multitude of Israel but must designate their tribal representatives, such as in Ex. 34:30–32, as v. 31 makes clear.

We need inspiration and direction simply insofar as we are created and living in community together.[10]

But sin did indeed enter the world, and with it came new requirements for government. To govern effectively, therefore, government needed energy and force. But because the sinners who so needed restraining and punishing were themselves in the government that was doing the restraining and punishing, the government itself required restraint.[11] As the Latins wisely warned, *Quis custodiet ipsos custodes?* Who will watch the watchmen?[12] Thus, that forceful, energetic government—necessary for containing within civilized limits the storm of sin within us—governs most safely and thus effectively when it is a decentralized system of constitutional, popular self-government. Those early heads of household would, like the elders of Israel, gather to decide matters of common concern to the community. What exact form that government would take would depend on the particular circumstances of the community. But after the fall, it would certainly involve the rule of law and a prudent system of checks and balances as the English developed and as their American colonies adapted. The redeemed man, thus, insists on these limits, vigilantly guards and defends them, and takes his place within them to serve his neighbors and their liberty. He does not trust bureaucracies to be enlightened and professional, nor elected officials to be good because they're from the right party. Only God is good. Men are entrusted with power and then distrusted by their vigilant voters. Even George Washington distrusted himself, limiting himself to only two terms as president.

As this is God's design for human government, Aristotle, by God's common grace a brilliant, albeit pagan, philosopher, identified the ideal

---

10. Innes, *Christ and the Kingdoms of Men*, 49.
11. Innes, *Christ and the Kingdoms of Men*, 120.
12. Juvenal, *Satires*, 6.347–48 (cf. insertion O 31–32), in *Juvenal and Persius*, trans. G. G. Ramsay, Loeb Classical Library (William Heinemann; G. P. Putnam's Sons, 1928), 110 (cf. 114–15).

government as what he called "political" government, ruling and being ruled in turn among equals, each man taking a hand in it in one way or another.[13] Ideal government is, therefore, popular self-government that is republican and constitutional.

Every redeemed man is called and equipped for this civic service. He has, first, the vocational right to citizen involvement. Everyone is called to govern himself and his wider sphere of responsibility for godly dominion (Gen. 1:28). He is called, that is, to govern his private affairs in vice-regency for the Creator-King. By extension, as we are thus equals in that calling, we are also called to govern with one another our broader affairs in that same King's name for establishing and securing the conditions that support everyone's vocational work.

The redeemed man has the spiritual equipment for this citizen involvement, and uniquely so, serving his neighbor in a civic capacity as faithful servant of the throne that is founded on justice and righteousness (Ps. 89:14). The spiritually dead are not. The redeemed man is alive to God, Ruler of the nations (22:28), and thus responsive to Him. He is spiritually equipped to hear the King and thus to receive orders from on high and respond in obedience. His heart is made new (Ezek. 36:26). He is born again (John 3:6–7), and so love is born in him, love for God and love for neighbor—his fellow citizen, the stranger within his borders and, as may be fitting, the stranger beyond his borders.

The redeemed man thus also has the moral preparation for citizen involvement. All government is God's government, a civic mediation of His goodness to us. The redeemed man as citizen knows in the marrow of his bones to consider others better than himself. Like his Savior, he knows that he lives to serve, not be served. Everyone who holds the office of civil

13. Aristotle, *Politics*, 1277b9–10, trans. Carnes Lord (University of Chicago Press, 1985), 91–92. He contrasts "political authority" with the authority of a master over the household slaves, for the former is "a sort of rule in accordance with which one rules those who are similar in stock and free."

magistrate, everyone in authority over his neighbors, should view the exercise of his authority the same way. The redeemed man, as God conforms him to the image of King Jesus, is morally equipped for this. Unlike the rulers of the earth, having as he does a higher "citizenship [which] is in heaven," he does not "set [his] mind on earthly things," so he can be trusted with civic authority to govern earthly things (Phil. 3:19–20).

Conclusion

There are those who warn men of Christian conscience and godly zeal that they should guard their hearts against political idolatry, saying, "This earth is not our home." This is true, and idolatry of any kind is sin. Political idolatry in particular is especially tempting as it offers a kind of worldly gospel. Passionate political commitments have a tendency to displace the eternal concerns of a greater kingdom.

But it does not follow that we should leave the politics of democratic self-government to the lost and the foolish. These critics of overtly Christian political life and of those who desire it tell us that we should, as God says, do justly, love mercy, and walk humbly with our God (Mic. 6:8). Certainly! But when given the choice, these critics mercilessly commend the institutions of justice into the hands of tyrants and wolves. Our place, they would have us believe, is to preach the gospel to the resulting oppressed multitudes. In effect, and no doubt unintentionally, their advice amounts to this: enable earthly slavery, then offer heavenly freedom. People of this apolitical, transpolitical, supposedly gospel-driven political theology would convince us that God who gives government for our good (Rom. 13:4) wants us to leave it in the hands of "those who call evil good, and good evil" (Isa. 5:20). But with neighbors like those, who needs enemies? The free Christian citizen must guard himself against earthly gospels, but equally also against being so heavenly minded as to be of no earthly good.

This world and the sojourning church in this world need men, godly men, who are strong and wise and faithful to form families, to cherish their wives, to train their children in godliness and model it, to have them regularly in Bible-teaching, Bible-obedient churches, to provide them with Christian schooling, and to train them in industrious habits through home and school. He, his children, and his children's children will strive to live and govern as free people—materially, morally, and spiritually prosperous—building God's kingdom among men and restraining man's government under God.

PART 4

A Godly Man's Finishing Well

CHAPTER NINETEEN

The Redeemed Man Sustaining His Health

Joseph Pipa

AS JOSHUA BEGAN his ministry, God commanded him to "be strong and very courageous" (Josh. 1:7). Of course, this commandment was to be strong in the Lord by observing the law of God, not turning from it to the right or the left.[1] But as they were about to enter combat, Joshua and the men of Israel would need physical strength for the task before them.

Caleb is a good example of one who could fight the Lord's battle because he was physically strong. He said to Joshua, in claiming the inheritance God promised him,

> And now, behold, the LORD has kept me alive, as He said, these forty-five years, ever since the LORD spoke this word to Moses while Israel wandered in the wilderness; and now, here I am this day, eighty-five years old. As yet I am as strong this day as on the day that Moses sent me; just as my strength was then, so now is my strength for war, both or going out and for coming in. (Josh. 14:10–11).

---

1. For further treatment of Joshua as a model of a man committed to God's Word, see chapter 3.

At the time of this writing, most Christian men in the United States, Canada, and most of Europe are not fighting physical battles. However, we should be prepared for war or the physical rigors of persecution. Moreover, God calls us to the daily battle of providing for ourselves, families, and churches. Part of our covenant responsibility is to provide for our families (Eph. 4:28; 1 Thess. 4:11).

Moreover, our emotional and spiritual health is to a degree dependent on our physical stamina. Therefore, the theme of this chapter is important. The redeemed man is responsible to maintain health and strength to the degree he is able under God's providence. I recognize that God gives various degrees of health and strength, but we need to maintain and, as we can, improve on our natural condition. For example, President Theodore Roosevelt in his youth was weak and asthmatic. He rigorously trained himself to overcome his physical weakness.

In this chapter, I intend to lay the exegetical and theological foundation for this responsibility and offer practical suggestions.

The Exegetical and Theological Foundations

We begin considering Paul's commandment in 1 Timothy 4:7b–8, "Exercise yourself toward godliness. For bodily exercise profits a little, but godliness is profitable for all things, having promise of the life that now is and of that which is to come." In this section, Paul depicts the habits of the godly minister. He begins by establishing the need to feed on the truth of orthodox theology and to reject all error (vv. 6–7a). Then, he calls him to discipline or "exercise" himself in godliness (v. 7b).

The term translated as *exercise* is the word from which we get our English word gymnasium or gymnast. It depicts rigorous athletic training. Paul then uses a preposition that here means "for the purpose of." It indicates the goal, which is "godliness." Godliness is Godlikeness, growing conformity to the image of Christ. As the Lord commanded Joshua to be strong and courageous, Paul orders Timothy to pursue godliness with the same rigor and discipline that the gymnast or the athlete approaches his sport.

One pursues this goal by a careful use of the means of grace and mortification of the flesh—seeking to put off sinful patterns, habits, thoughts, and actions in order that we may be conformed to the image of Christ in the whole person.[2] We often refer to the practice of these things as *spiritual disciplines*: Bible study, prayer, corporate worship with preaching and sacraments, fasting, meditation, Sabbath keeping, spiritual conversation, and so on.

In verse 8, Paul gives the ground for this exhortation: "For bodily exercise profits a little, but godliness is profitable for all things, having promise of the life that now is and of that which is to come." Here he contrasts the profit of bodily exercise with that of spiritual exercise. Although some writers take "bodily exercise" to refer to ascetic practices, Paul has in mind physical exercise. He is not teaching that there is no profit in bodily exercise. It is profitable, but one must keep it in perspective. In comparison to the exercise in godliness, it is of little profit. Bodily exercise is profitable for this age, but godliness for this age and the age to come. As the Savior says, "For what profit is it to a man if he gains the whole world, and loses his own soul?" (Matt. 16:26).

So, although care for the body is not as important as spiritual discipline, Paul states it is of some profit. Al Martin writes, "Yet the disciplines of godliness do not negate the disciplines of the body, which are profitable. The relative importance of something does not negate the validity, necessity, or even urgency of the thing, and this is the case here. Bodily training or discipline is an essential physical necessity."[3] Physical discipline was

---

2. On the means of grace, see the Westminster Larger Catechism 154, in *Westminster Confession of Faith* (Free Presbyterian Publications, 1994), 246.
3. Albert N. Martin, *Pastoral Theology, Volume 1: The Man of God: His Calling and Godly Life* (Trinity Pulpit Press, 2018), 309.

necessary for Paul to conduct his rigorous ministry. Think of the rigors of travel in those days as Paul delineates the toil he endured (2 Cor. 11:23–27).

The Holy Spirit gives three reasons in the Holy Scriptures why a redeemed man should be concerned about his health.[4]

First, the body is important because *God created us in His image with bodies as well as souls* (Gen. 1:26–28; 2:7). There is difference of opinion as to whether the body is part of the image. All, however, would agree with John Calvin: "Though the primary seat of the divine image was in the mind and the heart, or in the soul and its powers, there was no part even of the body in which some rays of glory did not shine."[5] The body is important, and God provided in the garden for it in a wonderful way (2:9, 15–16). Martin writes, "The Bible teaches that there is a powerful, delicate, and constant interplay between the body and the soul in man."[6] The soul affects the body, and the body the soul.

Second, *God redeemed people, not just souls*. Christ purchased our bodies as well as our souls (1 Cor. 6:20). Our bodies, not just our souls, are temples of the Holy Spirit (v. 19). We are to glorify God in our bodies as well as our souls. In Romans 12:1, the apostle commands us to present our bodies as living sacrifices to God.

Even in death the body, although decaying, remains in union with Christ. He will raise our bodies on the last day and transform them into a glorious body like His (Phil. 3:21). The Westminster divines said the following about the benefits that believers receive from Christ at death: "The souls of believers are at their death made perfect in holiness, and do immediately pass into glory; and their bodies, being still united to Christ, do rest in their graves till the resurrection."[7] At His return, Christ will

---

4. Martin develops these three reasons in *Pastoral Theology*, 1:303–9.
5. John Calvin, *Institutes of the Christian Religion*, trans. Henry Beveridge (Edinburgh, 1863), 1.15.3 (1:164).
6. Martin, *Pastoral Theology*, 1:304; cf. Prov. 3:7–8; 4:20–23.
7. Westminster Shorter Catechism 37, in *Westminster Confession of Faith*, 297–98.

raise our bodies, and "we shall be like Him, for we shall see Him as He is" (1 John 3:2).

Third, *the law of God requires the proper care of our bodies*. Among the duties required by the sixth commandment ("You shall not murder," Ex. 20:13), the Westminster Larger Catechism includes "a sober use of meat [food], drink, physic [medical care], sleep, labour, and recreations."[8] In other words, it is a sin not to care for our bodies.

Even though in our culture people make idols of the body, we must not overreact to that excess. We have a God-given responsibility to care for the body. What then are we to do?

Practical Suggestions

I offer four suggestions as practical guidelines for caring for our bodies.

Regular Medical Care

First, we are to take proper care of our bodies with regular medical care. By this I mean we are to take advantage of the wonderful provisions God has made for us in the day of modern medicine.

It is important to maintain a relationship with a physician and, according to age and the physician's protocol, have a regular physical examination. As we grow older, the scheduling of these examinations will increase. Again, according to the doctor's wisdom, the examinations should include prostate examinations and colonoscopies, as well as any other tests he thinks are appropriate.

Other regular examinations should include regular dental care. The health of our teeth affects the health of our entire body. Diseased teeth or gums can poison the body. My dentist, Dr. Tim Nary, highlights the importance of regular dental care:

---

8. Westminster Larger Catechism 135, in *The Westminster Confession*, 219.

Regular dental visits are essential for a healthy dentition, allowing us to properly eat, smile, communicate, and maintain our overall health. Periodic dental exams and imaging detect cavities when they are small and easily treated, detect periodontal or gum disease, which contributes to heart disease, and examine for oral, head, and neck cancers.[9]

It is also important to have regular eye examinations. Many eye diseases that cause blindness can be prevented or curtailed with a regular eye examination. Dr. Williams, a Christian ophthalmologist says,

> Jesus increased in wisdom, statue, and favor with God and man. A man must take time to feed his soul, as well as take care of his body, which is the temple of God. If he does not, he will lose the ability to unselfishly serve others. Over the years, I've realized the leading cause of blindness is not having a professional eye physician diagnosing and treating any early eye diseases. Often when a person notices a problem with their vision, especially with glaucoma, diabetes, or any family history of eye diseases, the damage is typically irreversible.

Most insurance plans and Medicare (in the United States) will cover regular eye examinations.

As we get older, we should seriously consider getting a hearing test. In 2019, when I was speaking at the Puritan Seminary Conference, my friend Joel Beeke noticed that I was straining to hear. He told me his physician said that straining to hear kills brain cells. My audiologist, Dr. Sandra Skipper, points to a new Johns Hopkins' study of a sample of more than 2,400 older adults that seems to confirm hearing loss may be

---

9. The medical authorities quoted in this section are from the author's personal interviews and correspondence.

a contributing factor over a period of time to dementia, and that treating hearing loss may lower the risk of dementia.

Also, I want you to consider three types of non-traditional medical care. The first is osteopathic medicine. My wife has gone to an osteopathic doctor for years and has profited from his care. The philosophy of an osteopathic doctor supplements the care of your physician. Her doctor, Dr. Kenneth Orbeck, defines his science as follows:

> As an osteopathic physician, I look at healthcare and body analysis with a holistic approach on how all organ systems interdependently work together. Understanding metabolic health and optimal metabolic balance allows individuals to age gracefully and continue to live quality lives. Structure and function are interrelated, and good body structure offers good functionality. Balancing fitness, nutrition, and cell signaling with proper hormones, allows the body to maintain an anabolic metabolism of growth and recovery rather than a catabolic metabolism of breakdown and decline. It's all about balance. Supporting the body with proper fuel, enhancing detoxification pathways, insuring proper communication pathways, and supplying the body proper building blocks for strength and recovery offers an individual optimal health.

The second non-traditional type of medical care is chiropractic medicine. Again, chiropractic care is a useful supplement to traditional medical care. Dr. Kevin Mobley defines chiropractic medicine as "a branch of health care in which adjustments are made to various joints in the body, but specifically to the spine, in order to restore greater nerve flow and increase mobility to the joint." Currently, he is treating me for neuropathy.

A third type of non-traditional care is natural healing. Don Partridge describes natural healing in this way:

> Natural healing is a broad subject that can be used to refer to many things from cleaning up your diet and avoiding processed foods, food additives, seeking organically grown and healthier food choices to support the immune system, to learning the use of things God put in creation for us like herbs, minerals, homeopathics, to prevent illness and support the body's innate ability to repair itself, to professionals trained in these modalities, like herbalists, nutritionists, naturopathic physicians.... The true essence of natural medicine is that it sees the body was created to heal and repair itself and that symptoms arise to warn us or as a result of damage resulting from some nutritional deficiency or toxic build up that is interfering with normal function and immune repair of the body.

Physicians, osteopathic doctors, and chiropractors also use natural supplements.

As I detail the useful options for medical care, I realize that for some readers the costs would be prohibitive. If you cannot afford regular medical insurance, use medical sharing programs such as Samaritan Ministries. Many Christians receive excellent medical care though these programs.

Moreover, I encourage deacons in the church to develop resources with Christian doctors in the various fields of medicine who will do *pro bono* work for the poorer members of their congregations. The church I am serving is currently compiling a list of such resources.

Healthy Habits

In order to sustain his health, the redeemed man needs to develop healthy habits. The top of the list is a healthy diet. We should follow our physician's recommendations as to a balanced diet and avoid immoderate use of junk food. We should maintain a proper weight for our height and frame. The Bible does not dictate ideal body weight. However, it is important that we do not impair our health and energy by being extremely overweight.

I place here the need for proper hygiene. Some annual viruses may be avoided by the practice of cleanliness. Moreover, we do not want to offend those around us with body odor. Regardless of how poor one is, there is no excuse for offensive body odor.

With respect to healthy habits, if we use caffeinated drinks such as coffee or sodas, or alcoholic beverages, we must do so in moderation. Paul, in exposing false teachers, teaches that God made all things, according to their nature and purpose, for man's good—including "foods which God created to be received with thanksgiving by those who believe and know the truth. For every creature of God is good, and nothing is to be refused if it is received with thanksgiving; for it is sanctified by the word of God and prayer" (1 Tim. 4:3-4)

Obviously, drunkenness or addiction to any substance is a sin (Prov. 23:29-35; Eph. 5:18). Nevertheless, God gave us wine to make glad our hearts (Ps. 104:15), and Paul commanded Timothy to use wine for stomach ailments (1 Tim. 5:23). God also permitted the use of alcoholic beverages at the tithe festival: "You shall spend that money for whatever your heart desires: for oxen or sheep, for wine or similar drink, for whatever your heart desires; you shall eat there before the LORD your God and you shall rejoice, you and your household" (Deut. 14:26).

The key is moderation. The important principle is nothing should master you. Paul writes, "All things are lawful for me, but all things are not helpful. All things are lawful for me, but I will not be brought under the power of any" (1 Cor. 6:12). This principle holds true of the use caffeine and other stimulants.

What about the moderate use of marijuana? Anything that alters our minds is sinful. There are those who insist one can smoke marijuana in the way one takes a drink of whiskey. The difference lies in the intention and the problem of addiction. As noted, Scripture allows moderate use of alcohol but forbids intoxication. It only takes a few puffs of marijuana to intoxicate. Studies also demonstrate that marijuana by nature is addictive and a gateway drug.

Life's Cycles

Another important aspect of sustaining health is the proper observance of what I call life's cycles. God has built into our lives a number of such cycles.

First, there is *the daily cycle of day and night*. In this cycle God designs time for work and time for rest. Job alludes to the fact that the slave or hired man has rest at the end of the day (Job 7:2). The psalmist reflects on the same cycle (Ps. 104:23). God has made us to work, and normally day is the time to work. Although some people will work night shifts as doctors, nurses, police officers, firefighters, and factory workers, the principle applies that God wants us to observe the cycle of work and sleep. Some need to beware of being work-alcoholics, driven by work, while others need to avoid sloth (Prov. 6:6–11; 24:30–34).

In the normal course of life, one should get regular hours of sleep. Again, the Bible does not say what amount that is. Some people require less sleep than others. Find out what is best for you. A couple of times in my life, I tried to train myself to get by on five hours or less of sleep, but I have learned that I am less efficient than if I get seven or seven-and-a-half hours of sleep.

You may be refreshed by a short nap in the afternoon. Our Savior, after a strenuous time of teaching, took a nap in the back of the boat (Matt. 8:23–24). Winston Churchill had the practice of working late at night but taking a nap in the afternoon.

Furthermore, make use of a schedule. Set aside daily times for private and family worship and quality time with your spouse and children. Schedule time for friends and create time for church work, prayer meeting, and so on.

Second, God has also given us *the weekly cycle of six days of work and one day of rest* (Ex. 20:8–11). The sabbath rest is primarily spiritual in its aims, but spiritual rest is also good for sustaining health. Furthermore, God also designed the sabbath to give physical rest, as Moses points out (Deut. 5:14).[10]

Third, another weekly cycle is *taking a day off*. Men should also regularly take a day off. The change of pace is important for maintaining efficiency and health. Charles Bridges wrote, "Neither mind nor body, indeed, can be sustained without moderate relaxation."[11] Some will use time off to do necessary chores or to maintain their house and property. Others will have hobbies—reading, wood working, golf, hiking, fishing, hunting, and so on.

Fourth, a man should also observe *yearly cycles of seasons*. Elihu teaches that God sovereignly sends snow and rain to give time for rest and contemplation: "For He says to the snow, 'Fall on the earth'; likewise to the gentle rain and the heavy rain of His strength. He seals the hand of every man, that all men may know His work" (Job 37:6–7). God's "seals the hand" of man by the weather to prevent him from working outside. By this cycle, God provides not only rest but time to meditate and commune with God. When I pastored in a farming community, I encouraged the men to use wintertime, when they could not work as much as other seasons, to spend that time in reading and studying.

Even though weather cycles do not affect most of my readers, God providentially provides times of inactivity—illnesses, vacations, weather delays in travel—to build into life's cycle time for rest and contemplation.

Sixth, another yearly cycle is *taking a vacation*. God uses these planned times away from our work to refresh us physically and spiritually.

Learn, as well, to pace yourself as you get older. Develop realistic

---

10. For a study of the Christian Sabbath and how to keep it profitably, see Joseph A. Pipa, Jr., *The Lord's Day* (Christian Focus, 1996).
11. Charles Bridges, *The Christian Ministry* (Banner of Truth, 1967), 135.

expectations. Pay attention to your body. For example, I have learned that I need a little more downtime when returning from overseas trips than in the past.

Physical Exercise

Finally, if your vocation does not include manual labor, build into your life weekly times of physical exercise. Find what works best for you. If nothing else, a man should walk 150 minutes a week. But I strongly recommend a combination of cardio activity and weight training. Of course, a hobby like golf or tennis provides good physical exercise. Such a regimen produces energy, stamina, and increased mental acuity.

Conclusion

I hope that, on the basis of the exegetical and theological foundation, I have motivated and encouraged you to do the things necessary to sustain your health. Take the suggestions for what they are: suggestions. But commit to a disciplined approach to sustain your health, for God's glory and your good. It is of some profit.

CHAPTER TWENTY

The Redeemed Man Persevering in His Faith

Geoff Thomas

REFORMED CHRISTIANS have long confessed, "Those whom God has accepted in the Beloved, effectually called and sanctified by His Spirit, and given the precious faith of His elect unto, can neither totally nor finally fall from the state of grace, but shall certainly persevere therein to the end, and be eternally saved."[1]

One should be careful not to summarize that enlightening statement as teaching a cliché, "Once saved, always saved," for those four words are both totally true and also erroneous in what they may suggest. It is true that if the Sovereign Ruler of heaven and earth begins a saving work in us that He will bring to bear all His irresistible resources needed to ensure that work to completion, overcoming the merciless devices of the Evil One, the pressures of a world system organized against Jesus Christ, and the power of remaining sin. As Augustus Toplady wrote, "The work

---

1. Second London Baptist Confession of Faith (17.1), in *Reformed Confessions of the 16th and 17th Centuries in English Translation: 1523–1693*, comp. James T. Dennison Jr. (Reformation Heritage Books, 2008–2014), 4:552. A virtually identical statement appears in the Westminster Confession of Faith (17.1), in *Westminster Confession of Faith* (Free Presbyterian Publications, 1994), 72.

which his goodness began the arm of his strength will complete."[2] By God's redeeming omnipotence every elect believer is assured of arriving at his heavenly home.

However, the slogan "once saved always saved" sometimes refers to a mere decision to become a saved person, expressed with outward gestures and words. This is not identical to a spiritual saving response to the gospel. If a person professes to love the Lord whom they claim has saved them, they will yearn to keep His commandments (John 14:21), which means they will continue to believe and to repent.

Christianity does require a life of decision-making as to the truth of the Bible. We must agree with the Bible's analysis of our fallenness and our sins in the eyes of a holy Creator. We must decide to set all our hope of eternal life on Jesus Christ, the Son of God, for what He has done in becoming the Lamb of God and achieving eternal redemption to reconcile the righteous God. Then, for the rest of our lives we go on committing ourselves to Him as the all-sufficient foundation of our eternal acceptance by Almighty God.

That is saving faith, and thus we battle on through "many dangers, toils, and snares" as John Newton put it.[3] We live in a world united in its indifference and hostility to the Lord Jesus Christ. We struggle on, experiencing fiery darts and Satan and battling with remaining sin. We persevere on and on in all the changing scenes of life, in our sufferings, in persecution, facing a legion of obstacles, at times scarcely saved (1 Peter 4:18). But we believe that the Scriptures very clearly affirm that all those saved by Christ will endure by the grace of a prayer-hearing and merciful Father, by the glorious, finished, saving achievements of the Son of God, and by the power of the indwelling Spirit of God.

---

2. Augustus Toplady, "A Debtor to Mercy Alone" (1771).
3. John Newton, "Amazing Grace, How Sweet the Sound" (1779).

The Perseverance of the Redeemed Man

Let us proceed to examine the plain teaching of the perseverance of every elect Christian. Some indestructible foundations are laid out by the Lord Jesus and His apostles that ensure that every true Christian who is resting on them will persevere in following Christ.

First, *God is true to Himself.* This is His freedom. He cannot change in Himself (Mal. 3:6). He does not wax and wane. He cannot deny Himself (2 Tim. 2:13). And He has made a covenant to save every one of His chosen people (Jer. 31:31–34; Eph. 1:4) so that our salvation hangs upon His faithfulness (1 Thess. 5:23–24). What He has planned, He will fulfil (Isa. 14:24). Unlike us and our arbitrary and capricious uncertainties, our salvation rests on our covenant fellowship with the nature and accomplishment of the triune God—our loving heavenly Father, our Savior's intercession, and the Spirit's constant work in our lives.

Second, *God does not lie*. He has affirmed, "I will be your God, and you shall be my people" (cf. Jer. 32:38–40; Heb. 8:10). That, again, is the attitude of Father, Son and Holy Spirit at this very moment even to the weakest Christian in the whole world. Though that person's faith is as thin as a spider's thread, if it is from his heart and rests in Christ alone, it is more unbreakable than the hawser that holds an aircraft carrier to the dock. It is not great faith that saves, but a great Savior who saves through a sinner's trust in Him. He chose sinners whom we could name Mr. Ready-to-Halt, Mr. Fearing, or Mr. Feeble Mind, men who are on their way to the Celestial City but who have problems about assurance, and who are prone to doubts and will foolishly focus on their great failings.[4] Yet "before the foundation of the world" (Eph. 1:4), God chose them.

Third, *God's will is our complete redemption.* He has made up His mind on this, and so salvation is inevitable for everyone whom our loving Father

---

4. These are characters in John Bunyan's timeless allegory, *The Pilgrim's Progress*.

chose and loves, the One who did not spare His own Son that we might be redeemed (Rom. 8:32). Robert Letham says, "From first to last, salvation is an exercise of God's grace to elect sinners and so redemption is lifted out of the realm of the merely possible. God's grace is given to us and maintained in us by the Holy Spirit, who does not leave things half done but brings to perfection those works he has begun (Phil. 1:6)."[5]

The key to assurance is perseverance. Hear now how one of the most searching preachers of our generation applies this truth,

> It is a perseverance in the ways of holiness and obedience, for Scripture says, "Follow . . . holiness without which no man shall see the Lord" (Heb. 12:14). "If ye continue in my word, then are ye my disciples indeed, and ye shall know the truth and the truth shall make you free" (John 8:31, 32). . . . Predestined to what end? "Whom he did foreknow, he also did predestinate to be conformed to the image of his Son" (Rom. 8:29). If so then I must ask a question of myself: is God's electing purpose being realised in me? He chose me in Christ that, being purchased in time and called in time, I might begin to be holy in time, and have that work perfected in eternity. The only assurance I have that I was purchased to be holy, and will be perfected in holiness, is that I am pursuing holiness here and now. . . . Do I confess that I am being preserved by God's keeping power? Then his preserving must come to light in my persevering. The only proof I have that he is preserving me is that by his grace I am enabled to persevere.[6]

Fourth, *God's promises to us are all in and through Jesus Christ His Son*. God not only has committed His omnipotence to glorifying each of us, but He has centered this commitment on His determination to honor Christ in

---

5. Robert Letham, *Systematic Theology* (Crossway, 2019), 745.
6. Albert N. Martin, *The Practical Implications of Calvinism* (Banner of Truth, 1979), 16–17.

the saving and keeping of every single one for whom our Lord Jesus shed His blood and endured their anathema. God rewards His sacrifice by glorifying all those for whom He died.

Each and every one of the redeemed will believe in Christ and will be raised from the dead on the last day (John 6:37–40). He knows each sheep for whom He, the good Shepherd, died (10:14–15). He calls each individual by name, giving each eternal life, and he will never perish in hell (vv. 27–28). They are all safe in the arms of Jesus. No one and nothing can pluck them out of His hands. The Lord Christ knew this and so prayed with thanks to His Father in His great prayer in John 17, that not one will be lost whom the Father has given to him (v. 12). God's purposeful policy in giving them to Jesus Christ is that He might save, sanctify, and beautify His church as a bride, uniting her with her Lord Jesus (1 Cor. 1:8–9; Eph. 5:25–27).

Every single aspect of our salvation is found in union with Christ; the whole gamut of redemption from eternity, through time, to its ultimate consummation is achieved through our being joined to Him (Eph. 1:3–14). The Father has chosen and ordained us to heaven through Christ (vv. 3–5). The Son Himself has redeemed us, and He is in charge of everything (vv. 7–10). The Holy Spirit is the earnest of the full inheritance (vv. 13–14). So, we are safe; we persevere through our Savior.

The Heidelburg Catechism declares, "He [Christ], all the time that He lived on earth, but especially at the end of His life, sustained in body and soul the wrath of God against the sins of all mankind."[7] To what end? Why was all that suffering essential? Robert Letham responds,

> The answer is the justice and righteousness of God, with whom as the eternal Son of God, he was fully and completely one. There was no other way, since God is just and true to himself. There

---

7. The Heidelberg Catechism (LD 15, Q. 37), in *The Three Forms of Unity* (Solid Ground Christian Books, 2010), 80.

was no other way than by taking into union our nature and in our nature repairing the damage done by the first man. There was no other way than by uniting us to himself through the Holy Spirit and thus restoring us to God—even more introducing us to something the first Adam never knew; union and communion with the holy Trinity in Christ.[8]

Fifth, *God's elect will heed the warnings of the danger of apostasy.* Some Jewish Christians lost heart. Their husbands had divorced them so that these women were penniless and homeless. Others were weary, missing attending the feasts in Jerusalem, the ceremonies, the holidays with their old friends, and the enthusiasm of a crowd. They were despised by family and former friends. They were meeting secretly in bare rooms behind locked doors. It proved all too much for some of them and they abandoned their profession of being followers of Christ.

The writer to the Hebrews deals with this calamity in two ways, chiefly by showing them the greatness and glory of Jesus Christ compared to the shadowlands of the Old Testament dispensation. He also solemnly warned them of the consequences of repudiating Him (Heb. 3:7– 4:10; 6:1–8; 10:26–39; 12:25–29). The author of Hebrews is asking these Jewish converts to consider the pressures their forefathers were under during their years of wilderness wanderings. They had seen the miracles, the parting of the Red Sea, the daily manna, and the water that flowed from the rock. They had tasted the Word of God; however, they were not believing His promise to bring them all into a land flowing with milk and honey. There was a superficial acquaintance with Jehovah's saving work that stopped short of saving trust. Those passages in the letter to the Hebrews suggest that, similarly, those people who had once professed to be followers of Christ now had made a once-for-all repudiation of God's promises

---

8. Letham, *Systematic Theology*, 748.

that through many tribulations He would bring them to a new heaven and earth. They had rejected Jesus as the Christ, the Son of the living God.

The apostle John also had to explain in his letter why people who once were church members now had forsaken their gatherings and renounced their former views of our Lord. John explained their conduct like this: "They went out from us, but they were not of us; for if they had been of us, they would have continued with us; but they went out that they might be made manifest, that none of them were of us" (1 John 2:19). Some apostates are named in the New Testament: Judas, Ananias, Sapphira, and Demas.

Consider how our forefathers seized upon this reality of professing Christians denying their Savior and in their preaching could address a congregation as Matthew Mead once did:

> You read in Hebrews 6:4 of some that were "once enlightened, and tasted of the heavenly gift, and were made partakers of the Holy Ghost." What work shall we call this? It could not be a *saving* work, a true change and conversion of state; for, notwithstanding this enlightening, and tasting, and partaking, yet they are here said to fall away (v. 6). Had it been a true work of grace, they could never have fallen away from that. A believer may fall, but he cannot fall away; he may fall foully, but he cannot fall finally; for, "underneath are the everlasting arms" (Deut. 33:27). His faith is established in the strength of that prayer of Christ, that our faith fail not (Luke 22:32); nay, he tells us expressly, that it is eternal life which he gives, from which we "shall never perish" (John 10:28). This work then here spoken of, cannot be any saving work, because it is not an abiding work; for they that are under it, are said to fall away from it.[9]

So, in those passages in Hebrews, in the writings of the apostle John,

---

9. Matthew Mead, *Almost Christian Discover'd*, 11th ed. (London, 1700), 94, Scripture references and capitalization modernized.

and in the preaching of Jesus in the parable of the sower (Mark 4:1–20), disciples are taught that there is such a thing as *temporary faith*. That is not true faith in Christ at all. We are warned of this that we may not be overwhelmingly discouraged when we are confronted by it. The London Baptist Confession of Faith of 1689 says, "Temporary believers and other unregenerate men may vainly deceive themselves with false hopes and carnal presumptions of being in the favor of God and state of salvation, which hope of theirs shall perish."[10]

How do we preach the perseverance of Christians? Do we both encourage them with the keeping power of a loving God but also by warning them of the possibility of falling away and going to hell? Yes, we do both. This is the view of the Canons of Dort: "And as it hath pleased God, by the preaching of the gospel, to begin this work of grace in us, so He preserves, continues, and perfects it by the hearing and reading of His Word, by meditation thereon, and by the exhortations, threatenings, and promises thereof, as well as by the use of the sacraments."[11]

Notice two things here. First, God causes us to persevere by several means. He makes promises to us, but He also threatens. He works by the hearing of the gospel and by the use of the ordinances. He has not bound Himself to one method. Surely, this helps us make sense of the warnings in Hebrews and elsewhere in the New Testament. Threats and exhortations do not undermine perseverance; they help to complete it. We gospel-centered Christians need to meditate on the "exhortations, threatenings, and promises" of the gospel.

Thus, we can sweetly say of all the elect of God, "once saved, always saved" and give thanks to our Savior that it is so.

---

10. Second London Baptist Confession of Faith (18.1), in *Reformed Confessions*, 4:553. Essentially the same statement is made in the Westminster Confession of Faith (18.1), in *Westminster Confession of Faith*, 75–76.
11. The Canons of Dort (Head 5, Art. 14), in *The Three Forms of Unity*, 158.

The Persevering of the Redeemed Man

Let me close with some applications for how the redeemed man must persevere by God's grace.

Perseverance Must Be Our Priority

There is nothing in life more important for the Christian than persevering in following the Lamb of God wherever we are and wherever He goes. This is not something for which a disciple of the Lord Jesus finds time in the midst of other engagements, preoccupations, and concerns. His walk with God controls his life. It is what daily living is built around, and his greatest longing is to be continually serving his Savior and to be conformed to the image of his God.

"This one thing I do," said the apostle Paul (Phil. 3:13), and again, "To me to live is Christ" (1:21). So, we must look at ourselves and challenge ourselves as to how things are in our relationship with our God. Is there one thing that the years have done, to change our scale of values and our sense of priorities? It is terribly easy to react against what could be dubbed religious fanaticism, in other words, the person whose only conversation is about religion and has nothing at all to say about anything else. There is something unbiblical about living in God's creation in all its divinely designed fullness and act as if we were bored with everything we see, hear, taste, smell, and feel.

There is, however, a far greater peril, and that is the reduction of religious aspirations, to demote them so that they are relegated from their proper primary place, and now they are no longer controlling our choices, convictions, and affections. And there is not a Christian who from time to time is shocked to consider whether this has happened to him or her, that, subtly, things that are indeed legitimate for every disciple—but secondary in value—have increasingly become his priority in life. His intercessions in the weekly prayer meeting no longer have the ring of earnest authority and heartfelt longing. He finds himself entertaining little observations, indicating almost a religious cynicism as if he is no longer sure of the value of knowing and enjoying God. We can visit a congregation on a Sunday and are alarmed to feel that such a spirit seems to be characterizing too many of the church—though they may inform you that they believe in the perseverance of the saints. An element of slackness and sloppiness has entered its corporate life. There are few whose personal conviction is "to live is Christ."

Unless individual Christians and united congregations hold to a non-negotiable testimony that they will persevere in believing that man's chief end in life is to glorify God and enjoy Him forever, they will face the most hopeless and appalling future.

Perseverance Is Neither Automatic nor Self Perpetuating

We cannot simply leave our souls to be self-nourishing, to fend and provide for themselves. We have to be sure that we are persevering in understanding, in obedience to God, in all the Christian graces—love, joy, peace, and so on—in serving the church, in bearing the burdens of the weak, in wisdom and usefulness, and that we are growing in all those graces. We have not arrived; we are a work in progress. The need to attend to the means whereby growth is achieved is evident in every form of life in the lesser creation. The very plants need cultivation and nutrition, while the whole animal world diligently seeks the right food every day. So it is with every single Christian on a natural level. We become what we imbibe. Our intellectual lives grow only by virtue of a diligent application to what benefits the mind and exercises our intellectual faculties—whatsoever things are true, noble, just, pure, lovely, of good report, if there is any virtue and if there is anything praiseworthy—to live on these things (Phil. 4:8). Neither our bodies nor our minds are able to look after themselves. The shepherd takes his sheep to green pastures and still waters, but the rams, ewes and lambs must individually eat every day of their lives if they are going to survive and grow

Our souls will not look after themselves. There has to be a deliberate concern, a program of care, a detailed and meticulous provision for the needs of our souls, or we are not going to be healthy and flourishing. If we are not caring for our souls, we will be led away into the attitudes, values, desires, and thinking of men and women who have no knowledge of the living God. The conviction that saints persevere is useless unless we are growing in our desire for God. Blessed are they that hunger and thirst after righteousness (Matt. 5:6), for they are the ones who persevere, and only they. We may possess a form of religion, but we will be strangers to that power that alone conforms us to the divine image (2 Tim. 3:5). Are not too many churches, while not blatantly worldly, yet in their presuppositions, aspirations, principles, and emotions indistinguishable from those who lack any holy thoughts of Jesus Christ?

Perseverance Requires Every Effort

Perseverance demands personal diligence. In what direction? One such as sitting under the best preaching you can possibly hear. There is no food so suitable for the soul as the genuine, pure milk of the Word of God. Nothing nourishes perseverance like the Bible, and we all have to be continually falling in love with it, searching its pages, ransacking it, memorizing it, hungering and thirsting for the true preaching of the gospel, delighting in discussing it among ourselves, meditating upon it, and coming upon it again, and examining it from every point of view, because the Christian will not grow in persevering grace without the food of the Word of God, and seeking the face of God, being conformed more and more closely to His image.

Again, it is in living communion with other Christians that we grow. There is a certain drop in the temperature when we sit alone in our homes and watch a service by ourselves on a screen. However powerful the sermon might be, it is enervated when we hear it alone. Preaching the Word is a corporate means of grace. We hear the Word for ourselves but also through the ears of all that are present, our family and friends and the stranger who has appeared that Lord's Day. Our blessing is greatly increased by the divinely appointed structures in which they are set. We must persevere in church attendance. There is an essential yet mysterious influence that one Christian has over another. We go to church to receive, but we also attend to be giving to others, even if it is by our mere presence. To persevere is to seek earnestly the society of our brethren in the Christian race.

Above all, perseverance entails seeking the blessing of God on our lives, because all the fellowship of other Christians, the hearing of the most searching and encouraging preaching, the reading of the most helpful books, the attention paid to the disciplines of godliness—indeed every single privilege the Christian meets as he perseveres on the narrow road—will be of no avail unless God blesses. May the Almighty bless every persevering Christian.

CHAPTER TWENTY-ONE

The Redeemed Man Entering Retirement

Derek W. H. Thomas

Retirement. "I can't wait," people say. "It's going to be fun: beach vacations, bucket-list destinations, yachts, new hobbies, and golf. Lots and lots of golf." This is how the world thinks of retirement. Of course, this assumes a healthy, well-planned, and carefully managed pot of money that will last the twenty or thirty years of retirement. Without Social Security, IRAs, and 401Ks, retirement may not be possible. And for those who are self-employed, retirement may not be desirable. But for most of us, preachers included, retirement in some form or another is a door through which we must eventually pass. I know, people have said to me, "Preachers never retire," but this is only half-true at best. Even preachers slow down, and although they may continue to preach somewhere, the pace of life changes.

Researching the topic of retirement, I found some who seemed to be militantly opposed to it. I also discovered that these were self-employed or in positions where their on-going presence was essential for the company's image. But realistically, most of us are not in such a position, and retirement is necessary.

A Personal Reflection on Retirement

As I write this chapter, I am a month or so into "my retirement." To be fair, I had three jobs (or callings): a part-time seminary professor, a Teaching Fellow with Ligonier Ministries, and the Senior Minister at First Presbyterian Church, Columbia South Carolina. I continue my responsibilities with the first two, but I am no longer in full-time "pastoral ministry." For a host of reasons (getting the church through the Covid-season, being one), I delayed my retirement until a few weeks shy of seventy-one.

I wasn't prepared for the reaction I constantly received when informing someone I had not spoken to in a while that I had retired. "Congratulations!" they said. In my mind I thought, "What have I done to be congratulated about?" Retirement simply came. I aged and found I needed to slow down, but I could have gone on longer. I wake up wondering, "What am I supposed to do today?" For those of us with zero do-it-yourself skills, and no desire to learn to paint or play golf five times a week, retirement feels a bit like purgatory!

Researching online what people think about retirement, it is fascinating (and troubling) that a robust (biblical) work ethic is a hindrance to the enjoyment of retirement. I read comments like these: *I am still feeling guilty about waking up later than I did and not going to work* and *my ingrained work ethic is looking for ways to be productive.*

I resonate with these observations. Many found the change so abrupt and disorientating that they returned to work in some form or another—in some cases, they have gone into the world of "consulting," whatever that means!

As I think about retirement, I am not doing it from the vantage point of experience; rather, I speak from aspiration. I do not yet know the shape of my retirement, though I have attempted to plan what it looks like. I have been told many times, by folk who have retired, that one does not retire "from something" but "to something." I have been given numerous knickknacks (coffee mugs, framed quotes, etc.) that suggest retirement is about relaxation, new hobbies, and road trips. Frankly, this iteration of my latter years brings no lasting comfort. After being in pastoral ministry for forty-five years, how does one stop? I cannot imagine, for example, not preaching on Sundays. There are aspects of every vocation that one does not miss, but preaching is not one of them. So how does one think biblically about retirement?

A Biblical Perspective on Retirement

To understand retirement, we must first contemplate what the Bible has to say about work. And we are barely only a few hundred words into the first book of the Bible, and we encounter God's plan for us: *work*! Before the creation of Adam's "helper" (Gen. 2:20), we are told, "The LORD God took the man and put him in the garden of Eden to tend it and keep it" (v. 15).

Later, after the fall, the work became difficult and, to some degree, fruitless. God said to Adam, "Cursed is the ground for your sake; in toil you shall eat of it all the days of your life. Both thorns and thistles it shall bring forth for you, and you shall eat the herb of the field. In the sweat of your face you shall eat bread till you return to the ground" (Gen. 3:17–19). Adam's disobedience brought about the *futility* of work (Rom. 8:20). Paul uses a word that suggests emptiness, fruitlessness, and possibly uselessness. The work is not only hard, but it does not fulfil. The "nine-to-five" routine is one we long to escape.

There was work for Adam to do in paradise, and, presumably, there will be work to do in the new paradise of the new heavens and new earth. His task was to make the whole of creation a paradise by fruitful and fulfilling toil. Work is to be viewed as a calling, a *vocation*. This was an issue so very important to Martin Luther and the early Reformation, that all work be understood as a calling from God. Rome viewed only the priesthood as a vocation, demeaning the contributions of farmers, woodworkers, and metalsmiths.

We already saw that God put the first man in the garden and commanded him to work to cultivate and keep it. Consider also the following statements of Scripture:
- "Six days you shall labor and do all your work, but the seventh day is a Sabbath to the LORD your God. . . . For in six days the LORD made the heavens and the earth, the sea, and all that is in them, and rested on the seventh day" (Ex. 20:9–11).
- "If anyone will not work, neither shall he eat" (2 Thess. 3:10).
- "Whatever you do, do it heartily, as to the Lord and not to men, knowing that from the Lord you will receive the reward of the inheritance; for you serve the Lord Christ" (Col. 3:23–24).

Work hard. Work as though God is your boss. And as it says in Colossians 3, work "heartily." Paul uses the Greek word *psychē*, meaning "soul, life." Put your *soul* into it. Don't view it as menial, robotic—a difficult command to fulfill if our work is making widgets! But we must try (or, if possible, get another job).

For us post-fall laborers, the experience of work is an experience of ineffectuality. Two extremes emerge from Adam's fall. One is the self-absorption that regards work as the end-all of our existence. These are the folks "who burn the candle at both ends," who have little or no time for relaxation or fun.

The opposite includes those who work to get to the weekend. Work becomes a necessary evil, a means of securing the required wage to pay for the pleasure that the weekend offers. Several European countries now advocate four-day working weeks allowing people to have longer weekends. Interestingly, as I write, an email has just popped into my inbox with the headline, "Get Away from it All. And Have it All." It was sufficiently alluring for me to pause and read what it was all about! (A cruise in the Mediterranean).

Between these two extremes lies the God-ordained rhythm of work and rest. As John Stott has written,

> The climax of Genesis 1 is not the creation of human beings as workers but the institution of the Sabbath for human beings as worshippers. The end point is not our toil (subduing the earth) but the laying aside of our toil on the Sabbath day. For the Sabbath puts the importance of work into perspective. It protects us from a total absorption in our work as if it were to be the be-all and end-all of our existence. It is not.[1]

The Sabbath mimics divine resting, when God finished His creation in six days and "rested . . . from all His work which He had done" (Gen. 2:2–3). In one sense, as the omnipotent God, He has no need of resting, for He does not experience the pain of labor. But accommodating to our finitude, God lowers Himself to suggest that He, too, requires "a day off." How extraordinary of Him to say that! First appearing in James Howell's *Proverbs* (1659), the proverb, "All work and no play makes Jack a dull boy," suggests that the need for a regular rhythm of time off work is universally felt. And God wrote it into our DNA.

The New Testament, no less than the Old, continues and underlines this necessary pattern of work followed by rest by making the Sabbath and the New Testament Lord's Day one and the same and by reversing the order to rest followed by work, thereby underlying the importance of the Sabbath rest (Acts 20:7; 1 Cor. 16:2). And Jesus's resurrection day would be marked as a day of rest and worship, continuing the appropriateness of the fourth commandment in the new covenant era.

The Bible says nothing about the modern concept of retirement. Some are adamant that retirement is therefore an unbiblical concept. The closest allusion is a statement in Numbers, "At the age of fifty years they [the

---

1. John Stott, *The Radical Disciple: Wholehearted Christian Living* (Inter-Varsity Press, 2010), 59–60.

Levites] must cease performing this work, and shall work no more" (8:25). Moving tabernacle furniture around was hard work, and the elderly would find it even harder to accomplish. The book of Numbers continues, "They may minister with their brethren in the tabernacle of meeting, to attend to needs, but they themselves shall do no work" (v. 26)—a hint that the Levites did not exactly "retire" in the modern sense but adjusted their labor to suit their aging disposition. Equally, Christians do not retire from work; they retire from one kind of work to take up another.

How then should we think through retirement? What biblical principles should guide us?

The first, and most obvious, is the doctrine of the fall. Adam's failure brought ruin upon us all. We inherit Adamic sin which renders us guilty before God. And though, wonderfully, the gospel cures the curse and sets us free, it does not prevent the curse of death and the wear and tear that age brings with it. Put simply, I cannot now do what I once did with efficiency and relative ease. Aches and pains, the inability to spring from a squatting posture to an upright one without groans and pain immediately reminds me that these bones of mine just do not respond the way they once did. Though, thankfully, I remain in relatively good health, I am no longer who I was when thirty-three. Thomas Aquinas surmised, "Man will rise again at the most perfect stage of nature. Now human nature is at the most perfect stage in the age of youth. Therefore all will rise again of that age."[2] We may not all have been afflicted with Job's malady when he said, "My bones are pierced in me at night, and my gnawing pains take no rest" (Job 30:17), but we can enter just a little into the spirit of his complaint. Our bodies cannot keep up the pace, and if we force them to comply, the cost may be severe. And then, the possibility of the terrible decline of one's mind, forgetfulness that can lead to severe memory loss and dementia. For some, then, continuing one's vocation is not an option.

2. Thomas Aquinas, *Summa Theologica*, trans. Fathers of the English Dominican Province (Burns, Oates, and Washbourne, 1921), III, suppl., q. 81, a. 1, s.c.

THE REDEEMED MAN ENTERING RETIREMENT

Consider the words of Solomon in Ecclesiastes:

Remember now your Creator in the days of your youth, before
the difficult days come [*old age*],
And the years draw near when you say,
"I have no pleasure in them"
[*I used to enjoy doing x or y, but I don't anymore*]:

While the sun and the light,
The moon and the stars,
Are not darkened, and the clouds do not return after the rain
[*before you get to the age when things are not as clear as they were*];

In the day when the keepers of the house tremble,
And the strong men bow down [*kyphosis or Dowager's hump*],

When the grinders cease because they are few
[*you have lost your teeth!*],
And those that look through the windows grow dim
[*failing sight*];

When the doors are shut in the streets,
And the sound of grinding is low [*deafness*];

When one rises up at the sound of a bird
[*sudden noises make you afraid*],

And all the daughters of music are brought low
[*music that once held you captive no longer charms as it once did*].

Also they are afraid of height [*lightheadedness*],

And of terrors in the way [*real or imaginary fears*];

When the almond tree blossoms [*your hair turns white*],

The grasshopper is a burden [*you need a cane or a walking frame*],

And desire fails [*you retreat into a dark place*].

For man goes to his eternal home, and the mourners go about the streets. *Remember your Creator* before the silver cord is loosed, or the golden bowl is broken, or the pitcher shattered at the fountain, or the wheel broken at the well. Then the dust will return to the earth as it was, and the spirit will return to God who gave it. "Vanity of vanities," says the Preacher, "All is vanity." (Eccl. 12:1–8)

Reading that Scripture passage makes it sound as though retirement is a curse that would not be necessary had Adam obeyed his test. Had he not worshipped the forbidden fruit and made an idol of it, we would have no need to retire due to the decline of body and mind. And this is true. But retirement need not be thought of as a curse, for, folk tell me, it can be enjoyed. The change of rhythms, the opportunity to exercise a theology of rest and play, the liberty of not having to serve a hard taskmaster and establish a lifestyle that can be liberating and refreshing.

Who knows how long we will retain our health and mobility? It is in the Lord's hands. If we are to enjoy retirement and make it productive, we need to seize the moment.

Retirement brings with it a different set of priorities. I am now free to choose how I wish to spend my time. But I am not free from the need "to glorify God and enjoy Him forever." There remains work for retirees to do, projects that were pushed aside because "there was no time." Aging, from a godless perspective (as the Preacher iterates it in Ecclesiastes 12 above), seems like an episode of vanity, fruitlessness, pointlessness, governed by the law of diminishing returns! But for the godly, aging can be utilized for much good.

Work—all work—is to be viewed as a service to God. Richard Baxter, suffering from poor health for most of his life, preached, "as never sure to preach again, and as a dying man to dying men."[3] He viewed his entire life as a service to the Lord. It was how he understood Paul's emphasis on "redeeming the time" (Eph. 5:16 KJV). William Tyndale said that if we look externally "there is difference betwixt washing of dishes, and preaching of the word of God; but as touching to please God, none at all."[4]

The danger in a man-centered approach to retirement is to view it as payback time. Having worked for a company all my life, I am now free to relax and enjoy life. Retirement is *me*-time! Thus, retirement becomes one long vacation. Though Solomon might have meant this cynically (the second half of the verse suggests that he did), there is truth in what he says: "Whatever your hand finds to do, do it with your might" (Eccl. 9:10). God has placed a rhythm of work and rest into our lives. The Sabbath is God's gift that frees us from labor to enjoy Him, in all his beauty. But Solomon's maxim applies to both: we work hard and rest hard. We labor for him and worship him *with all our might*.

At age eighty-eight, J. I. Packer wrote a book about aging.[5] Using what is probably a British-Canadian expression, he writes about living "flat out" for God. "My contention is . . . that, so far as our bodily health allows, we should aim to be found running the last lap of the race of our Christian life, as we would say, flat out."[6]

He amusingly referred to John Wesley's oft cited statement he made when age eighty-five that "the only sign of deterioration that he could see in himself was that he could not run as fast as he used to." With wry sarcasm, Packer commented, "With all due deference to that wonderful,

---

3. Richard Baxter, *The Poetical Fragments of Richard Baxter*, 4th ed. (Pickering, 1821), 35.
4. William Tyndale, *The Parable of the Wicked Mammon* (1528), Lectionary Central, www.lectionarycentral.com/trinity09/Tyndale.html.
5. J. I. Packer, *Finishing Our Course with Joy: Guidance from God for Engaging with Our Aging* (Crossway, 2014).
6. Packer, *Finishing Our Course with Joy*, 21–22.

seemingly tireless little man, we may reasonably suspect that he was overlooking some things."[7]

Packer drew attention to the image of running as central to Paul's understanding of his own life (1 Cor. 9:24–27; Gal. 2:2; Phil. 2:16), and said, "I urge now that it ought to be the central focus in the minds and hearts of all aging Christians, who know and feel that their bodies are slowing down."[8]

Paul would have been in his mid-sixties when Nero executed him, and did not experience the debilitating effects of aging as did the apostle John, who probably lived until he was in his eighties (the same age as Packer when he wrote this book!). Nowadays, with the advancements in healthcare and medicine, people live longer. There is talk online of advancements in slowing the aging process and of the viability of life to 120. That would mean that our retirement years would be greater than our working years! Be that as it may, how should godly Christians, intent on glorifying God in every stage of life, live? The world beckons us to a life of ease and relaxation, a lifestyle guaranteed to produce boredom and depression. Packer warns that Christians of any age, "exempt from the twin tasks of learning and leading, just because they do not inhabit the world of wage and salary earning any longer, and for aging Christians to think of themselves in this way, as if they have no more to do now than have fun, is worldliness in a strikingly intense and, be it said, strikingly foolish form."[9]

Retirement for the Glory of God

Let me suggest some principles that seem appropriate on how to live a God-honoring retirement.

First, *find something useful and God-honoring to do*. We were not created (or re-created) to amuse ourselves to death. We are made in the

---

7. Packer, *Finishing Our Course with Joy*, 44.
8. Packer, *Finishing Our Course with Joy*, 72.
9. Packer, *Finishing Our Course with Joy*, 68.

image of God to reflect Him who constantly works to uphold us and the universe in which we live (Gen. 1:26–27; 1 Cor. 11:7; Col. 3:10). Volunteer and help in some ministry that brings good to others. But be careful lest you find yourself too busy to do the other things that you want or need to do. Your body will tell you to slow down a little. And there may come a time when your body and mind will prevent you from accomplishing the things you wish to do. So don't leave off for tomorrow what can be accomplished today! "Do not boast about tomorrow, for you do not know what a day may bring forth" (Prov. 27:1; cf. James 4:14).

Second, *plan*! "The plans of the diligent lead surely to plenty, but those of everyone who is hasty, surely to poverty" (Prov. 21:5). Consider a project that will take a few years to accomplish. Be prepared to change your plans. Some plans may fail because they are not the Lord's plans: "There are many plans in a man's heart, nevertheless the LORD's counsel—that will stand" (Prov. 19:21). But few things are accomplished that were not planned. Without structure our lives collapse into hedonism.

Third, *consider retirement to be a season for getting to know God even better*. Spend time, quality time, in the Scriptures and prayer. Our working days were filled with busyness and appointments. I looked at my calendar for today and it was empty! I have no need to rush hither and yon. I am at no one's beck and call. (Well, except for my sweet wife, of course!) Return to reading the Bible in a structured and purposeful way. Get to know parts of the Bible that have been neglected. Read Christian books, such as commentaries, biographies, and books on Christian growth and nurture, for we are never too old to grow in grace and knowledge of our Lord Jesus Christ (2 Pet. 3:18). And God will be with us even in our "old age... and even to gray hairs" (Isa. 46:4). "Now also when I am old and grayheaded, O God, do not forsake me, until I declare Your strength to this generation, Your power to everyone who is to come" (Psa. 71:18).

Fourth, and, yes, *there is a place for leisure and pleasure*! Solomon says, "So I commended enjoyment, because a man has nothing better under the sun than to eat, drink, and be merry; for this will remain with him in his labor all the days of his life which God gives him under the sun" (Eccl. 8:15). Contempt for pleasure runs the risk of the Manichean heresy which Augustine was prone to follow, viewing the material, sensual world as essentially evil. When I was a very young Christian, a mentor urged me to get rid of my classical music LPs (given to me by my grandfather before he died), for he feared I loved them too much.[10] He should have counseled that I put them away for six months and then return to them with a more mature view of their place in my life. But he did not, and I obeyed, a decision I have now regretted for half a century.

Fifth, *finish well*. In my own experience, the term was used about my working life, but our entire life needs to finish well. Paul told the Philippians, "Brethren, I do not count myself to have apprehended [laid hold of it]; but one thing I do, forgetting those things which are behind and reaching forward to those things which are ahead, I press toward the goal for the prize of the upward call of God in Christ Jesus" (Phil. 3:13–14). Like a long-distance runner, Paul is tunnel-visioned on ending well and receiving the prize. He expands on it elsewhere: "Everyone who competes for the prize is temperate in all things. Now they do it to obtain a perishable crown, but we for an imperishable crown. Therefore I run thus: not with uncertainty. Thus I fight: not as one who beats the air. But I discipline my body and bring it into subjection, lest, when I have preached to others, I myself should become disqualified" (1 Cor. 9:25–27). There is intentionality and focus in this image. The author of Hebrews continues the idea:

> Therefore we also, since we are surrounded by so great a cloud of witnesses, let us lay aside every weight, and the sin which so

---

10. An LP is a long-playing phonograph record, a form of analog audio media, consisting of a grooved vinyl disc, that was especially popular in the latter half of the twentieth century and continues in use today.

easily ensnares us, and let us run with endurance the race that is set before us, looking unto Jesus, the author and finisher of our faith, who for the joy that was set before Him endured the cross, despising the shame, and has sat down at the right hand of the throne of God. (Heb. 12:1–2)

Run with endurance. Without stopping. With focus and tenacity. To the end.

CHAPTER TWENTY-TWO

The Redeemed Man Preparing for His Death

Ian Hamilton

THE REDEEMED MAN is a forgiven sinner, a child of God, a heaven-bound saint, and a joint heir with Christ of the glory of God (Rom. 5:2; 8:17; Eph. 1:7). The redeemed man is, therefore, the most blessed and privileged of men. He is loved by the living God who sings over him with joy (Zeph. 3:17). He is eternally secure in his salvation because God has loved him with "an everlasting love" (Jer. 31:3), and because God, through the perfect atoning work of Christ, has buried his sins in the sea of His forgetfulness (Isa. 43:25; Mic. 7:18–19; Heb. 8:12). This is glorious, but the redeemed man is yet a mortal man and must die (Heb. 9:27–28). Unless Christ returns, the redeemed man's death is inevitable and cannot be avoided or postponed—God has appointed the day.

The Word of God encourages every Christian to reckon with the inevitable fact of death. The Bible never indulges in wistful fancies but in facts. This fact, that death awaits everyone born of woman, is one that God Himself encourages us to face, but to face with faith, hope and calm assurance. How can that be done?[1]

---

1. For additional help, both spiritually and medically, on the topic of dying and death, see Joel R. Beeke and Christopher W. Bogosh, *Dying and Death: Getting Rightly Prepared for the Inevitable* (Reformation Heritage Books, 2018).

The Last Enemy

The Bible confronts us on almost every page with the reality of death. God's Word does not hide from us the ugly fact of death. On the contrary, the Bible tells us that "the wages of sin is death" (Rom. 6:23). Sin, Paul tells the church in Rome, came into the world through Adam's disobedience (5:12–14). God had warned Adam that, if he disobeyed Him, he would die (Gen. 2:17). Adam disobeyed God, and the rest is history. He ate the fruit of the forbidden tree and immediately died. He died spiritually and the process of physical death began to consume him. But more than that, because God had constituted Adam as a covenant head, his sin was our sin. "In Adam's fall, we sinned all."[2]

Death did not belong to God's original creation; all He made was "very good" (Gen. 1:31). This is why our Lord Jesus "groaned" with indignation at the tomb of Lazarus (John 11:33).[3] B. B. Warfield spoke of the "rage" that Jesus felt as he came to the tomb of his friend:

> The spectacle of the distress of Mary and her companions enraged Jesus because it brought poignantly home to his consciousness the evil of death, its unnaturalness, its "violent tyranny" as Calvin ([in his commentary] on verse 38) phrases it. In Mary's grief, he "contemplates"—still to adopt Calvin's words (on verse 33)—"the general misery of the whole human race" and burns with rage against the oppressor of men. Inextinguishable fury seizes upon him; his whole being is discomposed and

---

2. *The New-England Primer: A Reprint of the Earliest Known Edition, with Many Facsimiles and Reproductions, and an Historical Introduction*, ed. Paul Leicester Ford (New York, 1899), 14.

3. The verb translated as "groaned" (*embrimaomai*, John 11:33) means to express anger and displeasure. See Walter Bauer, *A Greek-English Lexicon of the New Testament and Other Early Christian Literature*, ed. William F. Arndt, F. Wilbur Gingrich, and Frederick W. Danker, 2nd ed. (University of Chicago Press, 1979), 254.

perturbed; and his heart, if not his lips, cries out. . . . It is death that is the object of his wrath, and behind death him who has the power of death, and whom he has come into the world to destroy. Tears of sympathy may fill his eyes, but this is incidental. His soul is held by rage: and he advances to the tomb, in Calvin's words again, "as a champion who prepares for conflict."[4]

Death may usher the redeemed man into God's nearer presence, but it is yet an enemy, indeed "the last enemy" (1 Cor. 15:26).

The redeemed man will therefore view the approach of death with two minds: He will, with the apostle Paul, say, "For to me to live is Christ, and to die is gain" (Phil. 1:21). But he will also see death for what it is, an enemy, the contradiction that reminds him of Adam's first sin and his own sin in Adam.

If this dread were all that there were, life would be unsupportable. But the redeemed man is a *redeemed* man. By His sin-vanquishing death and resurrection, Jesus Christ has redeemed believing sinners from the power of death and from him who holds the power of death, the devil (Heb. 2:14–15). Because of this, the redeemed man can face "the last enemy," knowing that it is a defeated enemy.

The Triumph of Christ

The Christian believer lives his life in the light of the cosmic triumph of his Savior, Jesus Christ. The apostle Paul wrote these richly encouraging words to the church in Corinth,

> O death, where is thy sting? O grave, where is thy victory? The sting of death is sin; and the strength of sin is the law. But thanks

---

4. B. B. Warfield, "On the Emotional Life of Our Lord," in *The Person and Work of Christ*, ed. Samuel G. Craig (Presbyterian and Reformed, 1950), 116–17.

be to God, which giveth us the victory through our Lord Jesus Christ. Therefore, my beloved brethren, be ye stedfast, unmoveable, always abounding in the work of the Lord, forasmuch as ye know that your labour is not in vain in the Lord. (1 Cor. 15:55–58)

Paul has been teaching the triumph of the risen Christ throughout this chapter. As our covenant Head, the Lord Jesus Christ entered the domain of death, paying in full the awful price our sin against God deserved. He bore God's righteous judgement in our place. But His death was the inevitable prelude to His triumph. As the apostle Peter told the Jewish crowd at Pentecost, "Him . . . ye have taken, and by wicked hands have crucified and slain: whom God hath raised up, having loosed the pains of death: because it was not possible that he should be holden of it" (Acts 2:23–24).

The bodily resurrection of Christ was the most inevitable fact in human history. But the Christian's hope is not simply in the fact of Christ's resurrection, but in the astounding truth that every believer has been raised with Him. Read Romans 6:3–5:

Know ye not, that so many of us as were baptized into Jesus Christ were baptized into his death? Therefore we are buried with him by baptism into death: that like as Christ was raised up from the dead by the glory of the Father, even so we also should walk in newness of life. For if we have been planted together in the likeness of his death, we shall be also in the likeness of his resurrection.

In life's struggles and tragedies and in death's relentless approach, the redeemed man looks to the triumph of his Savior and to his unbreakable union with Him. As death draws near—and we begin to die from the moment we are conceived—gospel truth is where the child of God anchors his mind and heart. Nothing will more prepare a believer to face death than a life lived in the light of the cosmic triumph of his Savior.

The resurrection of Christ was at the heart of the early church's gospel preaching. The resurrection was not simply the vindication of Christ's sin-atoning death, which of course it was; it was also the "firstfruits" of a new humanity (1 Cor. 15:22–23). The redeemed man is united indissolubly to his risen, exalted Head.

The Hope of Heaven

The Scriptures confront us with an inescapable fact: "It is appointed unto men once to die, but after this the judgment" (Heb. 9:27). The apostle Paul told the believers in Corinth, "We must all appear before the judgment seat of Christ; that every one may receive the things done in his body, according to that he hath done, whether it be good or bad" (2 Cor. 5:10). This is an awesome thought to reckon with. But the child of God can face that thought with calm assurance. In Christ, the child of God has a "lively hope" (1 Peter 1:3). Heaven with its unimaginable glories, not hell with its unimaginable torments and terrors, is the assured destiny of the redeemed man. Every Christian can prepare for death knowing that heaven is a "sure and stedfast" hope (Heb. 6:19).

Ponder with me what God has prepared for those who love Him:

- He has prepared an eternal home in the heavens not built by human hands (2 Cor. 5:1), "whose builder and maker is God" (Heb. 11:10). A home that will be forever *home*.
- He has promised to wipe away every tear from our eyes (Rev. 21:4). Sorrow, suffering, and death will be no more.
- He has promised to "make all things new" (Rev. 21:5). God will make a "new heavens and a new earth, wherein dwelleth righteousness" (2 Peter 3:13).
- He has promised that He will be the God of His people forever and ever: "I heard a great voice out of heaven saying, Behold, the tabernacle of God is with men, and he will dwell with them, and they

shall be his people, and God himself shall be with them, and be their God" (Rev. 21:3).

As death begins inexorably to invade our lives, the Lord makes us increasingly aware of our mortality. We read in God's Word that man is but a breath and life is swifter than a weaver's shuttle (Job 7:6; James 4:14). The psalmist captures the thought memorably: "LORD, make me to know mine end, and the measure of my days, what it is; that I may know how frail I am. Behold, thou hast made my days as an handbreadth; and mine age is as nothing before thee: verily every man at his best state is altogether vanity" (Ps. 39:4–5). It is from this humbling perspective that the hope of heaven, the hope of being forever with the Lord, becomes the redeemed man's increasing focus and anticipation. The sure and certain hope of being forever with the Lord, enjoying His nearer presence, and sharing in the pleasures at His right hand, support the redeemed man as the specter of death casts its dark shadow over his life.

Looking Back with Thankfulness

As Paul waited for the executioner's sword to end his life in this world, he wrote to his son in the faith, Timothy,

> For I am now ready to be offered, and the time of my departure is at hand. I have fought a good fight, I have finished my course, I have kept the faith: henceforth there is laid up for me a crown of righteousness, which the Lord, the righteous judge, shall give me at that day: and not to me only, but unto all them also that love his appearing. (2 Tim. 4:6–8)

The imminent prospect of death caused the apostle to look back and to look forward. He looked back to a life that was marked by faithfulness. He was faithful to "the faith." Paul is not speaking here about his personal faith, saving faith, but to "the faith," "the form of sound words" (2 Tim. 1:13), the body of doctrine that comprised the faith "once delivered unto the saints (Jude 3).

Looking back at one's life as death draws near can be deeply disheartening. We have not loved the Lord as we should have; we have failed to keep His commandments as we should have; we have sinned repeatedly in thought, word and deed. But the Lord is rich in mercy. He does not treat us as our sins deserve (Ps. 103:10). We can look back and bless the Lord for His forgiving and keeping grace. We can bless Him for the grace that enabled us to "fight the good fight of the faith" (1 Tim. 6:12). Looking back, unless we do so through the lens of the God of all grace, would be crushing. So, the approach of death has the potential to make us glory in the God who not only saved us, but who will certainly keep us to our last breath. The redeemed man can reflect with unceasing thankfulness to the Lord for His preserving and keeping grace all the days of his life.

Looking Forward with Expectation

But Paul also looks forward. He looks forward to "a crown of righteousness, which the Lord, the righteous judge, shall give me at that day: and not to me only, but unto all them also that love his appearing" (2 Tim. 4:8). A crown of life! What is Paul saying? Is he saying that a crown of life is merited by his faithful service? No. He is saying that God honors the faithfulness of His children, a faithfulness that He graciously enables them to fulfil. Read Philippians 1:6, "Being confident of this very thing, that he which hath begun a good work in you will perform it until the day of Jesus Christ." God accomplishes faithfulness in us by His grace, but not without our heart and soul engagement. Do you look forward to the crown of righteousness? Do you live as someone for whom the prospect of heaven will be all gain? The redeemed man has a glorious prospect waiting him at his death.

The Fellowship of the Church

The Christian life is a life lived in community and fellowship with other Christians. Every picture we are given of the church, in its Old Testament life or in its New Testament life, is corporate. The church is the body of Christ (1 Cor. 12:12); the church is the temple of God (3:16); the church is the bride of Christ (Rev. 21:2, 9); the church is the family of God (Matt. 12:48–50). These pictures of the church are deeply significant. For one thing, they impress on us that spiritual life is lived within the communion of the saints. Paul tells the church in Ephesus that only "with all the saints" will they comprehend "what is the breadth, and length, and depth, and height . . . know the love of Christ, which passeth knowledge . . . [and] be filled with all the fulness of God" (Eph. 3:17–19).

All this is to say that the redeemed man must till his last breath be committed to the fellowship of the people of God. Solitary Christianity is a contradiction. The new birth brings you into a new family, a new order of existence. The early church "continued stedfastly in the apostles' doctrine and fellowship, and in breaking of bread, and in prayers" (Acts 2:42). "Continued steadfastly" could be better translated "devoted." The fellowship of the church was not an option for believers; rather, it was the soil within which their new life in Christ was to be nourished. The redeemed man does not prepare for death in isolation from the rest of Christ's body. He cherishes its fellowship, its prayers, its ministry, its encouragements, its Christ-filled love.

Christians too often exalt their personal and private walk with God above the corporate and public "churchly" walk with God. I don't mean that the believer does not have a personal walk with God—every believer has. But the default of the life of faith is, "*Our* Father who art in heaven" (Matt 6:9). The redeemed man will cherish the fellowship of the saints and make the ordinary means of grace a non-negotiable priority as he walks through the valley of the shadow of death.

The Personal Return of Christ

The personal, visible, triumphant return of the Lord Jesus Christ is mentioned more than three hundred times in the New Testament. Christians are exhorted to wait expectantly and eagerly for their Lord's return. Jesus challenged His disciples to wait expectantly for His coming:

> But know this, that if the goodman [master] of the house had known in what watch the thief would come, he would have watched, and would not have suffered his house to be broken up. Therefore be ye also ready: for in such an hour as ye think not the Son of man cometh. Who then is a faithful and wise servant, whom his lord hath made ruler over his household, to give them meat in due season? Blessed is that servant, whom his lord when he cometh shall find so doing. (Matt. 24:43–46)

This note of believing, patient expectancy is found throughout the New Testament. The apostle Peter warned his readers not to become despondent or disheartened because Jesus had not yet returned:

> The Lord is not slack concerning his promise, as some men count slackness; but is longsuffering to us-ward, not willing that any should perish, but that all should come to repentance. But the day of the Lord will come as a thief in the night; in the which the heavens shall pass away with a great noise, and the elements shall melt with fervent heat, the earth also and the works that are therein shall be burned up. Seeing then that all these things shall be dissolved, what manner of persons ought ye to be in all holy conversation and godliness, looking for and hasting unto the coming of the day of God. (2 Peter 3:9–12)

Peter is not simply concerned that his readers believe in the Lord's coming; he wants the Lord's coming to provoke them unto godliness.

The coming of the Lord should inspire all God's people to live *sub specie aeternitatis,* in the light of eternity; or, to use John Calvin's oft used words, *coram Deo*, before the face of God. The apostle Peter is concerned that when Jesus returns, God's redeemed children will not shrink from Him in shame but rejoice with uninhibited delight. The apostle John put it thus,

> And now, little children, abide in him; that, when he shall appear, we may have confidence, and not be ashamed before him at his coming. If ye know that he is righteous, ye know that every one that doeth righteousness is born of him. Behold, what manner of love the Father hath bestowed upon us, that we should be called the sons of God: therefore the world knoweth us not, because it knew him not. Beloved, now are we the sons of God, and it doth not yet appear what we shall be: but we know that, when he shall appear, we shall be like him; for we shall see him as he is. And every man that hath this hope in him purifieth himself, even as he is pure. (1 John 2:28–3:3)

Too often Christians have argued over the details of the Lord's return. We divide into "eschatological groupings," identifying as premillennialists, postmillennialists, or amillennialists. No doubt each group can provide a biblical rationale for its chosen eschatological identity. However, the great concern of the New Testament is that God's redeemed children live godly and holy lives as they look to and prepare for the Lord's coming: "What manner of persons ought ye to be in all holy conversation and godliness, looking for and hasting unto the coming of the day of God" (2 Peter 3:11–12).

This the redeemed man will seek to do. The last thing he wants is to be ashamed when his Savior comes again. As the inexorable prospect of death begins to make its presence felt, as our bodies increasingly reveal their earthly fragility, the redeemed man will seek to finish his pilgrimage well by pursuing the "holiness, without which no man shall see the Lord" (Heb. 12:14).

No man knows the day or the hour of his death. God Himself has appointed the day and the hour. In the light of this certainty, it behooves the redeemed man to heed the exhortation of the writer of Hebrews to be "looking unto Jesus the author and finisher of our faith; who for the joy that was set before him endured the cross, despising the shame, and is set down at the right hand of the throne of God. For consider him that endured such contradiction of sinners against himself, lest ye be wearied and faint in your minds" (Heb. 12:2–3). In the Greek text there is a nuance that is rarely captured in our English versions. The force of the verb "looking unto" is more accurately "looking away to"—that is, looking away *from* yourself and looking away *to* Jesus. All the redeemed man's hope lies outside of himself. The devil is always seeking to turn God's people into themselves. The struggle of faith is to resist and refuse that temptation and look away from self to the Lord Jesus Christ, the author and finisher of faith.

The redeemed man, the man in Christ, has a glorious and living hope. Death will not, indeed cannot, extinguish that glorious and living hope. Jesus Christ will not lose one of those given to Him by His Father (John 10:27–30). So, the redeemed man will take to heart Paul's great words to the church in Corinth:

> Though our outward man perish, yet the inward man is renewed day by day. For our light affliction, which is but for a moment, worketh for us a far more exceeding and eternal weight of glory; while we look not at the things which are seen, but at the things which are not seen: for the things which are seen are temporal; but the things which are not seen are eternal. (2 Cor. 4:16–18)

May the Lord give us all the grace to do so.

"Examine yourself"
(2 Corinthians 13:5)

Contributors

Joel R. Beeke is chancellor and professor of homiletics and systematic theology at Puritan Reformed Theological Seminary, and a pastor at Heritage Reformed Congregation in Grand Rapids, Michigan.

Curt Daniel is the pastor of Faith Bible Church in Springfield, Illinois.

Kevin DeYoung is the senior pastor at Christ Covenant Church in Matthews, North Carolina, and associate professor of systematic theology at Reformed Theological Seminary, Charlotte, North Carolina.

Daniel Doriani is professor of biblical and systematic theology at Covenant Seminary and often has served as an interim pastor for churches.

Sinclair Ferguson is a teaching fellow at Ligonier Ministries and Chancellor's Professor of Systematic Theology at Reformed Theological Seminary. He has served as a minister in various churches in Scotland and the United States.

Ian Hamilton recently served as president and professor of historical theology at Westminster Seminary (UK) and also served as the pastor of Cambridge Presbyterian Church in England.

Michael A. G. Azad Haykin is professor of church history and biblical spirituality at the Southern Baptist Theological Seminary and director of the Andrew Fuller Center for Baptist Studies.

Jason Helopoulos is associate pastor at University Reformed Church in East Lansing, Michigan.

Gerard Hemmings is pastor of Amyand Park Chapel in London.

David C. Innes is associate pastor at Calvin Orthodox Presbyterian Church in Phoenix, Arizona, and served as professor of politics at The King's College for eighteen years.

Terry Johnson is senior Minister at Independent Presbyterian Church in Savannah, Georgia.

Conrad Mbewe is pastor of Kabwata Baptist Church in Lusaka, Zambia.

Jim Newheiser is professor of Christian counseling and pastoral theology at Reformed Theological Seminary (Charlotte) and served as preaching pastor at Grace Bible Church in Escondido, California.

Richard D. Phillips is senior minister at Second Presbyterian Church in Greenville, South Carolina, and serves as an adjunct professor at Westminster Theological Seminary.

Joseph Pipa is president emeritus and professor of systematic and applied theology at Greenville Presbyterian Theological Seminary and pastor of Antioch Presbyterian Church in Woodruff, South Carolina.

Paul M. Smalley is research and teaching assistant to Joel Beeke at Puritan Reformed Theological Seminary and a pastor at Grace Immanuel Reformed Baptist Church in Grand Rapids, Michigan.

David Strain is senior minister at First Presbyterian Church in Jackson, Mississippi.

Derek W. H. Thomas is Chancellor's Professor of Systematic and Pastoral Theology at Reformed Theological Seminary (Jackson, Mississippi) and a teaching fellow at Ligonier Ministries. He served as senior minister at First Presbyterian Church in Columbia, South Carolina.

Geoff Thomas served as the pastor of Alfred Place Baptist Church in Aberystwyth, Wales, for more than fifty years.